PENGUIN CLASSICS

ALL DESIRE IS A DESIRE FOR BEING

RENÉ GIRARD (1923–2015) was a French-born American historian, literary critic and philosopher of social science whose work belongs to the tradition of anthropological philosophy. He was elected to the elite Académie Française for his ground-breaking work in human nature after having spent nearly fifty years elaborating his theory of mimetic desire.

CYNTHIA L. HAVEN is a National Endowment for the Humanities Public Scholar, and author of *Evolution of Desire: A Life of René Girard*, the first-ever biography of the French theorist, and editor of *Conversations with René Girard: Prophet of Envy*. Her latest book is *Czesław Miłosz: A California Life*. She has been a visiting writer and scholar at Stanford.

RENÉ GIRARD

All Desire Is a Desire for Being

Essential Writings Selected by
CYNTHIA L. HAVEN

PENGUIN BOOKS

PENGUIN CLASSICS

UK | USA | Canada | Ireland | Australia
India | New Zealand | South Africa

Penguin Books is part of the Penguin Random House group of companies
whose addresses can be found at global.penguinrandomhouse.com

This selection first published in Penguin Classics 2023

003

Introduction and selection copyright © Cynthia L. Haven, 2023
Sources and Copyright information can be found on p. 301

The moral rights of the author and translators have been asserted

Set in 10.5/13pt Dante MT Std
Typeset by Jouve (UK), Milton Keynes
Printed and bound in Great Britain by Clays Ltd, Elcograf S.p.A.

The authorized representative in the EEA is Penguin Random House Ireland,
Morrison Chambers, 32 Nassau Street, Dublin D02 YH68

A CIP catalogue record for this book is available from the British Library

ISBN: 978-0-241-54323-8

www.greenpenguin.co.uk

MIX
Paper | Supporting
responsible forestry
FSC® C018179

Penguin Random House is committed to a
sustainable future for our business, our readers
and our planet. This book is made from Forest
Stewardship Council® certified paper.

Contents

Introduction: We Do Not Come in Peace   vii

1. Conflict   3
2. Violence and Foundational Myths in
   Human Societies   5
3. Is Oedipus Innocent?   9
   The Indispensable Victim in *Oedipus the King*   9
   A Crisis, a Plague, a Culprit: On the Innocence
   of Oedipus   15
4. The Founding Murder in the Philosophy of Nietzsche   21
5. Camus's Stranger Retried   41
6. Shakespeare in Comedy and Tragedy   73
   Myth and Ritual in Shakespeare:
   A Midsummer Night's Dream   73
   Collective Violence and Sacrifice in
   Shakespeare's *Julius Caesar*   98
7. Scandal and the Dance: Salome in the
   Gospel of Mark   119
8. Peter's Denial and the Question of Mimesis   137
9. Totalitarian Trials and the Obliteration of Memory   151
   The Totalitarian Trial   151
   Retribution   158
10. A Method, a Life, a Man   165
11. Violence and Religion: Cause or Effect?   189

Contents

12. Belonging   203
13. On Mel Gibson's *The Passion of the Christ*   217
14. The Mystic of Neuilly   227
15. Victims, Violence and Christianity   245
16. Literature and Christianity: A Personal View   259
17. Maxims of René Girard   273

Chronology   289
Books by René Girard   297
Acknowledgments   299
Sources and Copyright   301
Index   305

We Do Not Come in Peace

Cynthia L. Haven

It's been said that the universe is made up not of atoms, but of stories. Whether at a podium or over coffee with a friend, in the privacy of our thoughts or at an international summit, we tell stories pretty much all the time. We create ourselves out of the tales we tell – both individually and as a community, in our myths and in our histories. But who crafts the narrative, and with what motives and vested interests?

We deal in fictions. And yet we never stop asking what really happened.

The Avignon-born French theorist René Girard (1923–2015) had a keen ear for stories, and a remarkable way of coaxing the truth from them, the life out of the lies. He saw that conflict is a constant hum beneath human activity, an inevitable consequence of competing desires. When conflict causes crisis, a pattern of self-justification and cover-up follows. The long history of blame began the moment Adam bit the apple.

In this powder keg, Girard discerned patterns of social contagion, mob violence, and scapegoating. It begins with envy: 'All desire is a desire for being,' Girard wrote.* So we look with covetous eyes at someone we fantasize has it all, who represents our derivative aspirations. Imitation may be the sincerest form of flattery, but it tends to irritate the original. This metaphysical hunger attracts the resistance of the envied other and provokes heated competition. The enmity itself is the contagion, spreading until the

* René Girard, *When These Things Begin: Conversations with Michel Treguer* (East Lansing, MI: Michigan State University Press, 2014), p. 12.

whole community is in a mimetic meltdown. In an ugly attempt to end the escalating tit-for-tat reprisals as tensions rise, someone or some group is singled out as the cause of the mayhem. Although the target is innocent of the blame heaped on him, or her, or them – or at least no more blameworthy than anyone else in the community – people believe a problem has been solved by the elimination of the 'guilty.' As the community converges on the culprit, a new unity emerges. Condemnation is unanimous, or nearly so. No one is guilty because everyone is: 'It was a monster with one red eye,/A crowd that saw him die, not I.'* In some societies, the condemned faces lynching, exile, imprisonment (a modern version might be 'cancelling' the accused). It buys peace and reconciliation . . . for a while.

The scapegoat is not entirely random. Yet the process is unwitting – mobs don't *knowingly* pick a scapegoat. They believe in the culpability of the victim. Typically, the mob seeks someone who holds a more marginal place within the community, a person without allies, someone who cannot or will not retaliate. He, she, or they may be a foreigner, an ethnic minority, or someone so rich or renowned as to seem unreachable and alone – a president or pope, for example. Long before Oedipus headed for Colonus, the pattern was established: last year's hero becomes this year's sacrifice, first celebrated then defamed, revered then ridiculed. And we regularly – and unconsciously – seek new victims to focus our confusion, our envy, our anger, our blame.

Mob action is the origin of ritual and myth. In the archaic world, when society again faces an internal crisis, the scapegoating process is reenacted to evoke the dynamics that ended the fighting before. In a logic-defying turn, the eliminated victims are honored, sanctified, memorialized, even deified – they had brought peace and social cohesion, after all, which would seem to be a god-like power. How does one purify collective memory in this wilderness of lies?

Do these words sound atavistic in our up-to-date world – a

* W. H. Auden, *Horae Canonicae: Nones. Collected Poems*, ed. Edward Mendelson (New York: Modern Library, 2007), 632.

throwback to the Aztec rites, in which hundreds were slain to appease the sun/war god Huitzilopochtli? Think again. An eminent music scholar recently wrote about the links between rock music, violence, and sacrifice. Ted Gioia pointed out that modern rock makes use of these age-old practices, and that 'drums are linked to sacrificial ritual in every region of the world.' Today's twenty-first century inhabitants are not exempt from these timeless rituals; he suggests that some powerful modern equivalents continue to this day – for example, in the annual 'Burning Man' festival that attracts tens of thousands.*

No one took these lessons more to heart than René Girard himself. On occasion he showed it. Years ago at a Stanford conference, Girard faced a tough question about his unconventional methods. His research had involved a close reading of archaic texts – which is to say, stories. In them, he discerned hidden patterns of rivalry and the sacralization of violence to end strife, an unending sequence throughout the long night of humanity. His writing was seasoned with characteristic humor and insight – he had learned something about himself along his journey, and so didn't offer himself as a hero or an answer.

After the talk, one man asked a provocative question: 'Given that we can't entirely trust the veracity of ancient writings, how would you measure the success of your theory?'

Girard's answer was a thunderbolt in its directness and simplicity: 'You will see the success of my theories when you recognize yourself as a persecutor.'

That is not where most people begin. Yet there is nowhere else to begin.

The man dubbed 'the new Darwin of the human sciences'† started

---

* Ted Gioia, 'Why Do They Burn a Man at Burning Man?' 3 September 2021 https://tedgioia.substack.com/p/why-do-they-burn-a-man-at-burning
† Michel Serres, 'Receiving René Girard into the Académie Française,' in Sandor Goodhart, Jørgen Jørgensen, Tom Ryba, and James G. Williams, eds. *For René Girard: Essays in Friendship and in Truth* (East Lansing, MI: Michigan State University Press, 2009), 5.

his academic career in literature, not sociology, religions or anthropology. Though his dissertation at Paris' École des Chartes focused on Avignon's medieval history, he changed course in America, intellectually as well as geographically. Postwar GIs were flooding US campuses, and Girard was one of the many foreign teachers brought to fill the need. In 1947 he was appointed to teach French language and literature at Indiana University, tasked with teaching books he had yet to read himself. He gave himself a crash course, reading voraciously to stay one step ahead of his own class syllabus. And the more he read, the more he was spellbound by the interesting patterns that called out to him. As the lines of enquiry converged, the more he was driven by the need to comprehend the meaning of what he saw. He discovered that novels of the past were an important key, revealing the truth of human life that the 'official' records conceal – unintentionally, and sometimes intentionally, too. As Girard put it, 'The novel is the truth, and the rest is lies.'* His close reading showed that what we call 'fiction' preserves the social and psychological configurations of a time and place, the contexts that decode the human puzzle. The art of the novel is anthropology, he discovered. And elsewhere, 'My point of departure and my entire analysis are purely textual.'† He learned how to make the dead talk.

His first book, written at Johns Hopkins University, was 1961's *Mensonge romantique et vérité romanesque* (published in English as *Deceit, Desire and the Novel* in 1965), a study of the books and authors that fascinated him – Cervantes, Proust, Dostoevsky, Stendhal and Flaubert. Girard challenged the 'Romantic lie' – that is, the myth of personal autonomy, the 'authentic self' enshrined from Rousseau onward. The hero wants something, and it is really 'he' who wants it – unaffected by his friends, his family or public opinion. These works offered Girard a new concept of human wanting: our desires

---

* René Girard and Milan Kundera, transcript of radio conversation, 11 November 1989, 'Pleasure,' France Culture. Translation mine.
† Rebecca Adams, 'Violence, Difference, Sacrifice,' in Cynthia L. Haven, ed., *Prophet of Envy* (London: Bloomsbury, 2020), 56.

are not authentic and our own, he wrote. Instead, they are borrowed, 'mimetic.' Mimesis is the basic tool of human development: it's how we learn to eat and talk, the root of our ambitions, the fuel for our unquenchable longings and tormented romantic triangles. We learn what to want from each other, and our desires spread contagiously because we copy each other, hoping the people we admire hold the magic key to success and happiness. The more we imitate each other, the more we become the same – and it is our sameness, not our differences, that makes us fight.

The thesis that was swirling in his head was born this way: 'In autumn 1958, I was working on my book about the novel, on the twelfth and last chapter that's entitled 'Conclusion.' I was thinking about the analogies between religious experience and the experience of a novelist who discovers that he's been consistently lying, lying for the benefit of his Ego, which in fact is made up of nothing but a thousand lies that have accumulated over a long period, sometimes built up over an entire lifetime.'* His revelation was a revolution of the self – religious and literary and anthropological and deeply personal, and this conversion experience would be the basis of his thinking and writing. 'Everything came to me at once,'† he explained. He spent the rest of his life teasing out the substance and applications of that one compact vision, theoretically, exegetically, academically and personally.

Meanwhile, Girard continued to make the dead talk. He read the texts of ancient civilizations and considered the work of nineteenth-century anthropologists, who were working to build a new field of study, interviewing the last survivors of remote tribes that have long since vanished. Those accounts became the basis of his influential 1972 *La violence et le sacré* (published in English as *Violence and the Sacred* in 1977), exploring the role of ritual sacrifice in archaic societies. He maintained these early rites were a way to control violence within a society by channeling it.

---

* Cynthia L. Haven, *Evolution of Desire: A Life of René Girard* (East Lansing, MI: Michigan State University Press, 2018), 110.
† Ibid., 112.

His 1978 *Des choses cachées depuis la fondation du monde*, published in English as *Things Hidden since the Foundation of the World* in 1987, expressed more fully his deepening interest in biblical texts.

Girard contended that the scapegoat mechanism had been weakened and challenged in the Judaic tradition, with the gradual revelation of the scapegoat's innocence. It was broken at last by the Crucifixion, the cynical and opportunistic torture, beyond recognition, of an innocent man before a howling mob. We are living in the long aftermath: we still kill, but our hands are no longer clean, and we have little faith in our innocence.

More and more proof is emerging to support his wide-ranging hypotheses – even in the hard sciences, with the discovery of 'mirror neurons.' He anticipated that it would be so. However, the answers he found weren't merely artifacts of the past; they have vital meaning in the present. His thoughts continue to live powerfully, helping us to recover the words we have allowed to die and be forgotten within ourselves. ('Thou shalt not covet' among them.) His voice calls us to remember, so that, recovering and rediscovering them, *we* make the dead speak, too, with Girard's guidance.

This anthology shows the evolution of his thinking, bringing his work to bear on sources ranging from Sophocles to Shakespeare, Clausewitz to Camus, Nietzsche to Proust. His work encompasses mankind's violent history from early tribal warfare to modern terrorism and nuclear weapons. It shows how Job's 'comforters' prefigured the totalitarian trials of the twentieth century. It reveals why Salome's dance was not a sexual event, but a mimetic one – a crowd phenomenon, as was St Peter's betrayal in the courtyard. It includes Girard's surprising response to Mel Gibson's 2004 film *The Passion of the Christ*. We have also included the first English translation of Girard's sublime Académie Française address in English, on the occasion of his 2005 election to that august body, describing the nature of spiritual revelation in the life of Girard's predecessor for Seat #37 at the Académie, Père Ambrose-Marie Carré.

Girard's work took him into mankind's remotest past, examining the earliest human sacrifices to reconcile villages torn by internal strife. But in a sense, he probed our future, too, sometimes through the prophetic notes he heard in the writers he studied. Reading *Crime and Punishment*, he observed: 'Raskolnikov has a dream during a grave illness that occurs just before his final change of heart, at the end of the novel. He dreams of a worldwide plague that affects people's relationship with each other. No specifically medical symptoms are mentioned. It is human interaction that breaks down, and the entire society gradually collapses.'* Plagues had been a regular feature in mankind's history, and always threatened to return – though we had hoped modern medicine might banish them forever. Five years after Girard's death, we witnessed first-hand the effects of a pandemic, and the erosion of social order in its wake. We are mimetic creatures, after all, intimately tied with the past and future of each and every one of us.

We are all persecutors. That is one unpleasant, but practical and productive, takeaway from Girard's 'theory.' We are persecutors who see ourselves as victims. Our competitive and covetous quest for job perks, political clout, sexy bedfellows or an entrée into an élite clique spreads contagiously through a society and leads us to conflict and ultimately escalation – snubs, sackings, social ostracization, and violence. That imbroglio is still resolved, as it has been since time immemorial, by a scapegoating event that finds a target in someone who cannot or will not retaliate, someone who can plausibly be blamed for the troubles. Girard claims that this scapegoating process is the birth pangs of human culture, and also a page from the diary of our everyday lives.

The horror of this scapegoating, and our participation in it, is often overlooked when a study of his work becomes more and more theoretical, more and more abstruse. To comprehend it does not require workshops, support groups, spreadsheets or teams of experts – those approaches are subject to the very mimetic pitfalls Girard

---

* René Girard, 'The Plague in Literature and Myth,' in René Girard, *To Double Business Bound: Essays on Literature, Mimesis, and Anthropology* (Boston: Johns Hopkins University Press, 1978), 136.

describes. It begins instead in the loneliness of the human heart. You learn most about his ideas by observing them in your own choices and behaviors, and changing course – otherwise they pass unnoticed through your mind and days. Action works as a fixative to our understanding.*

His concepts must be understood from the inside – so that they become second nature, *felt*, a part of one's psychological makeup. Otherwise, you fall into the mimetic trap. To bypass this humbling step is to reenter the battle with the 'other,' the one who keeps us from consuming all we want (and we can want a lot). Clever ideas disconnected from action reap the questionable reward of self-satisfaction.

Girard's corpus is not just an erudite self-help manual, however; his intellectual landscape is not intended to be therapeutic, and yet it is. What he came to see was not a comfort, however, but something fierce and intractable. What he learned about the individual also limns the destiny of our species. Our impossible plight: the mechanism of scapegoat violence – whether on the level of the individual, or society, or epoch – is rooted in the very imitation that teaches us to love and learn, in fact, the very tissue that connects us with the rest of humanity.

His realm extends far beyond the personal, the 'me': his theories also anatomize political campaigns, world banking, international statecraft, and nuclear escalation; they illuminate our history from the beginning of time. The mystery of imitation is what threatens our survival and enables it, and for that reason alone it merits more careful study.

As we teeter on an existential brink, Girard invites us to be 'conscientious objectors' to the murderous sequence of mimetic events. This effort calls for more than reflection and study; it has seismic

---

* As Simone Weil wrote, 'Human nature is arranged in such a way that a desire of the soul that has not passed through the flesh by means of actions, movements or attitudes that correspond to it naturally, has no reality in the soul.' Simone Weil, 'Theorie des sacraments,' in *Pensées sans ordre concernant l'amour de Dieu* (Paris: Gallimard, 1962), 135.

implications. It sounds a note that extends backwards and forward through time, revolutionizing our past and determining our future. (The note was first struck at the killing of Abel, whose name means 'breath.' It has reverberated ever since.)

Girard's response at the Stanford conference – 'You will see the success of my theories when you recognize yourself as a persecutor' – was not just a clever way to turn a question on its head, though he often had that effect. Instead, his intuition was the first word of a personal *mea culpa*, the beginning of a vigilant internal pilgrimage that lasts a lifetime.

But it begins with the very necessary downfall of the self, the very come-uppance that marked Girard's own spiritual beginnings. The point is to see yourself as a questionable character. To look at yourself askance. In short, I am not a Savonarola, but a penitent who has blindly wished coals upon my enemies' heads. I carry my own personal stock of villains and whipping boys with me wherever I go.

The inevitable question follows: 'Is there a positive mimesis, a *good* mimesis?' Of course, anyone who has fallen in love – where kiss ignites kiss, lovers trade promises, and each tries to outdo the other in lavish adulation – knows the truth. But 'falling' is the operative word. It is something that happens to us, not something that is the effect of our will, and something that too easily flips into its mimetic opposite – such reversals are the stock-in-trade of melodrama and television sitcoms. How do we choose to accept the blame or insult that is heaped on us in such circumstances? How do we use our will to love the unlovable 'other'? Can we will the good of the other, even against our will? Or even against the will of the other? What would happen if we truly believed 'each of us is guilty before all for everyone and everything.' Those were the thoughts of Father Zosima, a Dostoevsky figure beloved of both Girard and the French philosopher Emmanuel Levinas, for whom these words were akin to a mantra or talismanic formula.* Could it break the cycle? Would

* Alain Toumayan, ' "I More than the Others": Dostoevsky and Levinas.' *Yale French Studies*, no. 104 (2004): 55. https://doi.org/10.2307/3182504.

it provide, perhaps, an even more durable 'high' than mind-bending designer drugs – or the next commercial rocket to the exosphere, the very rim of outer space?

René Girard was more to me than an object of study. He had been a personal friend even before *Battling to the End*, his final book, which I read in galleys before it was published. We can experience him today through what he wrote, but the firsthand effect of the living, breathing man – his deep courtesy, his affability, his gentle humor and hard-won restraint – is gone forever. I hope the section of 'maxims' I have included captures the spirit of his offhand aperçus and transformative insights. However, I would trade them all to enter the Girards' living room on Frenchman's Road, on the Stanford campus – with its old rose-colored armchair from Avignon, its bookcases with clay *ushabti* from Egypt lined up on the shelves – and to have René again invite me to sit down beside him on the white couch, and then ask me once more, 'What shall we talk about today?'

All Desire Is a Desire for Being

Conflict

Why do all people, myself no doubt included, have such a remarkable capacity for conflict? Why are our relations with one another so fragile, so easily damaged, so difficult if not impossible to repair?

The nuclear deadlock makes this question the most urgent one today. But it is not a new question. Paradoxically, its present urgency may hide rather than reveal its formidable scope. Let us suppose, for an instant, that America and Russia have succeeded in neatly annihilating one another without harming the rest of the world. Can one seriously believe that, with the two chief Satans gone (as the ayatollah would say), the world would finally be at peace? In the most optimistic hypothesis, there would be a resumption of the nuclear deadlock, with a different set of protagonists.

A political scientist will focus attention on America and Russia, on capitalism and Communism, but there is a broader question. It is so broad, indeed, that it seems abstract, and yet it is undoubtedly very concrete and very real: Why such a human capacity for conflict?

We can see in retrospect that all of human history (and prehistory) has been moving faster and faster toward a technical threshold beyond which the destructive power of weaponry, combined with the human genius for discord, leaves no alternative but the immediate destruction of life on this planet or its precarious continuation in a world permanently poised on the brink of total disaster.

Should we shift the blame to the national state as such, or perhaps to all forms of social organization, as Jean-Jacques Rousseau did? To do so is another recipe for evading the real question.

Can we blame our individual and collective divisiveness on some huge 'system' that manipulates us all for the sake of some obscure powers? Some systems are better than others, no doubt, but, except for universal death, we have yet to discover the one that will prevent the human genius for discord from reasserting itself. In my opinion, this genius is rooted in a form of alienation much more comprehensive and universal than anything discovered by Marx, Freud, et al.

Even the most passionate among us never feel they truly are the persons they want to be. To them, the most wonderful being, the only semi-god, is always *someone else* whom they emulate and from whom they borrow their desires, thus ensuring for themselves lives of perpetual strife and rivalry with those they simultaneously hate and admire.

In the old language of religious ethics, the sin of pride was said to be self-defeating. The more self-sufficient and autonomous man tries to be, the more intricate and perverse his foreign entanglements become.

No one, I feel, can study the formidable human capacity for conflict realistically unless he first recognizes that he is a part of the problem and that his worst impulses are inextricably mixed up with his best.

This irreducible personal involvement of the questioner as well as, at the other end, the all-embracing nature of the question, gives to my research a 'philosophical' and even a 'religious' twist that may forever prevent it from becoming 'scientific' in the eyes of the scientist. Does it mean that our scientific culture can ignore this question? Can it really afford to?

Violence and Foundational Myths in Human Societies

My interest in Christianity is not rooted in the Scriptures or theology. Strange as it may sound, it stems from Darwinism. This evolutionary theory assumes that human culture has evolved from what we call 'animal culture.' Can we develop a plausible genesis of what is not animal in our own culture – this 'supplement' that makes us human?

We can assume that hominization began when mimetic rivalries intensified so much that the animal dominance relationship collapsed. Mankind survived, no doubt, because religious prohibitions emerged early enough to prevent the new species from self-destructing.

But how to explain this emergence? To understand what happened, our only clues are the stories that tell the birth of the cults to which they belong. They are called founding myths or originary myths.

They usually begin with the story of a destructive crisis. In the Oedipus myth, it is a plague, elsewhere a cannibalistic monster. Behind these themes hides what Hobbes calls 'the war of all against all': explosions of rivalry intense enough to destroy communities. The thirst for revenge is concentrated on an increasingly small number of individuals. In the end, the community is united against one, the one I call the scapegoat. The group reconciles around this one victim, at a cost that seems miraculously low.

The problem that rationalist thinkers have vainly sought to solve through the hypothesis of the social contract, the origin of human societies, is thus solved without human intention, when the mimetic crisis is at its height.

The unconscious nature of the lynching is admirably illustrated by the phrase of Jesus on the Cross: 'Father, forgive them, they do not know what they do.' This sentence must be interpreted literally. For if the myths recognized the facts, the innocence of the scapegoat would become visible, and violence would lose its cathartic efficacy. The truth shines through if we ask ourselves about the recurring characteristics of mythical heroes.

Many of them are blind like Tiresias, one-eyed like Wotan or, more significantly, referred to as 'men from elsewhere.' The archaic communities were surely quite distant from each other. When a stranger made his appearance, people gathered around him with high hopes. The slightest unexpected gesture on his part could trigger panic, and death.

How are religious prohibitions put in place? We can assume that, in archaic communities, after the cathartic lynching ended the mimetic crisis, a new god emerged. And each time a fight broke out, the communities, remembering the ordeal of past rivalries, prohibited all contact between the people involved in the disorder. Each resumption of violence was interpreted as the expression of the anger of the god and, by virtue of his prestige, prohibitions appeared; prohibitions which slowly turned into a more or less coherent and definitive system.

Over time, the fear these prohibitions inspired probably lessened, and with it the power they had to prevent transgressions. Faced with this danger, archaic communities frantically sought new protection against their own violence. Since they had not forgotten the great catharsis that had saved them from a previous crisis, they must have asked if a new catharsis could be reproduced by replaying the process of the crisis, including the lynching. Many sacrificial rites thus begin with provoked disorders, which anthropologists have rightly defined as 'simulated crises.'

Two things suggest that religion (prohibitions and rituals) is thus the origin and the essence of human culture: we do not find the slightest trace of it in animal cultures; no human culture is totally devoid of it. Two ancient and powerful religions, the Greek and the Hindu, developed an incomplete but profound understanding of archaic systems, in their diversity as well as in their fundamental unity – systems that are regularly reborn from their ashes, but fail to eliminate, once and for all, mimetic rivalries. Doesn't an identical process play out in the Gospels, the same lynching leading to the same deification?

This is a fact that most Christians have not dared to explore further, fearing that the admission of these obvious resemblances would bring down the edifice of their faith. They were wrong, because a close comparison between the Gospels and mythology would turn to the advantage of Christianity. Myths take the scapegoating of the single victim very seriously. They think the victims really are guilty. On the contrary, the Gospels believe in the total innocence of Jesus and proclaim it.

Whereas in myth the victims are believed to have committed the crimes of which they are accused, in biblical and Christian tradition this verdict is often overturned. Many Bible stories condemn the crowd and rehabilitate the victim. As for the Psalms, they give snapshots of a lynching: a horrified narrator observes a band of individuals who try to surround him to kill him. Christ's situation recalls the many prophets who, after being idolized by the crowds, suddenly became their victims.

While archaic myths align with the crowd, and encourage their readers to do the same, the greatest texts of the Bible reverse the process, siding with the scapegoats in situations which, in the pagan world, would have led to the creation of a new myth. The Passion of Christ is a decisive illustration of this reversal.

The Bible therefore effects a radical departure from mythology: in the Old Testament, and even more spectacularly in the Gospels, the supremacy of the crowd, which dates back to the origins of humanity, is finally overthrown.

Translated by Cynthia L. Haven

Is Oedipus Innocent?

In the 1960s, René Girard became intrigued by Oedipus, the doomed Theban king – a passion he would share with anthropologist Mark Anspach. It was a fortunate collaboration: Girard later wrote a preface for Anspach's Œdipe mimétique (Paris: Éditions de L'Herne, 2010), a book which also included a conversation between Girard and Anspach. Both texts appear in English for the first time in this volume.

The Indispensable Victim in
Oedipus the King

The Oedipus that Mark Anspach gives us is not the Oedipus of the famous complex but the one the complex conceals. It is an Oedipus caught as we are in the blinding symmetries of mimetic desire.[*]

Unlike our needs, which make themselves felt in our body without any help from third parties, our desires have an irreducible social dimension. Behind our desires lurks a mediator or model who most often goes unrecognized by others, including the person doing the imitating. As a general rule, we desire what those around us desire. Our models can be real or imaginary, collective or individual. We imitate the desires of those we admire. We want to 'become like them', to spirit away their very being.

[*] Girard's opening discussion has been condensed and his praise for Anspach's book omitted.

Desire is not mimetic only in mediocre individuals, those whom the existentialists, following Heidegger, branded as inauthentic, but in everybody without exception, even in those who appear the most authentic in our own eyes, namely ourselves.

The more the modern world becomes spiritually if not materially egalitarian, the more the distance shrinks between mimetic models and their imitators. We are consequently free to desire the same object as our model and that is what we almost always do, without stopping to reflect upon the conflicts that we provoke. In what is known as the modern era, mimetic rivalries heighten and proliferate to such an extent that they modify the nature of existence.

To be sure, there is something positive in the intensification of mimesis: the competition that it fuels is inseparable from the extraordinary energy of our world and its enormous strides forward in science and technology. But the negative aspects increase concurrently. Violence is ever better armed, its destructive power growing to the point that it threatens humanity's very survival.

As a rule, mimetic competition makes people unhappy. One of the first to perceive this was Stendhal, one of the five novelists studied in my first book. Within a highly mimetic world, the only objects we desire intensely are those that a rival prevents us from possessing. And the converse is also true: we quickly lose interest in objects that nobody wishes to take from us. This dual phenomenon frequently suffices to render our lives hellish.

In the French title of my first book,* *Mensonge romantique et vérité romanesque*, the first part of the opposition, the 'romantic lie', designates the illusion under which we all labor that our desires are spontaneous, in other words that we are the sole authors and owners of our desires – an illusion that has its greatest hold over us precisely at those moments when it is furthest from the truth.

The second part of the opposition, 'novelistic truth', refers to the capacity of certain writers, novelists above all, to identify mimesis not only in others, where it is always easy to detect, but in themselves.

* This book was translated into English under the title *Deceit, Desire and the Novel*.

Nobody possesses this capacity from the start. It must be acquired at great cost, and novelistic masterpieces show us how it is acquired.

In *Oedipus the King* a reversal takes place that is more or less analogous to the reversal by which a novelist moves from the romantic lie to novelistic truth. In the face of the plague epidemic, Oedipus, who believes himself to be above suspicion, suspects everybody around him, until finally his anguished arrogance turns back against himself and he is 'hoist by his own petard'.

In an archaic community like the Thebes of the tragedy, an epidemic immediately suggests the wrath of the plague god, in this case Apollo, incensed by some crime left unpunished. Oedipus has every reason to believe himself innocent. Was it not he who, in the past, saved the city from an ordeal comparable to the one that he must now confront? Sophocles' Oedipus embodies the same crumbling of arrogance we see in the passage from the romantic lie to novelistic truth. In both cases, beyond the humiliation, the experience proves to be fruitful. To the novelist it brings the novel, to the mythic hero it brings the wisdom that triumphs in Sophocles' later tragedy *Oedipus at Colonus*.

The analysis of the hostile interaction between Oedipus and Tiresias is essential. Their relationship is manifestly a mimetic rivalry, one that produces an ever more violent symmetry between the two seers who perpetually imitate one another, their hatred redoubling with each exchange. The two men are already alike at the start and even more so at the finish. It is, one might surmise, to complete the resemblance with his blind rival that Oedipus gouges out his own eyes . . . We see the beginning of an analogous process with Creon. The more these characters seek to differentiate themselves, the more they come to resemble each other.

All the structural traits of mimetic conflicts are pushed to the extreme. The more the violence grows, the less it resolves. Tiresias or Creon could assume the role of the guilty party just as easily as Oedipus. The scales long remain equally balanced before they finally tilt against Oedipus, and if it is Oedipus who furnishes the indispensable victim, it is not because he deserves it more than the other two – it is for a reason which, I believe, Sophocles suspects but does not mention.

Far from being the most significant elements, the accusation of patricide and incest, the tale of the Corinthian 'messenger', all this is too stereotypical to really carry any weight. Contrary to what Freud thinks, nothing in myths is more banal than patricide and incest. There must be something else behind the final decision, and that can only be an irresistible impulse of the crowd. It is the crowd that decides, which is to say mimesis itself; it settles on the king but could just as well have settled on one of the other two men who manage to escape completely unscathed.

The crowd is even more crazily mimetic than the individuals who compose it. The decision can only flow from mimetic impulse, from an irresistible movement of collective violence. Certain textual clues suggest that Sophocles indeed sees things this way. Why then does he not say so explicitly? The tragic author is not free to say what he wants. The meaning of myths is fixed once and for all and he must not modify it.

By suddenly snowballing against Oedipus, mimesis transforms the impossibility of deciding into a unanimous decision at the expense of a single victim, the king. The crowd decides but does not realize it has done so. This decision, which arises spontaneously, is convenient for everyone – with the exception of the victim, of course.

In sum, what I see behind myths is a spontaneous phenomenon that is not unknown to us today. We refer to it by borrowing the term 'scapegoat' from the Hebrew ritual of Yom Kippur. Originally reserved for the ritual victim, the same term is now used for any innocent victim selected by a troubled community to deliver it from its anxiety at little cost.

The modern meaning is not unrelated to the ritual one, but it designates a spontaneous phenomenon. Mimesis intensifies within a group in crisis and, when it reaches a paroxysm, it stops dividing those it contaminates and becomes cumulative, snowballing against a member of the community such as Oedipus. The scapegoat ends up being unanimously expelled or lynched, at which point the violence comes to a halt. Ultimately appearing responsible for both the eruption of violence and its interruption, the scapegoat is perceived first as a fearsome threat and then as a source of succor. The archaic idea of the divine is rooted, I believe, in speculations inspired by this phenomenon.

I have been much reproached for turning from literary criticism to a subject as worn-out and wearisome as archaic religion. My critics have ascribed to me the ambition of building a system 'in the nineteenth-century sense'. This is not what I set out to do at all. In reality, my objective was always to go as far as I could in the exploration of mimetic desire and nothing more. I cannot help it if this exploration progressively led me first to mimetic crises and then to victimage mechanisms and sacrificial rituals – and thus to a definition of human cultures and religions as so many efforts to discipline mimetic rivalries and keep them from destroying the whole community. The only exception is the Biblical and Christian tradition and the modern world which sprang from it, and which alone sought to abolish blood sacrifices.

Far from being encyclopedic like the systems constructed by Hegel, Marx, and other nineteenth-century thinkers, my thesis deconstructs human culture, in a sense more radical than that of linguistic deconstructions. The violent structures of human societies are what it takes apart, scapegoating phenomena are what it reveals. After operating spontaneously throughout human history because they were not understood, these phenomena are more and more easily seen through in our world and consequently less and less effective.

That is not the only or even the most important discovery made by mimetic theory. The most important in my opinion is the fact that we are not the first to undertake this deconstruction, the fact that we are always already preceded in this path by the Hebrew Bible and the Gospels.

Modern anthropology has tried to prove that the Biblical religions, Judaism and Christianity, are very similar to all the others. There is a seemingly solid argument in favor of this position. Just like mythology, the Bible and Gospels are full of scapegoats, of victimary phenomena that begin with the murder of Abel by Cain and keep recurring until the crucifixion of Jesus, the most visible and explicit of all.

This is perfectly true but in no way settles the question of the relationship between mythology and the Bible. What anthropologists, philosophers and other scholars failed to notice is that the Bible and the Gospels do not treat scapegoats in the same way that myths do.

Never do myths cast doubt on the guilt of their victims. We see that in the case of Oedipus, for example. The same goes for all the other 'crimes' of the same kind supposedly committed by the victims of a thousand other myths. Such myths are thus the voice of religious and cultural systems founded on the unanimous belief in the guilt of an ultimately divinized victim. Archaic religious systems are never anything else.

All these mythical systems work less and less well in our day or no longer work at all because, by revealing the innocence of the Suffering Servant or of Jesus, the great Biblical dramas and the Passion of the Christ not only reveal the innocence of the victims whose innocence they proclaim directly, but, indirectly, they also proclaim the innocence of all the anonymous victims falsely condemned and massacred in archaic religions and all human cultures in general.

Translated by Mark Anspach

A Crisis, a Plague, a Culprit:
On the Innocence of Oedipus

Mark Anspach: Everyone thinks they know who Oedipus is: he's the fellow who killed his father and married his mother. You, René Girard, you say: not so fast! Oedipus is the fellow who is *accused* of killing his father and marrying his mother . . .

René Girard: He is accused of doing it, but he is only a scapegoat. You have to take into account the context of the accusation: there is a crisis, there is a plague in Thebes, they are looking for a culprit.

MA: They are trying to identify the murderer guilty of causing the plague, which does not bode well. From our point of view, it is hardly rational to ask what *criminal* caused the epidemic. The question is already poorly framed.

RG: Of course, that's the wrong question – it can only set off a witch hunt. But this wrong question was asked every time a plague raged in the West. We see exactly the same phenomenon occur in the Middle Ages, for example. The problem was that nobody knew how to fight a plague effectively, while they knew perfectly well how to pin the responsibility on a victim chosen more or less arbitrarily. In a crisis, the crowd is ready to incriminate anyone.

MA: Oedipus is not really just anyone, he is the ruler of Thebes.

RG: He is the ruler, but since he saved the city, there is no good reason *a priori* to suspect him of bringing about its downfall. Oedipus is a foreigner when he arrives in the city. Basically, he happens to be there by chance. And if the story of his origins is wrong . . .

MA: That is, if he is not really the son of Laius and Jocasta . . .

RG: Then he's anyone.

MA: In my writing, I underscore the relative fragility of the hypothesis which makes Oedipus the son of the king and queen of Thebes.

Obviously, Sophocles does not give us proof of his innocence, but he is careful not to provide irrefutable proof of his guilt. A reasonable doubt remains. We cannot be sure of the incest, the parricide, or even the regicide. At the outset, let us recall, Oedipus is trying to find out who killed his predecessor on the throne of Thebes, and even there I believe the answer is far from clear. But ultimately, all these questions are secondary to the real issue: the cause of the plague. Now, even if Oedipus were an incestuous and parricidal son, even if he had killed his predecessor on the throne, he still would not be the cause of the plague.

RG: He would still be a scapegoat.

MA: By saying, 'Oedipus is a scapegoat,' you are stating something very simple, even obvious, but which no one dared to say so clearly before. You could be compared to the little boy, if I may, from the tale 'The Emperor's New Clothes.' Everyone knows that the crimes of which Oedipus is accused could not cause a plague, but you are the first to proclaim: 'The Emperor is naked, these accusations are preposterous.' When it comes to the Oedipus myth, or other canonical myths, we are reluctant to state certain obvious things. It's as if we let our critical mind slumber.

RG: Yes, the critical mind gives way to the literary tradition. This could serve as an introduction to reexamining a great many attitudes towards literary texts. Certain texts, whatever the source of their prestige, come to serve as models. And, from that moment on, all questioning stops.

MA: In a sense, you place yourself in the same literary tradition – without ceasing to question it – because you developed your anthropological hypotheses starting from an in-depth rereading of *Oedipus the King*. In the 1960s, you devoted a series of articles to Sophocles's play. Those texts mark the transition from the theory of desire proposed in *Deceit, Desire and the Novel* to the theory of religion outlined in *Violence and the Sacred*, a book where the reinterpretation of both the Greek tragedy and the Freudian complex play an important role. It may be useful from a pedagogical standpoint to take an example that everyone knows, but isn't there the risk of reinforcing the idea that the myth of Oedipus enjoys a privileged status?

RG: The risk certainly exists. If I were to write again, I would try a different approach. One must avoid allusions to a sacralized Oedipus whose status is taken for granted when it ultimately rests only on Freud's dubious constructions, however relevant they may be from a certain point of view.

MA: Since you have devoted so much attention to Oedipus and the debate with Freud, some have suggested that the father of psychoanalysis was a sort of model or mimetic rival for you . . .

RG: That is considerably overstated. Freud was not really a model for me, much less an oppressive one. I never sought to break free of Freud, never having had a 'Freudian' period, either. I arrived at my approach to Freud a little at a time. I always went back and forth while reading him: I would admire certain things and then at other points say to myself 'what nonsense!' when it came to the properly psychoanalytic part. But Freud's textual analyses, for example in the beginning of *Totem and Taboo*, are always brilliant. *Moses and Monotheism* is, I think, Freud's best book. It's really full of insight.

MA: Let us come back to the psychoanalytic part of Freud's work. For him the libido is the driving force of the system; for you it is rather the propensity to imitate. You obviously recognize the importance of sexuality, but it is not sexuality that shapes human relationships in your theory. I wonder if you would go so far as to deny the existence of infantile sexuality, which is so decisive for the Freudian conception of the Oedipus complex?

RG: No, I wouldn't deny its existence, but I would probably say that it starts a little later than Freud says.

MA: Freud does tend to ferret out sexual impulses just about everywhere.

RG: He talks, for example, about the homosexual desire of little boys for their father. I think that is complete nonsense.

MA: The problem is that Freud doesn't know what to do with the positive side of emulation, the admiration that accompanies rivalry. You have your own version of the Oedipal triangle where imitation of the father precedes desire for the mother. The operation of the mechanism, its dynamics, is different with you, but the outward schema resembles Freud's.

RG: Freud brings together all the elements of the mimetic triangle, he comes very close. I would say he ends up with a mimetic triangle that he doesn't want to make a triangle of. The separate elements do not really form a coherent whole.

MA: You did not rely at all on the Oedipus complex to construct the mimetic triangle. You developed your theory of desire in *Deceit, Desire and the Novel* without considering the figure of Oedipus. It was not until later, when you began your study of mythology, that you took on the Oedipus myth.

RG: Yes. If I were to start over, I would insist more categorically the Oedipus story is just one myth among many.

MA: You could have begun with a completely different myth, an exotic myth that holds no special significance for the Western reader, and then show its affinities with the Oedipus myth at a later stage. Indeed, that is precisely what you do in *Violent Origins*, where you analyze a myth which, at first glance, has nothing to do with the Oedipus myth, that of Milomaki.

RG: It's a myth of the Yahuna Indians of Amazonia.

MA: The hero of the myth is a little boy, a stranger who arrives in the group and arouses admiration at first in virtue of his wonderful singing. People come from far and wide to listen to him. But afterwards, things take a turn for the worse . . .

RG: Because, once they are back home again, the people who had listened to him eat fish, get sick, and die. The others put the blame on the hapless Milomaki and kill him.

MA: The curious thing is that the narrative makes the connection between the illness and eating fish. For us, that would suffice as an explanation: we would say that the fish must have gone bad. But for the community behind the myth, some *person* had to be held responsible. And who else but this foreigner who stands out from the crowd, even if, like Oedipus, he had been received with favor upon his arrival? In both myths, then, a newcomer is arbitrarily blamed for a fatal illness afflicting the community. Although there is no incest in the case of Milomaki, would you put this Amazonian myth in the same category as the myth of Oedipus?

RG: Yes, it is arbitrary to regard the Oedipus myth as absolutely a case apart.

MA: It's as if we classify myths by the accusations they contain. If the hero is accused of incest or parricide, people say that it is an Oedipal myth. If he is blamed for food poisoning, one might call it a Milomakian myth! But that means taking the content of such accusations at face value.

RG: The circumstances in which the victim is condemned vary, but not the functioning of the mechanism. It is the unanimous belief in the victim's guilt, whatever the nature of the accusations against him, that allows the group to regain its unity. In retrospect, the victim will also be endowed with positive qualities, being perceived as responsible not only for the crisis, but for its resolution.

MA: In this context, we should recall how the myth of Milomaki ends. He is burned alive, and then a magnificent tree grows from his ashes: the first palm tree of a species whose wood will be used to make flutes. The music of these flutes replicates the marvelous song of the deceased.

RG: There you have it – collective murder produces a beneficial effect! The victim emerges transfigured, he becomes an object of worship, like Oedipus after his expulsion from Thebes.

MA: In 2009, we witnessed the posthumous transfiguration of an individual who became famous for his marvelous singing when he was little, like Milomaki, but was later accused, if not of incest like Oedipus, then of pedophilia, a rather equivalent crime: I am thinking of Michael Jackson, who, without being the object of a collective murder, was certainly a victim of his own celebrity. It was quite striking to see this fallen idol, on the verge of bankruptcy, turn into a focus of worship across the planet when he died. It was almost as though people were grateful to him for having offered, through his very death, a solemn occasion for everyone to unite around him.

RG: It does look like a phenomenon of that kind. In Oedipus's case, his metamorphosis into a positive god is suggested by the fact that he becomes a religious hero in Colonus. It is an innovation of Sophocles, who was born in Colonus, to say that this city welcomes Oedipus in his exile. He is hailed there as a star; it's a bit like the arrival of a first-rate football team in a city that did not have one!

MA: *Oedipus at Colonus* is Sophocles's final work, performed only after his death: his last testament, if you will. In this play, Oedipus defends himself and complains that he was mistreated. In short, he presents himself as a victim.

RG: Oedipus's self-defense is somewhat reminiscent of Job's. But the refusal of the persecutors' perspective is incomplete in Oedipus. The real hero of victimary knowledge is Job. By persisting in telling the truth, namely that he did nothing to deserve his misfortunes, Job effects a small epistemological revolution. Sophocles falls short of this revolution even if he sometimes departs from a purely mythological viewpoint.

MA: You brought up Job; for my part, I would like to offer you a somewhat novel comparison between the Oedipus myth and another biblical story: the destruction of Sodom. In the case of the plague in Thebes, the divine punishment strikes all the city's inhabitants indifferently due to the presence of just one man held to be guilty. Seen in this light, the people of Thebes are innocent victims, too, but the fact that they must suffer for the supposed crime of a single individual doesn't seem to shock anyone. In the case of Sodom, on the other hand, Abraham demands that God spare the innocent inhabitants. The Lord agrees that the presence of only ten righteous individuals will cause Him to restrain His wrath. In the end, Sodom is destroyed all the same, for not even ten righteous persons can be found there; there is only one, Lot, a stranger in the city. However, the angels of God take it upon themselves to save this stranger with his family, and when he hesitates to leave, he is taken by the hand and escorted out by force. In a word, he is *expelled*, but the expulsion of Lot has the opposite meaning to that of Oedipus; it aims to save a man who has done no wrong, to avoid making him an innocent victim.

RG: The biblical text is indeed characterized by a constant concern to distinguish the innocent from the guilty. That boils down to a concern to avoid scapegoating. The same concern is absent from mythical texts. This difference seems essential to me. In the Judeo-Christian universe, the expulsion of scapegoats does not disappear, but it no longer gives rise to myths like that of Oedipus.

Translated by Mark Anspach and Cynthia L. Haven

The Founding Murder in the Philosophy of Nietzsche

I stand revealed by these days of debate* as a man of few ideas, so simple in their principle that perhaps they amount to no more than a single idea. It would in that case qualify as an 'idée fixe'. The suggestion has been made . . .

It is well known that critics 'project' their own pet ideas onto the texts they claim to be criticizing. They exhibit their 'discoveries' triumphantly and rhapsodize over their relevance without ever suspecting that they have retrieved unaltered the very thing they fed the machine in the first place to ensure its functioning.

I understand all too well, then, the wariness that the 'surrogate system' inspires. Confronted with the breadth and perfection of what I call its power of *ratissage*, of sweeping up everything around it, I sometimes cannot help wondering about it myself . . . I am sure you divine my meaning . . . Send any masterpiece you like my way, literary, cultural or religious, and it will be quite a miracle if I do not come back to you, a month or a year later, with my mimetic desire, my sacrificial crisis and above all – give the Devil his due – that bloody atrocity with which I am infatuated, the primordial, founding act of violence: the collective murder of the deity.

Forgive me this spell of melancholy. All around me, everything is 'renewing' itself and I, too, dream of renewing myself. But I never succeed. Where might one find *something else* to talk about? What text might grant access to *something else*?

An idea comes to me: Nietzsche. I must have recourse to Nietzsche.

* René Girard's talk was given at an international symposium in Cerisy, France, in 1983. We have omitted some introductory text.

People have been talking about him constantly for a hundred years and nobody ever detects in his work the slightest collective violence, the faintest trace of a founding murder. Maybe he will cure me of my monomania. This is one philosopher who always has fashion on his side. Between 1930 and 1950 he had a few bad moments, but, thanks to our valiant critics, he always extricates himself admirably. Here he is among us once again, all freshened up and reinvigorated. Yesterday's somber thinker has been replaced by a merry '68-style dissident; this is the playful, insouciant and frisky Nietzsche whom neither Lou Salomé nor Cosima would recognize.

That is what I need. Without further ado, I turn to a text that should be just what the doctor ordered for my case of religious obsession, aphorism 125 of *The Gay Science*. This is the capital text, it seems, on the subject of the definitive demise of all religion.

I shall begin at the beginning:

Haven't you heard about the Madman who, having lit a lantern under the noonday sun, ran to the marketplace and cried incessantly, 'I seek God, I seek God!' As many of those who do not believe in God were standing around just then, he provoked much laughter. Why, have we lost him? said one. Did he lose his way like a child? said another. Or is he hiding? Is he afraid of us? Has he gone on a voyage? or emigrated? Thus they shouted and laughed.

This crowd is already modern because it is atheist. But it does not recognize its atheism in the Madman's message and that is why, from the start, it makes fun of him. The orator is 'mad' only from the point of view of the crowd. Foreseeing the misunderstanding, he does his best, curiously, to aggravate it. He provokes his listeners with his strange symbolism of the lantern lit under the noonday sun. By polarizing the many against him the Madman hopes to arouse the curiosity of the rare individuals liable to comprehend him: those who find themselves exposed, like him, to the hostility of mediocre minds.

On one side there is the atheism of the crowd, vulgar atheism, and on the other the presumed atheism of the Madman. The author himself sets the rules for the game of interpretation. He suggests we reject the vulgar atheism and embrace another, more distinguished brand which must be carefully defined.

That is how all the interpreters understand this exordium. Unfortunately, they go searching for their distinguished brand of atheism everywhere in the works of Nietzsche save in the aphorism itself. It would be better at least to begin with the latter and switch to other texts only as a last resort. The explicators conscientiously read the first lines, those I have just read you myself, but the next thing you know they are off in a cloud of dust, never to be seen by the aphorism again. Take a look, for example, at *Holzwege*, the celebrated essay by Heidegger. In principle its focus is aphorism 125. In reality the philosopher talks of everything but that.

This is a bad example, and I reject it. I have always been told that the conscientious critic deciphers his text word by word, and that is the example I am going to follow. Let me resume reading at the point where I left off:

The Madman burst into their midst and pierced them with his gaze.

'Whither is God!' he cried. 'I shall tell you. <u>We have killed Him</u> – you and I! All of us are His murderers.'

Alas, alas. . . . There it is, the trap: the collective murder! Exactly what I was dreading. And I have no one to blame but myself. If only I had done what everyone else does. My accursed presumptuousness has sunk me. I wanted to distinguish myself, to escape other critics' routine, and straight away I fell back into my own. Luckily, I warned you. That is my only consolation. Your expressions tell me that your surprise is not total.

You have to admire the sly obstinacy of the *idée fixe*. Nobody ever pulled the collective murder out of this text before. I grab hold of it and, in less time than it takes a psychoanalyst to say 'Oedipus complex', there it is, like the head of John the Baptist on its silver platter. It is no longer a success, it is a fatality. If I tried to extract from the aphorism the thousand and one amazing things our colleagues extract from it, I would fail miserably. The collective murder follows me like my shadow.

Perhaps the fault lies with the translation. When one does not find what one is looking for in a text in a foreign language, the translator, as a rule, serves as the scapegoat. Why not also when one finds what one is not looking for? Let us examine the original German: *'Wir haben ihn getotet – ihr und ich! Wir alle sind seine Morder.'* The idea of underlining we have killed Him – is not the translator's nor even mine; it is Nietzsche's. And it is Nietzsche who insists on the unanimity of the murder, with a heavy hand that reminds me of my own: *'We have killed Him – you and I! All of us are His murderers!'*

The translation is depressingly faithful. I feel as if I were going mad; maybe I am the Madman himself reincarnated, the one in the aphorism, of whom no one ever speaks. Things had none the less begun well. But my opening moves cannot be trusted. There is a first stage in which I often succeed in concealing what I am up to, in deluding myself if no one else, but after a few lines, infallibly, I fall back into my infernal orbit, the collective murder – my own personal eternal recurrence.

I envy those who do not share my obsession. The murder is spelled out clearly in my oddly distorted vision of the aphorism. It is totally absent from theirs. How do they manage? Their recipe is simple. Never do they quote the formulas Nietzsche uses here: 'we have killed Him', 'all of us are His murderers.' They carefully refrain from doing so. Something much better is at their disposal. They all go about very sweetly repeating, 'God is dead . . . God is dead . . .' without adding anything whatsoever.

It seems quite innocent, but it completely changes the meaning of the text. The formula 'God is dead' has enjoyed and will always enjoy an extraordinary success in our universe. It possesses a virtue so powerful that a thousand successors to Nietzsche – but are they really his successors? – seize on it every day and channel it towards new fields so that they may make a name for themselves among men. This tactic has long yielded spectacular results. Thanks to it, metaphysics is dead. We all kept vigil at its bedside. Next we went into mourning for philosophy as a whole. And since around 1890, once a generation, we are solemnly informed that man himself is dead. Every time, the news causes an enormous sensation. Truth is long dead, and sartorial fashion more recently deceased. I have myself said that the death of God is in the process of dying, and doubtless I am now in the process of repeating it. Nobody escapes this obituary itch.

Nietzsche entitled his aphorism 'The Madman,' but one would scarcely suspect it. Intellectual opinion knows it only under its own title: 'God is dead.' If you want to hear 'God is dead, God is dead' repeated in marvelously grave tones, the slightest reference to aphorism 125 will suffice, or even to Nietzsche's work in general . . . It is the Pavlovian reflex of modernity. Nietzsche is taken to be the great prophet of the *natural* death of God.

The formula 'God is dead' figures not only in the text but in the title of a considerable number of essays. I have already mentioned the one that is most in vogue, that of Heidegger. It is entitled, of course, *Nietzsche's Phrase 'God is Dead.'* It caps an immense body of literature that maintains only the most nebulous relationship with the text on which it pretends to be commenting.

This famous 'death of God' is not, however, the invention of the commentators. It does need to figure somewhere in aphorism 125. The transfiguring power of my obsession alone will not be enough, I hope, to conjure it away. If I look for it, I will find it in the end.

Let us read what follows . . . Nothing . . . But yes; ten lines further down, there is at last, the sentence so often repeated . . . Even here it is repeated: 'Gott ist tot! Gott bleibt tot!' God is in no danger, thank God, of reviving. This formula is the happiest day of my life. It may yet make of me a critic like any other.

Equipped with this philosophical life-buoy, I resume reading from the delectable 'God is dead . . .!'

God is dead! God remains dead! And it is we who have killed Him. How shall we, murderers among murderers, comfort ourselves? What was the holiest and most powerful of all that the world has yet possessed has bled to death under our knives. Who will wipe this blood from our hands?

This is most dismaying. The more I try to flee my obsession, the more it pursues me! Renewal, where are you? 'God is dead! God remains dead!' It was perfect . . . why couldn't Nietzsche have left it at that?

For a hundred years the best minds turn aphorism 125 round and about in every direction and never do they come upon the horrible bogey that haunts me unceasingly. The second apparition is more sinister than the first. The blood spilling . . . the knife . . . It is all in very bad taste. Nietzsche, decidedly, does it on purpose.

Having written 'God is dead,' Nietzsche returns immediately and overwhelmingly to his idea – or maybe to mine, I no longer know which. One would say that he is seeking to prevent the kind of falsification to which his aphorism has always been subjected. He can guess his readers' desire to escape the murder. Shrewd as they are, they will take advantage of the somewhat too-neutral formula 'God is dead' which the author has imprudently handed them. To forestall this danger, Nietzsche insists once again on the murder. The caricatural, *Grand Guignol* quality of the description contradicts categorically the connotations that the habitual consumers of the aphorism have always conferred on 'God is dead,' its connotations that exclude collective violence.

'God is dead' is not incorrect in its context. In writing this sentence, Nietzsche says nothing that contradicts his message or in any way attenuates it. Of someone who has got himself murdered one can always say, among other things, that he is dead. There is no risk of making a mistake. The passive formula is always accurate. Whether someone who dies is murdered or not, the result is the same. But, death from natural causes being the most common sort, that is quite obviously what is understood when it is said simply that somebody has died without its being specified how.

In the aphorism, 'God is dead' is framed by two thunderous announcements of collective murder. Taken out of context, 'God is dead' slips quietly back into meaning the natural death of God. The murder is dropped as if by an inadvertent gesture which passes without notice. One must admire the efficacy of the maneuver, which is all the more deft for being ignorant of its own cunning. A quotation from Nietzsche is provided which is in appearance accurate and complete but in reality truncated, due solely to the fact that it is emphasized separately, made into the title of the aphorism. The 'God is dead' which circulates in this world does not sum up the Madman's words, it grossly falsifies them.

For the philosophy of the Enlightenment, God can only die a natural death. Once the naive period of humanity is behind us religion ceases to be 'credible,' as we say these days. Rationalist optimism is supposed to be long dead, fallen victim in principle to the epidemic triggered by the death of God. In reality, it survives in the very idea of a God who dies of senile exhaustion. This first idea supposes a second: modern atheism is more *reasonable* than its predecessor, religion. For beings who have attained the 'maturity' on which we pride ourselves, such atheism alone is truly 'credible.' Other beliefs are purely medieval, not to say antediluvian.

The 'death of God' maneuver evacuates the Nietzschean idea to return on tiptoe to the easy idea, the banal idea, the *vulgar* idea. Nietzsche is careful not to cross his t's. Part of him fully enjoys being the misunderstood madman. The aphorism lays a kind of trap for us which everyone identifies but falls into all the same: the trap of vulgar atheism.

The real difference between the crowd's atheism and the Madman's thinking is none other than the difference between death and murder.

Through the intermediary of the formula 'God is dead,' all those who start out by making fun of the Madman end up co-opting the aphorism and cutting it down to the size of their own thinking. They claim to distance themselves from the vulgar atheism but then reinstall it serenely in the very text which repudiates it, with a mighty helping hand from the incantatory formula 'God is dead . . . God is dead.'

If the interpreters quote only the first lines of the aphorism that is because, in the rest, there is no longer any question of anything but collective murder. At the first appearance of the latter everyone runs away, like the disciples at the time of the Passion. And the same reasons which render this rout universal render it invisible to those who participate in it. Insist on the murder and you will immediately be taken for a 'madman.' It happens to me all the time . . .

You see . . . my obsession has triumphed. I have renounced resisting it. You can expect to see the rest of the aphorism blend itself into the rest of my system. You are familiar with all that, and I will spare you my commentary. The theory has its own ideas, and I will let it lead the way all by itself.

What does it demand, this theory, *before* the collective murder? The sacrificial crisis, of course, the abolition of differences. All that figures in the aphorism, but *after* the initial announcement of the murder. The crisis first appears as a consequence of this murder, not as a preliminary condition. That is a small anomaly, and I beg you to excuse it. In any case it is quickly rectified. *After* the sacrificial crisis comes the second announcement, the one I have just read to you, and in relation to this one our sacrificial crisis finds itself back where it belongs, right *before* the murder.

Let me read you the passage which appears between the two announcements, the one I skipped over a moment ago in the hope of arriving at a death that would not be the result of a murder:

But how have we done this? How were we able to drink up the sea? Who gave us the sponge to blot out the whole horizon? What did we do to unchain the earth from its sun? Where is the planet spinning to now? To what place is its movement carrying us? Far from all suns? Have we not tumbled into a continuous fall? A fall backwards, sideways, forwards, in every direction? Do high and low still exist? Are we not wandering as if across an infinite void? Do we not feel the breath of nothingness upon us? Is it not colder? Is it not night-time unceasingly and more and more night-time? Must we not light our lanterns even in the morning? Do we hear nothing yet of the noise of the gravediggers who have buried God? Do we smell nothing yet of the divine putrefaction?

We are often given *philosophical* commentaries on this text. It can be compared with Pascal. Two quite distinct infinities, the large and the small, still perpetuate the shadow of a fixed point, their point of intersection where man is situated. The spot from which we observe the real remains a kind of center. In our aphorism, even this ghost of a center has disappeared.

This state of affairs makes our aphorism very similar to myths, to rituals, to Greek tragedy. Everywhere, in 'primitive' texts, the collective murder is associated with the confusion of day and night, of the sky and the earth, of gods, men and animals. Monsters swarm. Everything begins with the abolition of differences, the monstrous twins, the 'evil mixture' of Shakespeare, the mixing of what should be distinguished.

It is indeed the sacrificial crisis described a thousand times, but no longer quite the old carnival masquerade, the inversion of roles and hierarchies during a brief festival period, strictly delimited. The affair appears more serious; all guideposts are gone, in time as well as in space. There is no longer either difference or deferral, no more horizon, no more fixed point anywhere to provide sense or direction. It is on the former God that the *humanization* of the real rested, and what little remains of this is in the process of rotting.

Everything is presented in the form of questions; no affirmation is possible. One is tempted to conclude that it is a version of the crisis that is 'more radical' because it is 'modern' and more modern because it is radical. But perhaps it is simply our own particular version, one we are incapable of relativizing. We cannot yet ritualize it . . . Maybe all we need is the collective murder once more . . .

We have our sacrificial crisis, we have our collective murder . . . To complete the cycle of violence and the sacred, we now need the return to the ritual order. Can one really demand that of an aphorism said to be devoted exclusively to the disappearance of religion in the modern world? It is doubtless asking too much, but you may count on the *idée fixe* to cause everything it needs to spring up around it.

The second description of the murder opens on to a passage that is the opposite of the one which followed the first description – in other words, it is exactly what we are looking for:

How shall we, murderers among murderers, comfort ourselves? What was the holiest and most powerful of all that the world has yet possessed has bled to death under our knives. Who will wipe this blood from our hands? What lustral water is there to cleanse us? What ceremonies of atonement, what sacred games shall we have to invent?

How can the lustral water, the ceremonies of atonement and the sacred games be defined, if not as ritual procedures rising out of the collective murder and so hard to distinguish from it to begin with, like the gesture of washing one's hands, that the description of the murder itself must be quoted again to be sure none of them is left out?

The murder is commemorated 'to comfort ourselves,' the drama is replayed to render the memory of the event tolerable by transfiguring it. And suddenly, we have before us a new religion. The destruction of the old religion culminated in the collective murder and the collective murder, through the intermediary of the rites, produces the new religion. Ritual reproduction and religious production are one and the same:

what sacred games shall we have to invent? Is not the greatness of this deed too great for us? Must we not become gods ourselves to appear worthy of such a deed? There never was a greater deed than this – and whoever is born after us shall belong, by virtue of this same deed, to a history superior to everything that history ever was until then!

Quite obviously, it is a question here of Zarathustra and of the superman, who are in the process of germinating in Nietzsche's thought. If the licensed Nietzscheans tell me that these themes must not be qualified as religious I will bow down low before their wisdom and take their word for it, but I am much too near-sighted, much too limited to the letter to go outside my aphorism. I want to hear nothing but the letter of the aphorism. It furnishes me with the exact word – 'gods' – at the precise moment when the theory of violence and the sacred requires it: 'Must we not become gods ourselves . . . ?'.

And that is not the end of it. The following passage brings us another cog in the mechanism of victimization, the paradoxical *misrecognition* (*méconnaissance*) of the murder by the murderers themselves:

Here the Madman fell silent and examined anew his listeners: they too were silent and watched him without understanding. Finally he hurled his lantern to the ground so that it broke and ceased shining. 'I come too early,' he said then, 'my time has not come yet. This tremendous event is still on its way, still wandering – it has not yet reached the ears of man. Lightning and thunder require time, the light of the stars requires time, deeds require time even after they are done, before they can be seen and heard. This deed is still more distant from them than the most distant stars – and yet it is they who have done it!'

The crowd knows nothing of the murder, yet it is itself the perpetrator. The commentators around the aphorism, like the crowd within the aphorism, fall back irresistibly into the attitude they seek to escape: vulgar atheism, that which consists in refusing the murder. The aphorism is therefore itself subject to the very type of misrecognition that the Madman denounces.

The natural death of God is the alibi of the murderers who deny the reality of their murder. How could we have killed the biblical God, they repeat, since He died without help from anyone, in the last stage of senility?

The only text constantly associated with 'the death of God,' the only truly memorable text, is aphorism 125. Other texts exist which genuinely say what the aphorism does not say; it is nevertheless the latter which is made to say it. Nobody is interested in the texts which genuinely speak of the death of God.

There is something surprising in the predilection of our atheists for a text which aims at subverting their own vision. Neither literary nor philosophical criticism can explain this paradox which in truth they do not see, convinced as they are that they respect the aphorism in extracting from it their mealy 'death of God.'

If this strange phenomenon is to be located and understood, it must be seen that the usage made of the aphorism is ritual in the very sense of which Nietzsche has just reminded us. The rite consists in reproducing the collective murder without recognizing the event reproduced. That is exactly the type of relationship which exists between the modern intelligentsia and the aphorism, but at the level of representation rather than of action.

The murder is indispensable to ritual practice as long as it remains unrecognized. To be made sacred, the text must conceal the collective murder in the precise sense of dissimulating it. It remains unrecognized. If you draw attention to it, it will be granted importance only on the plane of aesthetics or, better yet, of rhetoric. You will be told that its *language* confers on the aphorism a type of superiority which should not or cannot be defined with precision. The aesthetic quality is ineffable.

One must rid oneself of the murder, *but without eliminating it entirely*. It is therefore made into a dramatic and moving manner of speaking, the metaphor of a reality deemed utterly banal. In sum, the natural death of God alone appears real. One always comes back to that. Modernist tradition favors only those approaches destined to dissimulate the murder behind its harmless 'death of God.'

We maintain with Greek tragedy a ritual relationship analogous to this one. It passes for 'critical' but, in truth, nothing is less critical than the rite. The collective murder of Pentheus cannot be foreign to the fascination exercised by Euripides' *Bacchae*, but if you examine the matter too closely you transgress the imperative of dissimulation and your 'discourse' will not be 'acceptable.'

Aphorism 125 owes its places among us to a misunderstanding of which it is systematically the object. It fascinates for the same reasons as tragedy. It lets modern intelligence mime its own tragedy. One must burn one's fingers a little bit on the collective murder, but not too much. A century after the aphorism, the Madman's moment has not yet arrived. He will have to break his lantern one more time.

To exorcize the horrible murder, the veil of fashionable philosophies is thrown over it. The religious character of the operation is betrayed in the solemn, almost sacramental style that is unconsciously adopted as soon as reference is made to 'the death of God.' The ritual consumption is an inverted Eucharist.

The ritual process does not take only the text as its victim. It rebounds onto the person of Nietzsche himself; it is repeated in our relations with the author, in a weakened form, of course, as with all the rites of modernity. There is nothing original about it. It reproduces the classic schema of great men who serve as scapegoats in their own lifetime, the better to be converted into sacred figures after their death.

The process unfolds over two generations. The first curses the living geniuses, the second makes sacred the dead amid unanimous indignation against the murderers. Each generation believes it redresses the injustices of the generation before without committing equivalent ones. But it will itself appear to the following generation as the pitiless persecutor of its unappreciated great men. It is the old process of the primitive sacred which perpetuates itself among us while fragmenting and 'deferring' itself more and more. This is the process which was defined for the first time in the lightning words of the famous 'Curses against the Pharisees':

Woe unto you, scribes and Pharisees, hypocrites! Because ye build the tombs of the prophets, and garnish the sepulchres of the righteous, And say, If we had been in the days of our fathers, we would not have been partakers with them in the blood of the prophets. Wherefore ye be witnesses unto yourselves, that ye are the children of them which killed the prophets. Fill ye up then the measure of your fathers. (Matthew 23:29–32)

The posthumous sanctification does not bring genuine understanding. The way in which the crowd greets the Madman's message can be read as a sketch of the twofold process of persecution and sanctification which the Nietzsche of *The Gay Science* has begun to undergo.

The opening gibes give way, after the Madman's speech, to an embarrassed but already respectful silence. The crowd still does not understand the message but it is transfixed by the strange eloquence of the messenger; it is already ripe for veneration.

Elsewhere than in the aphorism, Nietzsche reveals clearly the ritual character of his relations with the public. Not without coquetry he protests against his future canonization, but he prepares the way for it by setting out to become a living scandal. He behaves like a proper sacrificial beast. He spontaneously, or rather mimetically, commits provocations which render him fully 'sacrificeable' to begin with, and thus canonizable later. The fact that Nietzsche voluntarily cooperates with the sacrificial system for which he serves as victim does not keep him from suffering terribly. In the language of pious biographers, that is called scorning immediate success for true glory.

The requirement for transgression, preliminary to immolation, appears aberrant and unintelligible to us when we observe it in the context of human sacrifice 'in the strict sense,' yet it figures in the literary rites which moderns play out themselves every time they canonize a 'damned' poet or demented philosopher. The process remains rooted in the collective murder which it reproduces ritually in a form that is simultaneously caricatural and attenuated: 'This deed is still more distant from them than the most distant stars – and yet it is they who have done it.'

Nietzsche is an expiatory victim in the place of God. He is that madman who cannot announce the murder of God without exposing himself to murder, at least symbolically. The aphorism closes on a collective expulsion of the Madman that reproduces, one more time, the original matrix of all religion:

The story has it that same day the Madman entered different churches in which he intoned his *Requiem aeternam Deo*. Thrown out and enjoined to explain himself, he retorted incessantly, 'What good are these churches, if they are not the vaults and tombs of God?'

From the remotest prehistory, through the Egyptian or Aztec pyramids, to all the cults of the dead in antique or primitive societies, the funerary and the religious have always been indistinguishable. All the tombs are temples and all the temples are tombs.

Notice that it is a liturgical chant which the Madman intones. The attitude presented as blasphemous, as negational of religion, is none other than the fundamental religious attitude. And the Madman is the object of a properly religious expulsion. It is impossible to call up the forces which weaken or destroy religion without simultaneously calling up those which restore it. They are the same forces, as we have occasion to observe once more.

From start to finish, aphorism 125 is identical with the 'victimage theory of religion.' The Nietzscheans will unanimously call me mad, but the letter of the text vindicates me. The letter vindicates violence and the sacred. In order never to have to take account of it the letter is sometimes neglected completely; while sometimes, inversely, it is fetishized, which amounts to the same thing.

The perspective of violence and the sacred is needed to reveal a religious anthropology which is not even latent in the aphorism but fails to appear clearly because the text has been cornered by a philosophy that negates its true content.

In a few sentences, Nietzsche defines in rigorous fashion the passage from disorder to the sacrificial order through the mediation of the collective murder and the rituals which spring from it. One cannot kill the gods, any gods, without engendering new ones.

What is the relationship of Nietzsche himself to what is said here? I will spare you references to the 'unconscious.' The thinking expressed is real, but it is not quite like the rest of Nietzsche's thinking and does not necessarily correspond to all his opinions on the subject of religion. In Nietzsche's intellectual panoply, a philosophy that satisfies the desired conditions does, in effect, exist. It sometimes happens that Nietzsche designates it as 'the most elevated philosophy,' the philosophy of eternal recurrence.

By taking up the eternal recurrence in a philosophical perspective, one may tangle the problem up to one's heart's desire. One cannot resolve it, and often one does not wish to. One seeks to give the impression that fathomless depths lie hidden here, infinitely superior to the linear vision of history or to Judaeo-Christian 'simple-mindedness.'

This confusion must be replaced by the true context of the eternal recurrence in pre-Socratic thought or in post-Vedic India: the mythic and ritual context. The philosophy of the eternal recurrence is a reflection on the identity of the forces of life and death in antique and primitive religion. Every dissolution is a new creation, and vice versa. Everything is always in the process of beginning and finishing. The belief in an absolute end and beginning is the illusion of individuals who accord too much importance to the cycle of which they are a part. One must lift oneself above current history to see the totality of cycles and to recognize linear time as illusory.

In the second half of the nineteenth century ethnologists discovered the unity of the central drama at the heart of the world's religions: the extreme frequency with which violence appears, often in collective manifestations, in the myths and rites of the whole planet. They also perceived that the most violent rites, those which they judged to be the most primitive, were the ones which were structurally closest to the

Christian Passion. Everywhere the language of *sacrifice* is present. From Frazer to Marcel Mauss, without of course forgetting Freud, every thinker emphasized the symbolic analogies between primitive sacrifices and the Christian theology of sacrifice.

The influence of this ethnology combines with his knowledge of Greek mythology and pre-Socratic philosophy to enable Nietzsche to elaborate his synthetic vision of the eternal recurrence. The lyricism of the eternal recurrence should not keep us from seeing that the synthesis is faithful to antique sources and compatible with the rationalism of modern ethnology, and even the positivism which says: 'All religions resemble each other and in consequence all religions are of equal value.'

Nietzsche does not betray the traditional idea of the eternal recurrence. The aphorism demonstrates this. Life and death are reciprocally exchanged. The one passes eternally into the other. The idea would be as banal in Nietzsche as everywhere else if there were not something more in the aphorism, the idea of making the collective murder into the engine of perpetual movement. Before *Totem and Taboo*, this idea appears nowhere but here, I think, in such explicit form. Nietzsche precedes Freud by nearly thirty years.

If the gods are born from the collective murder which aphorism 125 describes, they die from its absence. They die from living too long in the peaceable universe which the regularity of worship ensures for their devotees. In a universe with no mimetic and sacrificial crisis, the gods appear useless and their existence becomes problematic. But their very disappearance plunges everything into a violence and disorder from which, finally, new gods arise.

If religion once again dies a violent death in our world it will certainly be reborn in another form, it matters little which. The crisis of the modern world is but an episode in the middle of an unending process. The prodigious importance which we attach to our history is due to the narrowness of our vision.

If it is permissible to see even in the decline of the Christian God a murder rather than the sempiternal death of the rationalists, the symbolic functioning will reproduce itself. Modern irreligion constitutes only a particular variation on a drama which stays essentially the same through every repetition. The decisive break which Christian rationalists, then deists, and then atheists have thought they recognized in our own history, the history of the modern West, is but an insignificant fold in the gown of Maya. Nietzsche writes his aphorism in a timeless and parabolic style which heralds that of *Zarathustra*.

The eternal recurrence crushes all claims to absolute singularity. It relativizes our world in the midst of an infinity of worlds. It contradicts the Judeo-Christian conception of a unique history dominated by the divine determination to ensure the salvation of humanity. There is no alpha and omega.

The weapon is so powerful that in truth it is hardly usable. It empties all oppositions of their content. It destroys all concrete polemics; it deprives cultural analysis of its piquancy. Ultimately it reestablishes between Dionysus and the Crucified an equality which most often Nietzsche abhors, even if he occasionally accepts its principle in very special moments of enthusiasm or resignation. An absolute weapon can really serve only as a means of deterrence. Nietzsche keeps it in reserve but almost never resorts to it.

Most often, what renders all religions similar and makes them all perpetually spring one out of the other is less interesting to Nietzsche than the opposite: what differentiates them, what renders pagan religions, symbolized by Dionysus, incomparable to Judaism and above all to Christianity.

The aphorism is a remarkable but veiled exception. Neither Dionysus nor the Crucified is mentioned, for they figure here on an equal footing. Heidegger is wrong to assert that only the Christian God is referred to in the aphorism. How could this be true, since it is a question of the eternal recurrence?

In the final period, in *The Anti-Christ* and above all in the *Fragments* of 1888, Nietzsche is no longer interested in anything but the irreducible opposition of two religions. But this opposition does not contradict the universality of the collective murder, as aphorism 125 defines it. Quite the contrary. It is grafted on to the identity of the central drama in the myth of Dionysus and in the Christian Passion:

Dionysus versus the 'Crucified': there you have the antithesis. It is *not* a difference in regard to their martyrdom – it is a difference in the meaning of it. Life itself, its eternal fruitfulness and recurrence, creates torment, destruction, the will to annihilation . . .

In the other case, suffering – the 'Crucified as the innocent one' – counts as an objection to this life, as a formula for its condemnation. (*The Will to Power*, no. 1052)

The difference is not in the martyrdom . . . In other words, the collective murder is present in both cases. But the positivists who deduce from this identity the equivalence of all religions neglect, as always, the role of interpretation. Collective violence speaks powerfully, but it does not say the same thing to those who inflict it and to those who suffer it.

Christianity represents the viewpoint of the *innocent* victim concerning a collective murder which Dionysus and all of paganism conceive from the perspective of the persecutors.

The viewpoint of the Passion is not only the opposite of that of Dionysus, it is an engine of war against the latter and against all paganism; it is an effort to discredit the collective murder, to ruin its basis, to destroy all non-Christian religions by showing that they are founded on an arbitrary violence.

Far from taking Christianity to be just another sacrificial religion, Nietzsche reiterates several times that its great fault is to 'prevent sacrifice,' to render impossible the acts of violence necessary to the smooth functioning of society. Nietzsche is very close to seeing the *mechanisms* and the *effects* of the surrogate victim, and above all to seeing that the Gospels see them and, seeing them, discredit and derail them. The Gospel reveals 'things hidden since the foundation of the world,' and through the intermediary of Nietzsche this revelation begins to become self-aware.

Christianity is always accused of justifying suffering, of glutting itself on it. Nietzsche sees quite well that nothing of the sort is true. It is pagan religion which 'affirms even the harshest suffering: it is sufficiently strong, robust and divinizing for that' (op. cit.). The greatness of Nietzsche is that he apprehends the truth of Christianity with incomparable force. Nietzsche's drama, and his madness, is his obstinate preference for Dionysus, his conscious choice of violence, pursued with too much intellectual rigor not to culminate in the atrocious texts of the *Twilight of the Idols* and other writings:

The individual was taken so seriously, he was posited as such an absolute principle, that he could no longer be *sacrificed*: but the species only survives thanks to human sacrifices . . .

The conception of aphorism 125 could not have been simple. It must have been transformed during the course of its elaboration. I would readily accept the supposition that Nietzsche started out from the modern situation. He was thinking first of all of the death of the Christian God, in a banal sense analogous to that of the aphorism's exegetes.

The death changes on the way into a murder by virtue of the Christian Passion, a true object of 'repression' that accomplishes its return. A moment ago, I pointed out an anomaly. The first death of God does not lead to the restoration of the sacred and of the ritual order, but to a decomposition of meaning so radical and irremediable that a bottomless abyss opens beneath the feet of modern man.

The aphorism gives one the impression that this abyss closes up again when the second announcement leads this time to the order of Zarathustra and the superman. The aphorism affirms the eternal recurrence. But it reveals its engine, the collective murder of arbitrary victims. It goes too far in its revelation. It destroys its own foundation.

The engine driving the cycles is of course the surrogate victim whose innocence, once revealed, prevents our believing in the soundness of the basis for other victims' suffering and, breaking thereby the mainspring of the eternal recurrence, leads us this time to the idea of an end without a new beginning.

The knowledge is not quite present in the aphorism, yet it is already there implicitly in the role of scapegoat which the Madman plays *because he reveals the truth of the collective murder.* The Madman is an image of himself which Nietzsche only appears to control. Like all images of himself, it transforms itself irresistibly into an *imago Christi* of unusual relevance.

Aphorism 125 proclaims the victory of the eternal recurrence over Christianity. But by the very fact that it founds the eternal recurrence on the collective murder, its true foundation which must remain hidden if it is to remain foundational, the victory is undermined, secretly subverted by the very Christianity over which it believes it has triumphed. At the first announcement of the murder, the world spins out of its orbit *because the collective murder has been revealed.*

The power of the aphorism derives from its hesitation between the solution that is adopted and the opposite resolution. I perceive in it a kind of muted premonition of the 'God of the Jews, you have won' which Nietzsche strives desperately to reduce to silence in the last fragments but which resounds from them none the less like the trumpet of the Last Judgment.

The two announcements of the murder are not quite on the same plane. They do not really have the same meaning; the first is infinitely formidable because it is the Christian one; the second alone carries the reassurance of the eternal recurrence. In the end Nietzsche understands that the revelation of the innocent victim marks the definitive end of the eternal recurrence. The first announcement cancels the second. The eternal recurrence is the past which Christianity has abolished. History from now on treads the bottomless spaces of Christian knowledge.

One finds the same ambiguity at the conclusion of the *Twilight of the Gods.* One does not know if the colossal finish marks the end of a cycle only, the promise of a thousand renewals, or if it is truly the end of the world, the Christian apocalypse, the bottomless abyss of the unforgettable victim.

Translated by Mark Anspach

Camus's Stranger Retried

I have always pictured Meursault as a stranger to the sentiments of other men. Love and hatred, ambition and envy, greed and jealousy are equally foreign to him. He attends the funeral of his mother as impassively as he watches, on the following day, a Fernandel movie. Eventually, Meursault kills a man, but how could I feel that he is a real criminal? How could this man have any motive for murder?

Meursault is the fictional embodiment of the nihilistic individualism expounded in *Le mythe de Sisyphe* and commonly referred to as *l'absurde*. Meursault is possessed by this *absurde* as others, in a different spiritual context, are possessed by religious grace. But the word *absurde* is not really necessary; the author himself, in his preface to the Brée-Lynes edition of the novel, defines his hero as a man 'who does not play the game.' Meursault 'refuses to lie' and, immediately, 'society feels threatened.' This hero has a positive significance, therefore; he is not an *épave*, a derelict; 'he is a man poor and naked who is in love with the sun.'

It is easy to oppose *L'étranger* to a novel like *Crime and Punishment*. Dostoevsky *approves* the sentence which condemns his hero, whereas Camus *disapproves*. *L'étranger* must be a work of innocence and generosity, soaring above the morass of a guilt-ridden literature. But the problem is not so simple as it looks. Meursault is not the only character in the novel. If he is innocent, the judges who sentence him are guilty. The presentation of the trial as a parody of justice contains at least an implicit indictment of the judges. Many critics have made this indictment explicit and so has Camus himself in the preface to the American edition of *L'étranger*. After presenting the death of his hero as the evil fruit of an evil collectivity, the author concludes:

'In our society, a man who does not cry at the funeral of his mother is likely to be sentenced to death.' This striking sentence is really a quotation from an earlier statement; it is labeled 'paradoxical,' but it is nevertheless repeated with the obvious intent to clear all possible misunderstanding as to an interpretation of *L'étranger* which, in a sense, is beyond questioning.

The American edition of *L'étranger* was published in 1955 and *La chute* in 1956. A fashionable Parisian lawyer named Clamence has made a great reputation defending those criminals whom he could, somehow, picture as victims of the 'judges.' Clamence has a very high opinion of himself because he has always sided with the 'underdog' against the iniquitous 'judges.' One day, however, he discovers that moral heroism is not so easily achieved in deeds as it is in words and a process of soul searching begins which leads the 'generous lawyer' to abandon his successful career and take refuge in Amsterdam. Clamence realizes that mercy, in his hands, was a secret weapon against the unmerciful, a more complex form of self-righteousness. His real desire was not to save his clients but to prove his moral superiority by discrediting the judges. Clamence, in other words, had been the type of lawyer whom Salinger's hero, in *The Catcher in the Rye*, would hate to become:

Lawyers are all right . . . if they go around saving innocent guys' lives all the time, and like that, but you don't *do* that kind of stuff if you're a lawyer . . . And besides. Even if you *did* go around saving guys' lives, and all, how would you know if you did it because you really *wanted* to save guys' lives, or because what you *really* wanted to do was be a terrific lawyer, with everybody slapping you on the back and congratulating you in court when the goddam trial was over . . . How would you know you weren't being a phony? The trouble is, you *wouldn't*.

The 'generous lawyer' wants to be *above* everybody else and to sit in judgment over the judges themselves; he is a judge in disguise. Unlike the ordinary judges who judge directly and openly, he judges indirectly and deviously. When anti-pharisaism is used as a device to crush the Pharisees, it becomes another and more vicious form of pharisaism. This point is a pertinent one, especially in our time, but it is not new and it would not be so striking if Camus, in order to make it, did not return to the themes and symbols of his earlier works and in particular of *L'étranger*.

In *La chute* as in *L'étranger*, we have a court, we have a trial, we have the accused and, of course, we have the inevitable judges. The only new character is the generous lawyer himself who defends his 'good criminals' just as Camus, the novelist, defended Meursault in *L'étranger*. The good criminals lose their cases, and so did Meursault, but the loss, in either case, is more than regained in the wider court of public opinion. When we read *L'étranger*, we feel pity for Meursault and anger at his judges, the very sentiments which the 'generous lawyer' is supposed to derive from his practice of the law.

The pre-*chute* Camus is quite different, of course, from his hero Clamence, but the two have a common trait in their contempt for the 'judges.' Both of them have built an intellectually complex and a socially successful life around this one hallowed principle. The contemporary advocate of literary 'revolt' is perpetually challenging social institutions and values, but his challenge, like that of the lawyer, has become a part of the institutions themselves; far from entailing any personal risks, his activities bring fame and comfort in their wake.

If Camus had conceived any doubts as to the validity of his ethical attitude and if he had wanted to express these doubts in another work of fiction, he could not have hit upon a more appropriate theme than that of *La chute*. All the earlier works of the author are based upon the explicit or implicit tenet that a systematic hostility to all 'judges' provides the surest foundation for an 'authentic' ethical life. *La chute* openly derides this tenet. It is natural, therefore, to conclude that the work contains an element of self-criticism.* It is no less natural to reject a conclusion which threatens all established ideas concerning Camus, the writer and the man.

* Of *La chute*, Jacques Madaule writes: 'En un certain sens, c'est comme une réplique et une réponse à *L'étranger*.' In 'Camus and Dostoevski,' La table ronde, CXLVI (1960), 132. See also the article of Quilliot in *Camus, A Collection of Critical Essays*, ed. Germaine Brée (Englewood Cliffs, NJ: 1962).

We live in an age of middle-class 'individualism' in which self-consistency is rated as a major virtue. But a thinker is not bound by the same rules as a statesman or a banker. We do not think less of Goethe because he repudiated *Werther*. We do not blush at the thought of Rimbaud repudiating his whole work, or of Kafka refusing to have his manuscripts published at the time of his death. Progress in matters of the spirit is often a form of self-destruction; it may entail a violent reaction against the past. If an artist has to keep admiring his own works at all times in order to remain admirable, Monsieur Joseph Prud'homme, the caricatural French bourgeois, is certainly greater than Pascal, Racine, Chateaubriand, or Claudel.

A writer's creative process has become a major, if not the major literary theme of our time. The lawyer of *La chute*, like the doctor of *La peste*, is, at least to a certain extent, an allegory of the creator. Can this assertion be denied on the grounds that it involves a 'naive confusion' between the author and his fictional work? Fear of the 'biographical fallacy' must not be an excuse to evade the truly significant problems raised by literary creation. This fear is itself naive because it conceives the rapport between an author and his work as an all or nothing proposition. When I say that Clamence is Albert Camus, I do not mean that the two are identical in the sense that an original document is identical to its carbon copy, or that a traveler is identical to the snapshot which figures on the first page of his passport. When a work is really profound, the existential significance of its characters and situations can never be stated in terms of straight biography, but why should it have to be so stated?

I may admit that Camus's past is present in *La chute* and still evade the most difficult consequences of this discovery. By placing the emphasis upon the political and social allusions, I may interpret the confession of Clamence as an attack against whatever is implied in the word engagement. Camus's quarrel with Sartre as well as his restrained public attitude during the last years of his life could provide some additional evidence for this view. If *La chute* is a reaction against the recent past only, is it not, as such, a return to the earlier past and a vigorous – if enigmatic – restatement of the positions defended in *Sisyphe* and *L'étranger*? This minimal interpretation is attractive; unfortunately, it rests not on internal evidence but on the implicit assumption that Camus's entire itinerary can and must be defined in terms of that *engagement/dégagement* polarity which reigned supreme a dozen years ago. The trouble with this polarity is that it excludes the one possibility which is actually realized in *La chute*, that of a change in vision radical enough to transcend both the *engagement* of *La peste* and the dégagement of *L'étranger*.

Engagement can rarely be distinguished from the other targets of satire in *La chute* because, from the standpoint of Clamence, it no longer constitutes a truly autonomous attitude. The first Camus, as well as the later advocate of *engagement*, can fit the description of the 'generous lawyer.' The only difference is that the 'clients' are characters of fiction in the first case and real human beings in the second. From the cynical perspective of Clamence, this difference is unimportant. To the generous lawyer, the clients are never quite real since they are not an end in themselves, but they are never quite fictional since they are a means to discredit the judges. Engagement represents only a variation on the theme of 'bad faith,' one of the many forms which a secretly self-seeking dedication to the downtrodden can assume. Behind the clients, therefore, we can see the characters created by the early Camus, such as Caligula, the two women murderers in *Le malentendu*, and, preeminently, Meursault, no less than the real but shadowy people whose cause a writer is supposed to embrace when he becomes *engagé*.

The passage in which Clamence describes his kindness to old ladies in distress and other such people is, probably, the one direct reference to engagement in *La chute*. And we may note that this boy-scoutish behavior is presented to us as nothing more than an extension of the lawyer's professional attitude. Clamence has become so engrossed in his legal self that he goes on playing the part of the generous lawyer outside the court; the comedy gradually takes over even the most ordinary circumstances of daily life. Literature and life have become one, not because literature imitates life but because life imitates literature. Unity of experience is achieved at the level of an all-pervasive imposture.

La chute must be read in the right perspective, which is one of humor. The author, tired of his popularity with all the *bien-pensants* of the intellectual elite, found a witty way to deride his quasi-prophetic role without scandalizing the pure at heart among the faithful. Allowance must be made for overstatement, but the work cannot be discounted as a joke or safely extolled as art for art's sake. The confession of Clamence is Camus's own, in a broad literary and spiritual sense. To prove this point, I shall turn first to *L'étranger* and uncover a structural flaw which, to my knowledge, has not been previously detected. The significance of that structural flaw will provide the evidence we need to confirm the reading of *La chute* as self-criticism.

On the purely phenomenological level, Meursault's condemnation is almost unrelated to his crime. Every detail of the trial adds up to the conclusion that the judges resent the murderer not for what he did but for what he is. The critic Albert Maquet expressed this truth quite well when he wrote: 'The murder of the Arab is only a pretext; behind the person of the accused, the judges want to destroy the truth he embodies.'

Let there be no murder and a good pretext to get rid of Meursault will, indeed, have been lost, but a pretext should be easy to replace, precisely because it does not have to be good. If society is as eager to annihilate Meursault as it is pictured by Maquet, the remarkable existence of this hero should provide more 'pretexts' than will ever be needed to send an innocent to his doom.

Is this assumption well founded? We ask this question in all awareness that we are abandoning, for the time being, pure literary phenomenology for common sense realism. If we feel, when we are reading the novel, that Meursault lives dangerously, this impression evaporates under examination. The man goes to work regularly; he swims on the beaches of the Mediterranean and he has dates with the girls in the office. He likes the movies but he is not interested in politics. Which of these activities will take him to a police station, let alone the guillotine?

Meursault has no responsibilities, no family, no personal problems; he feels no sympathy for unpopular causes. Apparently he drinks nothing but *café au lait*. He really lives the prudent and peaceful life of a little bureaucrat anywhere and of a French petit bourgeois into the bargain. He carries the foresight of his class so far that he waits the medically recommended number of hours after his noonday meal before he plunges into the Mediterranean. His way of life should constitute a good insurance against nervous breakdowns, mental exhaustion, heart failure, and, *a fortiori*, the guillotine.

Meursault, it is true, does not cry at his mother's funeral, and this is the one action in his life which is likely to be criticized by his neighbors; from such criticism to the scaffold, however, there is a distance which could never be bridged if Meursault did not commit a murder. Even the most ferocious judge could not touch a single hair on his head, had he not killed one of his fellow men.

The murder may be a pretext, but it is the only one available, and upon this unfortunate event the whole structure of meaning erected by Camus comes to rest. It is very important, therefore, to understand how the murder comes to pass. How can a man commit a murder and not be responsible for it? The obvious answer is that this murder must be an accident and many critics have taken up that answer. For Louis Hudon, for instance, Meursault is guilty of involuntary manslaughter at worst.* How could Meursault premeditate murder since he cannot premeditate a successful career in Paris or marriage with his mistress? Involuntary manslaughter, as everyone knows, should not send a man to the guillotine. This interpretation seems to clinch Camus's case against the 'judges.'

There is a difficulty, however. If Meursault must commit a crime, we agree that he must be an involuntary rather than a voluntary criminal, but why should he commit a crime in the first place? Accidents will happen, no doubt, but no general conclusion can be drawn from them or they cease, quite obviously, to be accidents. If the murder is an accident, so is the sentence which condemns Meursault, and *L'étranger* does not prove that people who do not cry at their mothers' funerals are likely to be sentenced to death; all the novel proves is that these people will be sentenced to death if they

---

* Louis Hudon, '*The Stranger* and the Critics,' *Yale French Studies*, xxv, 61.

also happen to commit involuntary manslaughter, and this 'if', it will be conceded, is a very big one. The accident theory reduces Meursault's case to the proportions of a pathetic but rather insignificant *fait-divers*.

Let a million devotees of *l'absurde* copy Meursault's way of life down to the last dregs of his *café au lait*, let them bury their entire families without shedding a single tear, and not one of them will ever die on the guillotine for the simple reason that their *imitatio absurdi* will not and should not include the accidental murder of the Arab; this unfortunate happening, in all probability, will never be duplicated.

The accident theory weakens, if it does not destroy, the tragic opposition between Meursault and society. That is why it does not really account for the experience of the reader. Phenomenologically speaking, once more, the relationship between Meursault and his murder cannot be expressed in terms of motivation, as would be the case with an ordinary criminal, but it is nevertheless felt to be essential, rather than accidental. From the very beginning of the novel we sense that something frightful is going to happen and that Meursault can do nothing to protect himself. The hero is innocent, no doubt, and this very innocence will bring about his downfall.

The critics who, like Carl Viggiani, have best captured the atmosphere of the murder reject all rational interpretations and attribute this event to that same *Fatum* which presides over the destinies of epic and tragic heroes in ancient and primitive literatures. They point out that the various incidents and objects connected with this episode can be interpreted as symbols of an implacable Nemesis.

We still invoke Fate, today, when we do not want to ascribe an event to chance, even though we cannot account for it. This 'explanation' is not meant seriously, however, when we are talking about real happenings taking place in the real world. We feel that this world is essentially rational and that it should be interpreted rationally.

An artist is entitled to disregard rational laws in his search for esthetic effects. No one denies this. If he makes use of this privilege, however, the world which he creates is not only fictional but fantastic. If Meursault is sentenced to death in such a fantastic world, my indignation against the iniquitous judges must be fantastic too, and I cannot say, as Camus did in his preface to the Brée-Lynes edition of *L'étranger*, that, in our society, people who behave like Meursault are likely to be sentenced to death. The conclusions which I infer from the novel are valid for this novel only and not for the real world, since the laws of this world have been violated. Meursault's drama does not give me the right to look with contempt upon real judges operating in a real court. Such contempt must be justified by a perfectly rational sequence of causes or motivations leading from the funeral of the mother to the death of the hero. If, at the most crucial point in this sequence, *Fatum* is suddenly brandished, or some other deity, as vague as it is dark, we must note this sudden disregard for the rational course of human affairs and take a very close look at the anti-social message of the novel.

If supernatural necessity is present in *L'étranger*, why should Meursault alone come under its power? Why should the various characters in the same novel be judged by different yardsticks? If the murderer is not held responsible for his actions, why should the judges be held responsible for theirs? It is possible, of course, to read part of *L'étranger* as fantasy and the rest as realistic fiction, but the novel thus fragmented presents no unified world view; even from a purely esthetic point of view it is open to criticism.

The fate theory looks satisfactory as long as the episode of the murder remains detached from the novel, but it cannot be integrated with this novel. Sympathy for Meursault is inseparable from resentment against the judges. We cannot do away with that resentment without mutilating our global esthetic experience. This resentment is present at the phenomenological level and we must somehow account for it even if it is not logically justified.

The search for the significance of Meursault's murderous gesture leads nowhere. The death of the Arab can be neither an accident nor an event inspired from 'above.' And yet it must be one of these two things if it is not voluntary. It is as difficult to ascribe an 'ontological status' to the murder as it is easy to ascertain its function in the story. Meursault, we found out, could never have been tried, convicted, and sentenced if he had not killed the Arab. But Camus thought otherwise, and he said so in the preface to *L'étranger*: 'A man who does not cry at the funeral of his mother is likely to be sentenced to death.' Is this an *a posteriori* judgment, deduced from the facts of the story, as everybody has always taken for granted, or is it an *a priori* principle to which the 'facts' must somehow be fitted? Everything becomes intelligible if we choose the second solution. Camus needs his 'innocent murder' because his *a priori* principle is blatantly false. The irritating cult of motherhood and the alleged profundities of *l'absurde* must not obscure the main issue. Let us translate the brilliant paradoxes of the author back into the terms of his story, let us remove the halo of intellectual sophistication which surrounds the novel and no one will take its message seriously. Do we really believe that the French judicial system is ruthlessly dedicated to the extermination of little bureaucrats addicted to *café au lait*, Fernandel movies, and casual love affairs with the boss's secretary?

One of the reasons we do not question the tragic ending of *L'étranger* is the lowly status of its hero. Little clerks are, indeed, potential and actual victims of our modern societies. Like the other members of his class, Meursault is vulnerable to a multitude of social ills, ranging from war to racial and economic discrimination. But this fact, on close examination, has no bearing on Camus's tragedy. The work is not one of social but of individual protest, even though the author welcomes the ambiguity, or, at least, does nothing to dispel it. The main point is that Meursault is the incarnation of unique qualities rather than the member of a group. The judges are supposed to resent what is most Meursault-like in Meursault. Unfortunately, the alleged uniqueness of this hero has no concrete consequences in his behavior. For all practical purposes, Meursault is a little bureaucrat devoid of ambition and, as such, he cannot be singled out for persecution. The only real threats to his welfare are those he shares with every other little bureaucrat, or with the human race as a whole.

The idea of the novel is incredible; that is why a direct demonstration is unthinkable. The writer wanted to arouse an indignation which he himself felt, and he had to take into account the demands of elementary realism. In order to become a martyr, Meursault had to commit some truly reprehensible action but, in order to retain the sympathy of the readers, he had to remain innocent. His crime had to be involuntary, therefore, but not so involuntary that the essential Meursault, the man who does not cry at his mother's funeral, would remain untouched by the sentence. All the events leading to the actual scene of the shooting, including that scene itself, with its first involuntary shot followed by four voluntary ones, are so devised that they appear to fulfill these two incompatible exigencies. Meursault will die an innocent, and yet his death sentence will be more significant than a mere judicial error.

This solution is really no solution at all. It can only hide, it cannot resolve, the contradiction between the first and the second Meursault, between the peaceful solipsist and the martyr of society; it is that contradiction in a nutshell, as revealed by the two conflicting words, 'innocent' and 'murder,' whose combination sounds unusual and interesting, somewhat like a surrealistic image, precisely because they cannot form a real concept and be fused together any more than a surrealistic image can evoke a real object.

The skillful narrative technique makes it very difficult to perceive the logical flaw in the structure of the novel. When an existence as uneventful as that of Meursault's is described in minute detail, without any humor, an atmosphere of tense expectation is automatically created. As I read the novel, my attention is focused upon details which are insignificant in themselves but which come to be regarded as portents of doom just because the writer has seen fit to record them. I sense that Meursault is moving towards a tragedy, and this impression, which has nothing to do with the hero's actions, seems to arise from them. Who can see a woman knitting alone in a dark house at the beginning of a mystery story without being led to believe that knitting is a most dangerous occupation?

In the second half of *L'étranger*, all the incidents recorded in the first half are recalled and used as evidence against Meursault. The aura of fear which surrounds these incidents appears fully justified. We are aware of these trifles as trifles but we have been conditioned to regard them as potentially dangerous to the hero. It is natural, therefore, to consider the attitude of the judges both unfair and inevitable. In a mystery story, the clues ultimately lead to the murderer; in *L'étranger*, they all lead to the judges. The murder itself is handled in the same casual and fateful manner as the other actions of Meursault. Thus, the gap between this portentous action and an afternoon swim in the Mediterranean or the absorption of a cup of *café au lait* is gradually narrowed, and we are gently led to the incredible conclusion that *the hero is sentenced to death not for the crime of which he is accused and which he has really committed, but for his innocence, which this crime has not tarnished and which should remain obvious to all people at all times, as if it were the attribute of a divinity.*

L'étranger was not written for pure art's sake, nor was it written to vindicate the victims of persecution everywhere. Camus set out to prove that the hero according to his heart will necessarily be persecuted by society. He set out to prove, in other words, that 'the judges are always in the wrong.' The truth deeply buried in *L'étranger* would have been discovered long before it became explicit in *La chute* if we had read the tragedy of Meursault with truly critical eyes. A really close reading leads, indeed, to questioning the structure and, beyond it, the 'authenticity' of *L'étranger* in terms identical to those of Clamence's confession. The allegory of the generous lawyer stems from the structural flaw of *L'étranger*, fully apprehended for the first time and interpreted as the 'objective correlative' of the author's 'bad faith.' Further evidence can be provided by the explication of some obscure passages and apparent contradictions in the text of *La chute*.

Here is a first example. At one point in the description of his past professional life Clamence remarks: 'Je ne me trouvais pas sur la scène du tribunal mais quelque part, dans les cintres, comme ces dieux que, de temps en temps, on descend, au moyen d'une machine, pour transfigurer l'action et lui donner un sens.' Readers acquainted with the terminology of post-war French criticism will remember that Sartre and his school accuse novelists of mistaking themselves for 'gods' when they warp the destiny of a character and when, consciously or not, they lead him to some pre-ordained conclusion. If we recognize the figure of the writer behind the mask of the lawyer we shall immediately perceive, in this bizarre statement, an allusion, and a very pertinent one, to the wrong kind of novelist. Can this same statement be made meaningful if *La chute* is not understood as an allegory of the writer's own literary past?

The image of the god is originally Sartrian, but the Greek element brings us back to those critics who have rejected all rational interpretation of the murder. They themselves are solely concerned with problems of esthetic symbolism, but their writings may well have helped Camus realize what he now implicitly denounces as the 'bad faith' of his own creation. The murder of the Arab, in a novel otherwise rational and realistic, is a *deus ex machina*, or rather a *crimen ex machina* which provides the author not with a happy ending but with a tragic one which is really precluded by the character he himself has given to his hero.

Here is a second example. Clamence tells us that he chose his clients 'à la seule condition qu'ils fussent de bons meurtriers comme d'autres de bons sauvages.' This sentence is absolutely unintelligible in a non-literary context. It is a thinly disguised reference to Meursault who plays, in his fictional world, a role similar to that of the good savage, a well-known pre-Romantic stranger, in the world of eighteenth-century literature. Here again, the image may have been suggested by Sartre, who, in his *Situations* article, defined *L'étranger* as a twentieth-century *conte philosophique*.

Like the 'bon sauvage,' Meursault is supposed to act as a catalyst; his sole presence reveals the arbitrariness of the values which bind the 'insiders' together. The *bonté* of this abstract figure is an absolute which no amount of *sauvagerie* can diminish. Meursault's excellence has the same quality. He is no less innocent and the judges no less guilty for punishing him, a confessed criminal, than if no crime had been committed. Innocence and guilt are fixed essences; they cannot be affected by the vicissitudes of existence any more than Ormazd and Ahriman can exchange their roles as the principle of good and the principle of evil.

In *La chute*, the author questions his own motives for writing fiction within the framework of this fiction itself. Meursault, as a 'client' of Clamence, has retreated into the background and become anonymous, but he is still a *dramatis persona*, and the structural incoherence of *L'étranger* must be expressed primarily in terms of his personal motivations. In order to denounce what he now regards as his own moral illusions and creative weakness, Clamence must say, as he does, that his clients were not so innocent after all. Their allegedly spontaneous and unmotivated misdeeds were, in fact, premeditated. If Camus is to abide by the rules of the fictional game initiated in the first novel, he must attribute to the hero the 'bad faith' which really belongs to his creator, and this is precisely what he does. The 'good criminals' killed, not for any of the ordinary reasons, as we are well aware, but because they wanted to be tried and sentenced. Clamence tells us that their motives were really the same as his: like so many of our contemporaries, in this anonymous world, they wanted a little publicity.

Meursault, however, is a character of fiction; responsibility for his crime lies, in the last resort, with the creator himself. The present reading would be more convincing if Clamence, instead of placing the blame upon his 'clients,' had placed it squarely upon himself. But Clamence is already the lawyer; how could he be the instigator of the crime without absurdity? Such transparent allegory would deal the last blow to *La chute* as art for art's sake and the present exegesis would be pointless. Let us apologize, therefore, for belaboring the obvious since Clamence does, indeed, present himself both as the passionate defender and as the accomplice of his good criminals. He does not hesitate to assume these two incompatible roles. If we reject the obvious implications of this inconsistency, we must dare condemn *La chute* as an incoherent piece of fiction.

This is a curious lawyer, indeed, who manipulates the court from high above, as he would a puppet show, and who discovers the guilt of his clients after they are sentenced, even though he himself had a hand in their crimes. We must observe, on the other hand, that this collusion with the criminals should destroy the image of the generous lawyer as a stuffy, self-righteous, upper middle-class man if the reader did not realize, subconsciously at least, that these criminals are only paper ones. The account of Clamence's law career is really a collection of metaphors, all pointing to 'unauthentic creation,' and Camus uses them as he sees fit, tearing as he goes the thin veil of his fiction. Clamence really suggests that the author of *L'étranger* was not really conscious of his own motivation until he experienced his own 'chute.' His purpose, which disguised itself as 'generosity,' was really identical with egotistical passion. *L'étranger* must not be read as a *roman à thèse.* The author did not consciously try to deceive his audience, but he succeeded all the better because he managed to deceive himself in the first place. The dichotomy between Meursault and his judges represents the dichotomy between the Self and the Others in a world of intersubjective warfare.

L'étranger, as the expression of egotistical values and meanings, forms a structure, a relatively stable 'world view.' Camus 'sincerely' believed in his and, consequently, in Meursault's innocence, because he passionately believed in the guilt of the 'judges.' The incoherence of the plot does not stem from an awkward effort to prove something which was only half believed or not believed at all. On the contrary, the author's conviction that the iniquity of the judges can always be proved was so strong that nothing could shake it. The innocent will inevitably be treated as a criminal. In the process of proving this point, Camus had to turn his innocent into a real criminal, but his faith was such that he did not perceive the tautology. We can understand, now, why the 'generous lawyer' is presented to us both as the sincere defender of his clients and as the accomplice of their crimes.

As long as the egotistical Manicheism which produced *L'étranger* held its sway over him, the author could not perceive the structural flaw of his novel. All illusions are one. They stand together and they fall together as soon as their cause, egotistical passion, is perceived. The confession of Clamence does not lead to a new 'interpretation' of *L'étranger* but to an act of transcendence; the perspective of this first novel is *dépassée.*

The rejection of the world view expressed in *L'étranger* is not the fruit of an empirical discovery but of an existential conversion, and it is, indeed, such a conversion which is described ironically, but unmistakably, throughout the novel, in terms of an ego-shattering 'chute.' This spiritual metamorphosis is triggered, so to speak, by the incident of the drowning woman but, basically, it has nothing to do with exterior circumstances. Neither can our own re-evaluation of *L'étranger* in the light of *La chute* rest on external evidence such as scholarly arguments and 'explications de textes,' however extensive the material proof available through these channels. The evidence will not be judged convincing until there is a willingness to go along with the self-critical mood of the creator. I, the reader, must undergo an experience, less profound to be sure, but somewhat analogous to that of this creator. The true critic must not remain superbly and coldly objective; he is the one most profoundly affected and transformed by the work of art; he truly *sympathizes*, suffers with the author. I, too, must fall from my pedestal; as an admirer of *L'étranger*, I must accept the risk of an exegetical *chute*.

A refusal to probe the confession of Clamence must not be rationalized on the grounds that it makes the literary reputation of Camus more secure. It is the reverse which is true. The fact that *La chute* transcends the perspective of *L'étranger* does not mean that, in a comparison with other works of recent fiction, the earlier work ranks lower than had been previously thought; it certainly means, however, that *La chute* ranks higher.

A gingerly approach to *La chute* obscures the true greatness of Camus. This work can already be defined as a forgotten masterpiece. Camus is praised to the high heavens by some, while others deride his role as 'directeur de conscience' of the middle class, but all this is done with only passing reference, or no reference at all, to *La chute*. Most people ignore the fact that Albert Camus was the first one to react against his own cult. Here and there, some voices are raised in defense of a truth which no one, it seems, is really eager to hear. Philippe Sénart, for instance, maintained in *La table ronde* (July 1962) that Camus refused to be the infallible pope of his own new neo-humanism:

Il ne voulait être que le *pape des fous* et il écrivait *La chute* pour se tourner en dérision et il s'accusait en se moquant. Clamence, avocat déchu, qui avait 'bien vécu de sa vertu,' qui se trouvait, avec coquetterie, 'un peu surhomme,' était, dans le bouge où il se déguisait en juge pour mieux rire de lui, le Bouffon de l'humanité, d'aucuns disaient le Singe de Dieu, comme Satan. Clamence, l'Homme-qui-rit, c'était l'Anti-Camus.

In one of the speeches pronounced when he received his Nobel Prize, Camus opened still a new line of investigation to the critics of his work:

Le thème du poète maudit né dans une société marchande (Chatterton en est la plus belle illustration), s'est durci dans un préjugé qui finit par vouloir qu'on ne puisse être un grand artiste que contre la société de son temps, quelle qu'elle soit. Légitime à son origine quand il affirmait qu'un artiste véritable ne pouvait composer avec le monde de l'argent, le principe est devenu faux lorsqu'on en a tiré qu'un artiste ne pouvait s'affirmer qu'en étant contre toute chose en général. (*Discours de Suede*)

Throughout the *Discours de Suede*, Camus dissociated himself from his own past as much as the occasion permitted. Here, he relates the type of literature he himself had practiced for so long not to an awe-inspiring philosophical tradition, as in *L'homme révolté*, but to French romanticism. He chooses as the archetype of 'révolte' *Chatterton*, the one work of Alfred de Vigny with which contemporary readers are likely to find most fault. He suggests that the tragic conflicts set forth in his own early works are really a *degraded* form of Vigny's romantic drama.

An earlier Camus would certainly have rejected this *rapprochement* out of hand in spite or rather because of its extreme relevance. *L'étranger* is really much closer to *Chatterton* than to the *conte philosophique* because the *conte* has a concrete content and it fights for definite objectives whereas *Chatterton* like *L'étranger* is primarily an abstract protest of the discontented ego. A work which is against everything in general is really against nothing in particular and no one actually feels disturbed by it. Like Dostoevsky's Underground Man, Meursault says: 'I am alone and they are together.' The work spells the final democratization of the romantic myth, the universal symbol of the separated ego in a world where almost everyone feels like an 'outsider.'

Chatterton, like Meursault, was conceived as a lonely figure, as a man who refuses 'to play the game.' Both men live in a world of their own which contrasts with the unauthentic world of other men. Both of them suffer and die because society makes it impossible for them to live according to their own lonely, infinitely superior ways.

There is a difference, however. When Chatterton is offered the same type of third-rate job Meursault holds, he refuses haughtily. In his eyes, this menial way of life is incompatible with his mission. We find it rather easy to interpret Chatterton's destiny in terms of romantic pride. Camus's hero appears very humble by contrast; he does not view himself as a man with a mission; he has no visible pretensions and he is ready to do whatever is necessary to sustain his mediocre existence.

This modest appearance really hides a more extreme form of romantic pride. Between Chatterton and other men there is still a measure of reciprocity, whereas none is left in the case of Meursault. Chatterton gives his 'genius' and the community must give him food and shelter in return. If society does not fulfil its share of the contract, the poet cannot fulfil his role as a great poet; the crowd grows spiritually hungry and the poet grows physically hungry. This general starvation is less tragic, no doubt, than Greek or classical tragedy and it is so because Chatterton is less deeply involved with his fellowmen than earlier tragic heroes. Real tragedy demands genuine involvement. It is somewhat ironic, let us note in passing, that a doctrine with such ethereal pretensions as 1830s romanticism could produce only alimentary tragedies of the Chatterton type. But this last meager resource is still truly present, whereas it is gone in the case of Camus. The poetic life cherished by Chatterton has become a part of the shameful game which the real individual must refuse to play in order to remain 'authentic.' *L'étranger* should not end in a Chatterton-like tragedy; it should revolve around the closed circle of a perfectly self-sufficient personality. An endless succession of *cafés au lait*, Fernandel movies, and amorous interludes should provide a scale model of the Nietzschean eternal return.

Romantic pride separates Chatterton from his fellow men; greater pride cuts Meursault off so completely that no tragic possibilities remain. In order to grasp this point, we may compare Meursault with another romantic in disguise, Monsieur Teste, the solipsistic hero of Valéry's youth. Monsieur Teste is infinitely brilliant and original but he alone is aware of his own worth. He is satisfied, like Meursault, with a third-rate job; he does not mind looking *quelconque* and remaining unknown. He will never be a *grand homme* because he refuses to sacrifice anything to the spirit of the crowd. Meursault is really a Teste without a PhD, a Teste who prefers *café au lait* to higher mathematics, a super-Teste, in other words, who does not even bother to be intelligent.

The idea of turning Teste into a martyr of society would have sounded ludicrous to Valéry. The only thing a solipsist is entitled to ask of society is indifference, and indifference he will get if he behaves like a Teste or a Meursault. Valéry was perfectly aware that, as individualism becomes more extreme, the possibilities offered to a writer shrink; and he rejected as 'impure' all types of dramatic literature.

L'étranger begins like *Monsieur Teste* and it ends like Chatterton. Unlike Valéry, Camus does not perceive or he refuses to assume the consequences of his literary solipsism. He resorts to the device of the 'innocent murder' in order to retrieve the structure of the 'poète maudit' or, more generally, of the 'exceptional man persecuted by society.' The *crimen ex machina* saves the author from the limitations of his own attitude.

Contemporary readers sense that there is something contrived in *Chatterton*, and yet Vigny did not have to turn his exceptional man into a murderer in order to present him as a martyr of society. *L'étranger* should appear even more contrived, but we do not understand the disturbing role which violence plays in it, probably because the novel is the latest successful formulation of the myth of the romantic self.

Chatterton already prefers to be persecuted rather than ignored, but we cannot prove the point because it is plausible that society will prevent a poet from fulfilling his destiny as a poet. In the case of Meursault, this same preference for egotistical martyrdom can be proven, because it is not plausible that society will prevent a little bureaucrat from fulfilling his destiny as a little bureaucrat. Camus takes his hero out of society with one hand only to put him back with the other. He wants Meursault to be a solipsist, then turns him into the hero of a trial, that quintessence of diseased human relations in our modern society.

Why does Camus crave solitude and society at the same time; why is he both repelled and fascinated by *les autres*? The contradiction is really inherent in the romantic personality. The romantic does not want to be alone, but to be seen alone. In *Crime and Punishment*, Dostoevsky shows that solitary dreams and the 'trial' are the two inseparable facets, the dialectically related 'moments' of the romantic consciousness. But this proud consciousness refuses to acknowledge openly the fascination it feels for the others. In the days of Vigny a discreet return to society was still possible because a few bridges were left between the individualist and his fellow men. The 'mission of the poet' was one, romantic love another. Camus has destroyed these last bridges because the urge to be alone is stronger in him than ever before. But the unacknowledged urge to return to other men is also stronger than ever. And this second urge can no longer be satisfied within the context created by the first.

The murder is really a secret effort to re-establish contact with humanity. It reveals an ambivalence which is present in all art with solipsistic tendencies but which has probably never been so visibly written into the structure of a work. This contradiction is also present in *Monsieur Teste* because it can never be eliminated completely. Monsieur Teste lives and dies alone, but not so much alone that we, the readers, are left in the dark about his superhuman and invisible qualities. The egotistical *Deus* is never so *absconditus* that it does not have its priests and mediators. The ambiguous narrator plays the part of the 'innocent murderer' in *L'étranger*. He is an artificial bridge between the solipsist and ordinary mortals. He is close enough to Teste to understand him and close enough to us to write for us. Such a man, by definition, should not exist and the work should never have been written. Valéry was so aware of it that he remained silent for twenty years after writing *Monsieur Teste*.

Camus, too, should be silent and he is at least partly aware of it since, in *Sisyphe*, he discusses literature and concludes that it is a fitting pastime for the knight-errant of *l'absurde* – provided, of course, it is not oriented to *les autres*. This *a posteriori* justification must be read primarily as evidence that the problem was a significant and an important one for Camus at the time. The pure doctrine of solipsism is not in *Sisyphe* but in *L'étranger*. Meursault does not read or write; we cannot imagine him submitting a manuscript to a publisher or correcting galley proofs. All such activities have no place in an 'authentic' existence.

Both the young Valéry and the young Camus cherished literature; both knew that it offered an avenue of escape from their equally mediocre station in life. And yet both of them held views which made the practice of their art almost impossible. Romantic individualism becomes so exacerbated with these writers that it verges on a certain type of neurotic behavior.

We all know, outside literature, that certain people are too proud to acknowledge a situation as painful. These people may even do their utmost to perpetuate or even aggravate this situation in order to prove to themselves that it is *freely chosen*. The creation of Meursault certainly reflects an attitude of this type. The life of this hero is objectively sad and sordid. The man is, indeed, a derelict; he has no intellectual life, no love, no friendship, no interest in anyone or faith in anything. His life is limited to physical sensations and to cheap pleasures of modern mass culture. The uninformed readers – American undergraduates, for instance – often perceive this essential wretchedness; they grasp the *objective* significance of the novel because the *subjective* intention of the creator escapes them. The 'informed' reader, on the other hand, rejects the objective significance as naive because he readily perceives the subjective intention, and he feels very sophisticated – until he reads and understands *La chute*. Clamence alone is aware that there are two layers of significance, subjective and objective, and he picks the latter as the essential one when he states that his 'good criminals' were wretched people *at bottom*. The most lucid view justifies the most naive; the truth belongs to the reader who takes *nothing* or *everything* into account, and to no one in between.

The undergraduates quickly learn, of course, that it is not smart to pity Meursault, but they vaguely wonder, for a while, why his living hell should be interpreted as paradise. This hell is the one to which, rightly or wrongly, Camus felt condemned in the years of *L'étranger*. There are psychological, social, and even metaphysical reasons, as well as literary ones, for *L'étranger*'s mood of repressed despair. These were troubled times; opportunity was scarce; the health of the young Camus was not good; he was not yet a famous writer and he had no assurance that he would ever become one. He *willed*, therefore, as many did who came before and after him, the solitude and mediocrity from which he did not see any escape. His was an act of intellectual pride and desperation reminiscent of Nietzschean *amor fati*. Valéry's *Monsieur Teste* stems from a comparable experience in a world somewhat less harsh. A young man who feels doomed to anonymity and mediocrity is compelled to repay with indifference the indifference of society. If he is very gifted, he may devise a new and radical variety of romantic solipsism; he may create a Teste or a Meursault.

Even more relevant here than a purely psychiatric interpretation are the passages of *The Sickness unto Death* dedicated to what Kierkegaard calls 'defiance,' or 'the despair of willing despairingly to be oneself.'

. . . this too is a form of despair: not to be willing to hope that an earthly distress, a temporal cross, might be removed. This is what the despair which wills desperately to be itself is not willing to hope. It has convinced itself that this thorn in the flesh gnaws so profoundly that he cannot extract it – no matter whether this is actually so or his passion makes it true for him – and so he is willing to accept it as it were eternally. So he is offended by it, or rather from it he takes occasion to be offended at the whole of existence. . . . To hope in the possibility of help, not to speak of help by virtue of the absurd, that for God all things are possible – no, that he will not do. And as for seeking help from any other – no, that he will not do for all the world; rather than seek help he would prefer to be himself – with all the torture of hell, if so must be. . . . Now it is too late, he once would have given everything to be rid of this torment but was made to wait, now that's all past, now he would rather rage against everything, he, the one man in the whole of existence who is the most unjustly treated, to whom it is especially important to have his torment at hand, important that no one should take it from him – for thus he can convince himself that he is in the right.*

The absurd of which Kierkegaard is speaking, needless to say, is not Camus's *absurde*. It is rather the opposite of it, since it is the final rejection of nihilism, rejected by Camus himself and dismissed as facile optimism in *Sisyphe*. The young Camus thought he could dispose of Kierkegaard in a few sentences but Kierkegaard on Camus goes much deeper, paradoxically, than Camus on Kierkegaard: 'such self-control, such firmness, such ataraxia, etc., border almost on the fabulous. . . . The self wants . . . to have the honor of this poetical, this masterly plan according to which it has understood itself. And yet . . . just at the instant when it seems to be nearest to having the fabric finished it can arbitrarily resolve the whole thing into nothing.'†

This highest form of despair, Kierkegaard informs us, is encountered solely in the works of a few great poets and we perceive the bond between the Vigny of *Chatterton*, the Valéry of *Teste*, and the Camus of *L'étranger* when the philosopher adds: 'one might call it Stoicism – yet without thinking only of this philosophic sect.' The genius of Kierkegaard cuts through the maze of minor differences which help a writer assert his own individuality, thus obscuring the fundamental significance of his literary posture. The whole spiritual structure is grasped through a single act of intuition. The essential features are revealed, common, as a rule, to two or more writers. The following passage enables us, for instance, to account for the similarities between Teste and Meursault:

One might represent the lower forms of despair by describing or by saying something about the outward traits of the despairer. But the more despair becomes spiritual, and the more is the self alert with demoniac shrewdness to keep despair shut up in close reserve, and all the more intent therefore to set the outward appearance at the level of indifference, to make it as unrevealing

* Søren Kierkegaard, *Fear and Trembling and The Sickness unto Death* (New York: Doubleday, 1954), 204–205.
† Ibid., 203

and indifferent as possible. . . . This hiddenness is precisely something spiritual and is one of the safety devices for assuring oneself of having as it were behind reality an enclosure, a world for itself locking all else out, a world where the despairing self is employed as tirelessly as Tantalus in willing to be itself.*

This last reference might as well be to Sisyphus rather than to Tantalus. Camus's *Sisyphe*, like *Teste*, is a 'rationalization' of Kierkegaardian despair, whereas *L'étranger* is the esthetic, or naive and, as such, most revealing expression of that same despair.

Here again, we must not let the hollow specter of the 'biographical fallacy' interfere with our comprehension of an author's fundamental problems. We do not confuse the creator with his creation. The relationship is not a simple one. Meursault is the portrait, or even the caricature, of a man Camus never was but swore to be, at the end of his adolescence, because he feared he could never be anyone else. The scene with the employer is revelatory. Meursault, as we all know, is offered a trip to Paris and the possibility of a permanent job there. He is not interested. The incident has only one purpose, which is to demonstrate Meursault's total lack of ambition. And it does what it is supposed to do; it does it, in a sense, too well; it is just a little too pointed. Why should *any* little clerk with a penchant for sun bathing want to move to Paris, with its dreary winter climate? At the lower echelon, which is Meursault's, sunny Algeria offers the same possibilities for advancement as the French capital. As Meursault refuses, with studied indifference, to live in Saint-Germain-des-Prés, we can hear Camus himself protesting that he has no literary ambitions.

Camus left Algeria for Paris; he wrote and published quite a few books; he submitted, at least for a few years, to the various indignities which the fabrication of a *grand homme* demands. The conclusion is inescapable: Camus, unlike his hero, was not devoid of ambition, especially literary ambition. This truth is as obvious as it is innocuous, but it sounds almost blasphemous: we are still living in the atmosphere of puritanical egotism which fosters such works as *L'étranger* and which prevents us from reading them critically.

* Ibid., 206–207.

The urge to escape solitude was stronger than the self-destructive dynamism of repressed pride. But this urge had to prevail in an underhanded fashion. Camus could not contradict himself too openly. The style of the novel reveals how he managed to deceive himself. Rhetorical ornaments are systematically avoided; the author uses none of the gestures which serve to emphasize a good point. We feel that he is not looking at us and that he hardly unclenches his teeth. He rejects even the affectation of vulgarity and profanity which the preceding generation had adopted in an earlier attempt to destroy rhetoric – with the sole result, of course, of creating a new one. The famous rejection of the preterite – or of the present – the two tenses of formal narration, for the *passé composé* which is a conversational tense, amounts to an abandonment of all approved techniques of story telling. The author refuses to be a 'raconteur' who performs for an audience. His *écriture blanche* gives an effect of greyish monotony which is the next best thing to silence, and silence is the only conduct truly befitting a solipsist, the only one, however, which he cannot bring himself to adopt.

This style bears a striking resemblance to the style of Meursault's actions prior to the murder. We feel that someone, on some fine day, handed Camus a pen and a piece of paper, and Camus did the natural and mechanical thing, in such circumstances, which is to start writing, just as Meursault did the natural and mechanical thing to do, when you receive a gun, which is to start shooting. The book, like the murder, appears to be the result of fortuitous circumstances. The overall impression is that *L'étranger* was written in the same bored, absent-minded, and apathetic fashion as the Arab was murdered. We have a crime and we have no criminal; we have a book and we have no writer.

Camus and his hero have sworn to forsake all but the most superficial contacts with their fellowmen. Overtly, at least, they both kept their oaths. Meursault refused to go to Paris; Camus criticized writers and thinkers naive enough to believe in communication. But the oath was not kept so firmly that Meursault refrained from killing the Arab or Camus from writing *L'étranger*. A murder and a book are not superficial contacts but, in the case of the murder, the destructive nature of the contact as well as the casual way in which it was obtained make it possible to deny that there is any contact at all. Similarly, the antisocial nature of the book, as well as the furtive nature of its creation, make it possible to deny that the solipsist is really appealing to other men.

Camus betrays solipsism when he writes *L'étranger* just as Meursault betrays it when he murders the Arab. The close analogy between the murder of the Arab and the style of the novel is not difficult to explain; every aspect of the work bears the imprint of a single creative act which stands in the same relation to its own consequence, the book, as Meursault's behavior to his murder. The 'innocent murder' is really the image and the crux of the whole creative process. Clamence is aware of that fact when he insists that he, as a lawyer, had the same hidden motives as his clients. He, too, craved publicity but he did not have to pay as dearly as the actual criminals for the satisfaction of that impure desire. He should have shared in the punishment as he had shared in the crime, but he was acclaimed, instead, as a great moral leader:

Le crime tient sans trêve le devant de la scène, mais le criminel n'y figure que fugitivement pour être aussitôt remplacé. Ces brefs triomphes enfin se paient trop cher. Défendre nos malheureux aspirants à la réputation revenait, au contraire, à être vraiment reconnu, dans le même temps et aux mêmes places, mais par des moyens plus économiques. Cela m'encourageait aussi à déployer de méritoires efforts pour qu'ils payassent le moins possible; ce qu'ils payaient, ils le payaient un peu à ma place.

Camus does not want us to believe that his motives, as a writer, were those of a literary opportunist writing cheap best-sellers. From the higher standpoint of *La chute*, he realizes that his own involvement in the tragic conflicts represented in his work was rooted in his own ambitions and in that stubborn need for self-justification to which we all succumb. *L'étranger* is a real work of art since it can be apprehended as a single structure; its stylistic features are reflected in its plot and vice versa. We must not speak of the novel's unity, however, but of its consistent duality and of its radical ambiguity. How could the novel be one when its creative process is truly 'divided against itself'? Every page of the work reflects the contradiction and the division inherent in the murder; every denial of communication is really an effort to communicate; every gesture of indifference or hostility is an appeal in disguise. The critical perspective suggested by *La chute* illuminates even those structural elements which the esthetic approach makes its essential concern but which it ultimately leaves out of account because it isolates them from the content of the work and its many-sided significance.

Can we really understand the murder of the Arab, the structure of the novel, its style, and the 'inspiration' of the novelist as a single process? We can if we compare this process to certain types of immature behavior. Let us imagine a child who, having been denied something he wanted very much, turns away from his parents; no blandishments will make him come out of his retreat. Like Meursault, like the first Camus, this child manages to convince himself that his sole desire is to be left alone.

If the child is left alone, his solitude quickly becomes unbearable but pride prevents him from returning meekly to the family circle. What can he do, then, to re-establish contact with the outside world? He must commit an action which will force the attention of the adults but which will not be interpreted as abject surrender, a punishable action, of course. But an overt challenge would still be too transparent; the *punishable* action must be committed covertly and deviously. The child must affect toward the instruments of his future misdeed the same casual attitude as Meursault towards his crime or as Camus towards literature.

Look at Meursault: he starts mingling with underworld characters inadvertently and casually, just as he would associate with anyone else; the matter is of no real consequence since other people do not really exist for him. Meursault, gradually, becomes involved in the shady dealings of his associates but he is hardly aware of this involvement. Why should he care since one action is as good as another? The child's behavior is exactly the same; he picks up, for instance, a box of matches; he plays with it for a while, absent-mindedly; he does not mean any harm, of course, but all of a sudden, a match is aflame, and the curtains too if they happen to be nearby.

Is it an *accident*, or is it *fate*? It is 'bad faith' and the child feels, like Meursault, that he is not responsible. Objects, to him, are mere fragments of substance lost in a chaotic universe. The *absurde*, in the sense popularized by *Sisyphe*, has become incarnate in this child.

L'étranger was written and is usually read from the warped perspective which has just been defined. The secretly provocative nature of the murder is never acknowledged, and the reprisals of society are presented as unprovoked aggression. The relationship between the individual and society is thereby turned upside down; a lonely individual, Meursault, is presented to us as completely indifferent to the collectivity, whereas the collectivity is supposed to be intensely concerned with his daily routine. This picture is false, and we all know it. Indifference really belongs to the collectivity; intense concern should be the lot of the lonely and miserable hero. The real picture is found in the few truly great works of fiction of Cervantes, Balzac, Dickens, Dostoevsky, and, we might add, the Camus of *La chute*.

The truth denied in *L'étranger* is really so overwhelming that it comes out almost openly at the end of the novel, in Meursault's passionate outburst of resentment. Many readers have rightly felt that this conclusion rings more true than the rest of the novel. The resentment was there all along but pride silenced it, at least until the death sentence, which gave Meursault a pretext to express his despair without losing face in his own eyes. The child, too, wants to be punished, in order to express his grief without confessing its real cause, even to himself. In the last sentence, Meursault practically acknowledges that the sole and only guillotine threatening him is the indifference of *les autres*. 'Pour que tout soit consommé, pour que je me sente moins seul, il me restait à souhaiter qu'il y ait beaucoup de spectateurs le jour de mon exécution et qu'ils m'accueillent avec des cris de haine.'

The structural flaw in *L'étranger* becomes intelligible when the novel is assimilated to a type of behavior which has become very common, even among adults, in our contemporary world. Meursault's empty life, his sullen mood, his upside-down world, no less than his half-hearted and secretly provocative crime are typical of what we call 'juvenile delinquency.' This social aspect can easily be reconciled with the ultra-romantic conception of the self which underlies the novel. Observers have pointed out the element of lat-terday romanticism in juvenile delinquency. In recent years, some novels and films dealing openly with this social phenomenon have borrowed features from *L'étranger*, a work which, outwardly at least, has nothing to do with it. The hero of the film *À bout de souffle*, for instance, half voluntarily kills a policeman, thus becoming a 'good criminal' after Meursault's fashion. The theme of juvenile delin-quency is absent from *L'étranger* because the novel is the literary equivalent of the action, its perfect *analogon*.

L'étranger is certainly no accurate portrayal of the society in which it was created. Should we say, therefore, as the formalists do, that it is a 'world of its own,' that it is wholly independent from this society? The novel reverses the laws of our society but this reversal is not an absence of relationship. It is a more complex relationship which involves negative as well as positive factors and which cannot be expressed in the mechanical terms of the old realism or positiv-ism. It is a dialectical relationship which must be apprehended if we want to apprehend the esthetic structure itself. We have just seen that the only way to illuminate the esthetic structure of *L'étranger* as an integrated structure is to resort to the social phenomenon called 'juvenile delinquency.' *L'étranger* is not independent from the social reality it overturns, since this overturning is a social attitude among others and a very typical one. The autonomy of the structure may appear absolute to the writer at the time of his writing, and to the uncritical reader, but it is only relative. *L'étranger* reflects the world view of the juvenile delinquent with unmatched perfection precisely because it is not aware of reflecting anything, except, of course, the innocence of its hero and the injustice of his judges.

Camus wrote *L'étranger* against the 'judges' or, in other words, against the middle class who are his sole potential readers. Instead of rejecting the book as the author had half hoped, half feared, these bourgeois readers showered it with praise. The 'judges,' obviously, did not recognize their portrait when they saw it. They, too, cursed the iniquitous judges and howled for clemency. They, too, identified with the innocent victim and they acclaimed Meursault as a Galahad of sun-worshiping 'authenticity.' The public turned out, in short, to be made not of judges, as the author had mistakenly believed, but of generous lawyers like the author himself.

Since all the admirers of the early Camus share, to some extent, in the guilt of the 'generous lawyer,' they, too, should be present in *La chute*. And they are, in the person of Clamence's silent listener. The man has nothing to say because Clamence answers his questions and objections almost before they are formulated in our minds. At the end of the book, this man confesses his identity; he, too, is a generous lawyer.

Thus, Clamence is addressing each one of us personally, leaning toward me across a narrow café table and looking straight into my eyes. His monologue is dotted with exclamations, interjections, and apostrophes; every three lines we have an 'allons,' 'tiens,' 'quoi!' 'eh bien!' 'ne trouvez-vous pas,' 'mon cher compatriote,' etc. The style of *La chute* is the exact antithesis of the impersonal and antirhetorical *écriture blanche*. Gone is the false detachment of Meursault. We have shifted from the 'restrained indignation' of the generous lawyer, as Clamence aptly defines it, to the open theatricality of a self-confessed and yet insurmountable bad faith. The studiously cheap and cacophonic symbolism of *La chute* is a parody of the serious symbolic works of the past.

As he questions the authenticity of *L'étranger* and similar works, Camus questions the question itself. *La chute*, no less than *L'étranger*, is directed against all potential readers since it is directed against the lawyers in a world where only lawyers are left. The technique of spiritual aggression has become more subtle but its aim has not changed.

Why does Clamence point out to us that his new posture is still one of bad faith? He undermines his own position in order to prevent others from undermining it. After deriding the generous lawyer, he mockingly describes himself as a penitent-judge. Slyly anticipating his readers whom he knows to be adept at gleaning moral comfort from the most sinister parables, he gives a new twist to the now familiar serpent, hoping to keep one step ahead of everybody else in a game of self-justification which has turned into a game of self-accusation.

Let the judge repudiate judgment and he becomes a judge in disguise, a lawyer; let the lawyer repudiate the disguise and he becomes a penitent-judge; let the penitent-judge ... We are spiraling down the circles of a particularly nasty hell, but this more and more pre-cipitous 'chute' is perhaps not so fatal as it seems. The penitent-judge does not believe in his role half as much as the generous lawyer did. The conclusion of *La chute* is a final pirouette, as well, perhaps, as the image of what may happen to a world entirely given over to the lawyers and the penitent-judges.

The universal need for self-justification haunts all modern trial lit-erature. But there are different levels of awareness. The so-called 'myth' of the trial can be approached from several mutually exclusive perspectives. In *L'étranger*, the real question is that of the innocence and guilt of the protagonists. The criminal is innocent and the judges are guilty. In the more conventional ego-nourishing fiction, the crimi-nal is usually guilty and the judges innocent. But this difference is really secondary. In both cases, 'good' and 'bad' are rigid concepts; the verdict of the judges is challenged but not their vision.

La chute goes higher and deeper. Clamence is still busy proving that he is 'good' and that other people are 'bad,' but his systems of classification keep breaking down. The real question is no longer 'who is innocent, who is guilty?' but 'why do we, all of us, have to keep judging and being judged?' It is a more interesting question, the very question of Dostoevsky. In *La chute*, Camus lifts trial litera-ture back to the level of this great predecessor.

The first Camus did not realize how far-reaching, how pervasive the evil of judgment is. He felt that he was outside judgment because he condemned those who condemn. Using Gabriel Marcel's terminology, we may say that Meursault viewed evil as something outside himself, a problem that concerned the judges alone, whereas Clamence knows that he, himself, is involved. Evil is the mystery of a pride which, as it condemns others, unwittingly condemns itself. It is the pride of Oedi-pus, another hero of trial literature, always uttering the curses which result in his own undoing. Reciprocity between the I and the Thou asserts itself in the very efforts I make to deny it: 'The sentence which you pass against your fellow men,' says Clamence, 'is always flung back into your face where it effects quite a bit of damage.'

The outsider is really inside, but he is not aware of it. This lack of awareness determines the esthetic as well as the spiritual limitations of *L'étranger*. A man who feels the urge to write a trial novel is not really 'in love with the sun.' He does not belong to the sunny Mediterranean but to the fogs of Amsterdam.

The world in which we live is one of perpetual judgment. It must be our Judeo-Christian heritage, still active within us. We are not healthy pagans. We are not Jews, either, since we have no Law. But we are not real Christians since we keep judging. Who are we? A Christian cannot help feeling that the answer is close at hand: '. . . thou art inexcusable, O man, whosoever thou art that judgest; for wherein thou judgest another, thou condemnest thyself; for thou that judgest doest the same things.' Did Camus realize that all the themes of *La chute* are in Paul's *Epistles*? If he had, would he have drawn from the analogy, and from the answers of Paul, the conclusions which a Christian would draw? Nobody can answer these questions.

Meursault was guilty of judgment but he never found out; Clamence alone found out. The two heroes may be viewed as a single one whose career describes a single itinerary somewhat analogous to the itinerary of the great Dostoevskian heroes. Like Raskolnikov, like Dmitri Karamazov, Meursault-Clamence first pictured himself as the victim of a judicial error, but he finally realized that the sentence was just, even if the judges were personally unjust, because the Self can provide only a grotesque parody of Justice.

The universal dimension of *La chute* can be reached only through its most personal, almost intimate dimension. The two are really one; the structure of the work is one and its significance is one. Openly, at least, this significance is entirely negative. But the positive aspects are summed up in one sentence of the Nobel Prize acceptance speech. Camus opposes, in their order, his two fundamental attitudes, as a creator and as a man, leaving no doubt as to the personal significance of Clamence's confession:

L'art . . . oblige . . . l'artiste à ne pas s'isoler; il le soumet à la vérité la plus humble et la plus universelle. Et celui qui, souvent, a choisi son destin d'artiste parce qu'il se sentait différent, apprend bien vite qu'il ne nourrira son art, et sa différence, qu'en avouant sa ressemblance avec tous.

Shakespeare in Comedy and Tragedy

René Girard became interested in Shakespeare after watching A Midsummer Night's Dream, *probably the 1969 televised Royal Shakespeare Company production directed by Sir Peter Hall. His many essays, written in English, were a gift of love not only to the English bard, but to the language that had become his own.*

Myth and Ritual in Shakespeare: *A Midsummer Night's Dream*

'*I have* considered our whole life is like a *Play*: wherein every man forgetfull of himselfe, is in travaile with expression of another. Nay, wee so insist in imitating others, as wee cannot when it is necessary returne to ourselves; like Children, that imitate the vices of *Stammerers* so long, till at last they become such; and make the habit to another nature, as it is never forgotten.' – Ben Jonson, *Timber: Or, Discoveries*

The opening scene of *A Midsummer Night's Dream* leads the audience to expect an ordinary comedy plot. Boy and girl love each other. A mean old father is trying to separate them, with the help of the highest authority in the land, Theseus, duke of Athens. Unless she gives up Lysander, Hermia will have no choice but death or the traditional convent. As soon as this formidable edict is proclaimed, the father figures depart, leaving the lovers to their own devices. They launch into a duet on the impediments of love: age difference, social conditions, and, last but not least, coercion by those in authority.

The two victimized youngsters prepare to flee their ferocious tyrants; they plunge into the woods; Hermia is pursued by Demetrius, himself pursued by Helena, Hermia's best friend, whom, of course, he spurns. The first couple's happiness appears threatened from the outset, but the second couple, even from the start, insist on being unhappy by themselves, always falling in love with the wrong person. We soon realize that Shakespeare is more interested in this systematically self-defeating type of passion than in the initial theme of 'true love,' something unconquerable by definition and always in need of villainous enemies if it is to provide any semblance of dramatic plot.

It quickly turns out that self-defeating passion dominates the relationship of not just one but both couples, involving them in a four-way merry-go-round that never seems to allow any amorous reciprocity even though partners are continually exchanged. At first the two young men are in love with Hermia; then, during the night, both abandon that girl and fall in love with the other. The only constant element in the configuration is the convergence of more than one desire on a single object, as if perpetual rivalries were more important to the four characters than their changing pretexts.

Although the theme of outside interference is not forgotten, it becomes even more flimsy. In the absence of the father figures, the role is entrusted to Puck, who keeps pouring his magical love juice into the 'wrong' eyes. When Oberon rebukes Puck for his mistake, he does so with a show of emotion, in a precipitate monologue that ironically reflects the confusion it pretends to clear, thereby casting doubt upon the reality of the distinctions it pretends to restore:

What hast thou done? Thou hast mistaken quite,
And laid the love juice on some true love's sight:
Of thy misprision must perforce ensue
Some true love turned, and not a false turned true. [III, ii, 88–91]

Who will tell the difference between *some true love turned* and *a false turned true*? We may suspect a more serious rationale for the four protagonists' miseries, for the growing hysteria of the midsummer night. A close look reveals something quite systematic about the behavior of the four, underlined by more than a few ironic suggestions. The author is hinting at something which is never made fully explicit, but which seems cogent and coherent enough to call for a precise formulation.

The midsummer night is a process of increasing violence. Demetrius and Lysander end up in a duel; the violence of the girls' rivalry almost matches that of the boys. Their fierce quarreling certainly contradicts – or does it? – Helena's earlier expression of unbounded admiration for her friend Hermia:

Your eyes are lodestars, and your tongue's sweet air,
More tunable than lark to shepherd's ear,
When wheat is green, when hawthorn buds appear.
Sickness is catching. O! were favour so,
Yours would I catch, fair Hermia, ere I go;
My ear should catch your voice, my eye your eye,
My tongue should catch your tongue's sweet melody.
Were the world mine, Demetrius being bated,
The rest I'd give to be to you translated. [I, i, 183–191]

This is a strange mixture of quasi-religious and yet sensuous worship. The last line admirably sums up the significance of the passage. Desire speaks here, and it is the desire for another's *being*. Helena would like to be *translated*, metamorphosed into Hermia, because Hermia enjoys the love of Demetrius. Demetrius, however, is hardly mentioned. The desire for him appears less pressing than the desire for Hermia's being. In that desire, what truly stands out is the irresistible sexual dominance that Hermia is supposed to exert upon Demetrius and all those who approach her. It is this sexual dominance that Helena envies: 'O teach me how you look and with what art/You sway the motion of Demetrius' heart' (I, i, 192–3). Helena sees Hermia as the magnetic pole of desires in their common little world, and she would like to be that. The other three characters are no different; they all worship the same erotic absolute, the same ideal image of seduction which each girl and boy in turn seems to embody in the eyes of the others. This absolute has nothing to do with concrete qualities; it is properly metaphysical. Even though obsessed with the flesh, desire is divorced from it; it is not instinctive and spontaneous; it never seems to know directly and immediately where its object lies; in order to locate that object, it cannot rely on such things as the pleasure of the eyes and other senses. In its perpetual *noche oscura*, metaphysical desire must therefore trust in another and supposedly more enlightened desire on which it patterns itself. As a consequence, desire, in *A Midsummer Night's Dream*, perpetually runs to desire just as money runs to money in the capitalistic system. We may say, of course, that the four characters are in love with love. That would not be inaccurate; but there is no such thing as love or desire in general, and such a formulation obscures the most crucial point, the necessarily jealous and conflictual nature of mimetic convergence on a single object. If we keep borrowing each other's desires, if we allow our respective desire to agree on the same object, we, as individuals, are bound to disagree. The erotic absolute will inevitably be embodied in a successful rival. Helena cannot fail to be torn between worship and hatred of Hermia. Imitative desire makes all reciprocal rapports impossible. Shakespeare makes this point very clear, but for some reason no one wants to hear. The audience resembles the lovers themselves, who talk ceaselessly of 'true love' but obviously do not care to understand the mechanisms of their own feelings.

Metaphysical desire is mimetic, and mimetic desire cannot be let loose without breeding a midsummer night of jealousy and strife. Yet the protagonists never feel responsible for the state of their affairs; they never hesitate to place the blame where it does not belong, on an unfavorable fate, on reactionary parents, on mischievous fairies, and on other such causes. Throughout the play, the theme of outside interference provides much of the obvious dramatic structure; and we must suspect that it is not simply juxtaposed to the midsummer night which, in a sense, it contradicts: the two may well be in a more complex relationship of disguise and reality, never clearly spelled out and formalized, allowing enough juxtaposition and imbrication so that the play, at least in some important respects, can really function as two plays at once. On one level it is a traditional comedy, destined for courtly audiences and their modern successors; but, underneath, mimetic desire holds sway, responsible not only for the delirium and frenzy of the midsummer night, but also for all the mythical themes which reign supreme at the upper level.

The real obstacles are not outside the enchanted circle of the lovers: each of them is an obstacle to the others in a game of imitation and rivalry that is their mode of alienation, and this alienation finally verges on trance-like possession. The outside obstacle is an illusion, often a transparent one, a telltale disguise of the real situation, constructed so that it can serve as an allegory. It even happens that absolutely nothing has to be changed in order to pass from the truth to the lie and back again to the truth: the same words mean both the one and the other. Shakespeare loves to play on these ambiguities. I have already mentioned the love duet between Lysander and Hermia: most critics would agree that it constitutes a parody of fashionable clichés, and they are no doubt correct; but we cannot view this parodic character as sufficient justification in itself. The real purpose cannot be parody for parody's sake. There must be something more, something which Shakespeare definitely wants to say and which we are likely to miss because it will appear in the form of 'rhetoric.' In the duet part of that love scene, the first seven lines seem to mark a gradation which leads up to the eighth, on which the emphasis falls:

LYSANDER: The course of true love never did run smooth.
But either it was different in blood—
HERMIA: O cross! Too high to be enthralled to low.
LYSANDER: Or else misgraffèd in respect of years—
HERMIA: O spite! Too old to be engaged to young.
LYSANDER: Or else it stood upon the choice of friends—
HERMIA: O hell! To choose love by another's eyes. [I, i, 134–140]

The last two lines can only be read as one more 'cross,' the most relevant really, the one we would expect to see mentioned first in the present context. The reference to 'friends' is somewhat unexpected, but not so strange as to merit a second thought for most listeners.

But if we isolate these last two lines, if we replace the love mystique in the spirit of which they are uttered with the present context, the context of the preceding remarks and of countless Shakespearean scenes (not only in *A Midsummer Night's Dream* but also in almost every other play), another meaning will appear, a meaning more evident and infinitely more significant.

Everywhere in Shakespeare there is a passion which is primarily the copy of a model, a passion that is destructive not only because of its sterile rivalries but because it dissolves reality: it tends to the abstract, the merely representational. The model may be present in the flesh and strut on the stage of the theater; and it may also rise from the pages of a book, come out of the frame of a picture, turn into the worship of a phantom, verbal or iconic. The model is always a text. It is Othello's heroic language, the real object of fascination for Desdemona rather than Othello himself. It is the portrait of Portia which her lover chooses to contemplate in preference to the original. This metaphysical passion is a corruption of life, always open to the corruptive suggestions of mediators and go-betweens, such as the Pandarus of *Troilus and Cressida*. The paramount role that Shakespeare attributes to such desire, in an obviously calculated way, even in relationships where we may least expect it, is matched only in the works of such writers as Cervantes, Molière, or Dostoevsky. *O hell! To choose love by another's eyes.* Since the phrase is uttered in conformity with the ideology of 'true love,' surely appropriate to a royal wedding (the occasion of *A Midsummer Night's Dream*), the true Shakespearean meaning must dawn upon us, prompted by the events that follow but by a thousand echoes from all the other plays.

Mimetic desire remains unperceived even when it is most obvious. In the very process of being denied, displaced, reified, it still manages to proclaim its own truth. Almost every time they open their mouths, the lovers unwittingly proclaim what at the same time they ignore, and we generally go on ignoring it along with them. The midsummer night is a hell of the lovers' own choosing, a hell into which they all avidly plunge, insofar as they all choose to choose love by another's eyes. Hermia, talking about the turn of her love affair with Lysander has given her own life, naively recognizes that the hell is all hers, and that it was already there before the appearance of the parental and supernatural bugaboos that are supposed to be its cause:

Before the time I did Lysander see
Seemed Athens as a paradise to me.
O then, what graces in my love do dwell
That he hath turned a heaven unto a hell! [I, i, 204–207]

Shakespeare is making fun of us, of course. He seems intent on proving that you can say almost anything in a play as long as you provide the audience with the habitual props of comedy, the conventional expressions of 'true love,' even in minimal amounts, adding, of course, a ferocious father figure or two to satisfy the eternal Freudian in us. As long as the standard plot is vaguely outlined, even in the crudest and least believable fashion, the author can subvert his own myths and state the truth at every turn, with no consequences whatsoever. The audience will instinctively and automatically rally around the old clichés, so completely blind and deaf to everything which may contradict them that the presence of this truth will not even be noticed. The continued misunderstanding of the play throughout the centuries gives added resonance to the point Shakespeare is secretly making, providing ironic confirmation that the most worn-out myth will always triumph over the most explicit demythification.

If the subject persists in his self-defeating path, the rivalries into which mimetic desire inevitably runs must logically be viewed as glorious signs and heralds of the absolute that keeps eluding him. Mimetic desire breeds rejection and failure; it is rejection and failure that it must ultimately seek. The impossible is always preferred to the possible, the unreal to the real, the hostile and unwilling to the willing and available. This self-destructive character flows directly and automatically from the mechanical consequences of the first definition: *to choose love by another's eyes.* Are these consequences really spelled out in the play? They are in the most specific fashion, in perfectly unambiguous statements that somehow never manage to be heard; and even when they are noticed, a label is immediately placed on them, canceling out their effectiveness. The following lines, for example, will be labeled 'rhetorical,' which means that they can be dismissed at will, treated as insignificant. Recall that when Helena seeks the secret of Hermia's power over Demetrius, Hermia answers:

HERMIA: I frown upon him, yet he loves me still.
HELENA: O, that your frowns would teach my smiles such skill!
HERMIA: I give him curses, yet he gives me love.
HELENA: O, that my prayers could such affection move!
HERMIA: The more I hate, the more he follows me.
HELENA: The more I love, the more he hateth me. [I, i, 194–199]

It cannot be denied that there is a great deal of rhetoric in *A Midsummer Night's Dream*. Rhetoric in the pejorative sense means that certain figures of speech are repeated unthinkingly by people who do not even notice their meaning. The four protagonists of *A Midsummer Night's Dream* certainly are unthinking repeaters of modish formulas. But mere parodies of rhetorical vacuity would be themselves vacuous, and Shakespeare does not indulge in them. With him the most exhausted clichés can become bolts of lightning. When Helena calls Demetrius 'a hard-hearted adamant,' she speaks the most literal truth. Harshness and cruelty draw her and her friends as a magnet draws iron. The supposedly artificial figures of speech really describe the truth of desire with amazing exactitude. When an impeccably educated reader comes upon the lines, 'Where is Lysander and fair Hermia?/The one I'll slay, the other slayeth me' (II, i, 189–190), he feels a secret anxiety at the thought that a cultural monument like Shakespeare may be lapsing into less than impeccable taste. These lines are satirical; but, in order to be completely reassured, we have to know what the satirical intent is about. Shakespeare is not mocking a particular 'rhetoric' and a particular 'bad taste.' Considerations of 'style' are mainly relevant to professors of literature. It is rather the whole language of passion, with its constant borrowings from the fields of war, murder, and destruction, that Shakespeare is commenting upon. A book like de Rougement's *Love in the Western World* throws more light on the type of meditation that nourishes Shakespearean satire than all stylistics put together. Shakespeare is almost contemporary in his recourse to the debased language of degraded human relations. With us, however, debased language generally remains just what it is and nothing more; the work never rises above the mire it pretends to stigmatize, or else it immediately sinks gently back into it. Not so with Shakespeare. The interest of the so-called rhetoric is its frightening pertinence: the destiny it spells for the four lovers, the destiny they unthinkingly announce, is really the one that they are busily forging for themselves; it is a tragic destiny from which they escape only by the sheer luck of being in a comedy.

This ambiguous nature of 'rhetoric' is essential to the twofold nature of the play. As long as we listen as unthinkingly as the protagonists speak, we remain in the superficial play which is made up of 'figures of speech,' as well as of fairies and father figures. At the purely esthetic and thematic level of 'poetic imagination,' we operate with the same conceptual tools as Theseus and the lovers: good and bad metaphors, true love turned false and false turned true. We understand little more than the lovers themselves. If, on the contrary, we stop long enough to hear what is being said, a pattern begins to emerge: the disquieting infrastructure of mimetic desire, which will erupt into hysterical violence a little later.

One of the most striking features in the amorous discourse of the protagonists is the abundance of animal images. These images express the self-abasement of the lover in front of his idol. As he vainly tries to reach for the absolute that appears incarnated in the model, the lover exalts his successful rival to greater and greater heights; as a result, he feels degraded to lower and lower depths. The first animal images appear immediately after Helena's hysterical celebration of her rival's beauty:

No, no, I am as ugly as a bear,
For beasts that meet me run away for fear.
Therefore no marvel though Demetrius
Do as a monster fly my presence thus. [II, ii, 94–99]

We will be told once again that such images are 'pure rhetoric'; their source has been identified: most of them, it appears, come from

Ovid. This is true, but the existence of a literary source for a figure of speech does not necessarily imply that it is used in a purely formal and inconsequential manner, that it cannot be given a vital significance by the second writer. It can be shown, I believe, that the animal images are part of the process which leads from mimetic desire to myth; this process is a continuous one, but a certain number of steps can be distinguished which have an existential as well as a functional significance. Far from raising himself to the state of a superman, a god, as he seeks to do, the subject of mimetic desire sinks to the level of animality. The animal images are the price the self has to pay for its idolatrous worship of otherness. This idolatry is really 'selfish' in the sense that it is meant for the sake of the self; the self wants to appropriate the absolute that it perceives, but its extreme thirst for self-elevation results in extreme self-contempt, quite logically if paradoxically, since this self always meets and invites its own defeat at the hands of a successful rival.

Animal images are thus a direct consequence of the inordinate metaphysical ambition that makes desire mimetic. They are an integral part of the rigorous pattern I am trying to unravel; the law of that pattern could be defined by Pascal's aphorism, *Qui fait l'ange fait la bête* with Demetrius:

I am your spaniel, and, Demetrius,
The more you beat me I will fawn on you.
Use me but as your spaniel: spurn me, strike me,
Neglect me, lose me; only give me leave
(Unworthy as I am) to follow you.
What worser place can I beg in your love
(And yet a place of high respect with me)
Than to be usèd as you use your dog? [II, i, 203–210]

Partners in mimetic desire cannot think of each other as equal human beings; their relationship becomes less and less human; they are condemned to an angel–beast or superman–slave relationship. Helena's near worship of Hermia might be described, today, in terms of an 'inferiority complex.' But psychiatrists view their so-called complexes almost as physical entities, almost as independent and stable as the self they are supposed to affect. Shakespeare is alien to this substantial thinking; he sees everything in terms of relations. Helena's 'inferiority complex,' for example, is only the 'wrong' or the 'beast' end of her relationship with Hermia and Demetrius. Ultimately, everyone ends up with the same 'inferiority complex,' since everyone feels deprived of an absolute superiority that always appears to belong to someone else.

Being purely mimetic, this relationship is anchored in no stable reality; it is therefore bound to be unstable. The metaphysical absolute seems to shift from character to character. With each shift the entire configuration is reorganized, still on the basis of the same polarities, but reversed. The beast becomes a god and the god becomes a beast. Inferiority becomes superiority and vice versa. Up is down and down is up.

During the first scenes, Hermia, being worshiped by everyone, appears to be and feels divine. Helena, being truly rejected and despised, feels despicable. But then it is Helena's turn to be worshiped and Hermia feels like a despicable beast. After the initial moment of relative stability, the four lovers enter a world of more and more rapid reversals and inversions. The necessities of dramatic presentation force Shakespeare to be selective and somewhat schematic in his description of the process, but the principles at work are obvious. As soon as the midsummer night crisis begins in earnest, the animal metaphors are not only multiplied but turned upside down and jumbled together. As the reversals become more and more precipitate, we obviously move toward complete chaos. All this, of course, to the renewed chagrin of our guardians of 'good taste,' who do not see any purpose to this unseemly spectacle and view it as mere stylistic self-indulgence on the part of the author. The 'rhetoric' was bad enough before, but now it is going out of its rhetorical mind. Here is Helena, getting ready to chase Demetrius through the woods:

Run when you will. The story shall be changed:
Apollo flies and Daphne holds the chase;
The dove pursues the griffin; the mild hind
Makes speed to catch the tiger. [II, i, 230–233]

Reversal is so pervasive a theme in *A Midsummer Night's Dream*, as in most of Shakespeare's plays, that it finally extends to the whole of nature. Titania tells us, for example, the seasons are out of turn. Scholars assume that the weather must have been particularly bad in the year Shakespeare wrote the play; this, in turn, gives some clues to the dating of the play. It must be true, indeed, that Shakespeare needed some really inclement weather to write what he did; however, the bad weather serves a specifically Shakespearean purpose, providing still another opportunity for more variations on the major theme of the play, the theme of differences reversed and inverted:

> ... The spring, the summer,
> The childing autumn, angry winter, change
> Their wonted liveries, and the mazed world,
> By their increase now knows not which is which. [II, i, 111–114]

The very pervasiveness of reversal makes it impossible for commentators not to acknowledge the theme, but it also provides a means of minimizing its significance by shifting the emphasis where it should not be shifted, onto nature and the cosmos. This, of course, is exactly what myth itself does in its constant projection and expulsion of human violence. The nineteenth- and twentieth-century mythologists who asserted and still assert that myth is mostly a misreading of natural phenomena really perpetuate the mythical dissimulation and disguise of human violence. Shakespeare seems to be doing the same thing when he inserts his midsummer night into the poetic frame of a crisis of quasi-comic proportions. In that vast macrocosm, our four protagonists' antics appear as a tiny dot moved by forces beyond their own control, automatically relieved, once more, of all responsibility for whatever harm their even tinier components may be doing to one another and to themselves. Nature, in other words, must be included among other mythical excuses, such as the mean father and the fairies. Shakespeare certainly gives it a major poetic and dramatic role, in keeping with the principles of what I earlier called the surface play. This is true; but, as in the other instances, he also makes sure that the truth becomes explicit. The real Shakespearean perspective is clearly suggested immediately below the lines just quoted. Titania ascribes disarray neither to herself nor to Oberon nor even to both, insofar as they would remain serene divinities manipulating humanity from the outside, but to the *conflict* between them, a very human conflict, to be sure, which implies the same reversals of roles as the midsummer night and which duplicates perfectly the strife among the four lovers:

And this same progeny of evils comes
From our debate, from our dissensions;
We are their parents and original. [II, i, 115–117]

Reversals in nature are only reflections, metaphoric expressions, and poetic orchestrations of the mimetic crisis. Instead of viewing myth as a humanization of nature, as we always tend to do, Shakespeare views it as the naturalization as well as the supernaturalization of a very human violence. Specialists of the subject might be well advised to take a close look at this Shakespearean view; what if it turned out to be less mythical than their own!

The lopsided view that the lovers take of their own relationships keeps reversing itself with increasing speed. This constant exchange of the relative positions within the total picture is the cause of vertigo, the loss of balance which the four characters experience. That feeling is inseparable from the sense of extreme difference to which the same characters never cease to cling, even as this difference keeps shifting around at a constantly accelerating tempo. It is a fact, to be sure, that two characters who face each other in fascination and rivalry can never occupy the same position together, since they themselves constitute the polarity that oscillates between them. They resemble a seesaw, with one rider always going up when the other is going down and vice versa. Never, therefore, do they cease to feel out of tune with each other, radically different from each other. In reality, of course, the positions successively occupied are the same; whatever difference remains is a purely *temporal* one which must become smaller and, as the movement keeps accelerating, even tend to zero, though without actually reaching it.

Even though they persevere in difference (an evermore vertiginous difference to be sure, but difference nevertheless), the protagonists become more and more undifferentiated. We have seen that the seasons lose their relative specificity, but the true loss of differentiation comes from the crisis among men who are caught in the vicious circle of mimetic desire. Progressive undifferentiation is not an illusion but the objective truth of the whole process, in the sense that reciprocity becomes more and more perfect. There is never anything on one side of a rivalry which, sooner or later, will not be found on the other. Here and there it is exactly the same mixture of fascination and hatred, the same curses, the same everything. It can be said that mimetic desire *really works*: it really achieves the goal it has set for itself, which is the *translation* of the follower into his model, the metamorphosis of one into the other, the absolute identity of all. As the climax of the midsummer night approaches, the four protagonists lose whatever individuality they formerly appeared to have; they wander like brutes in the forest, trading the same insults and finally the same physical blows, all drugged with the same drug, all bitten by the same serpent.

The more our characters tend to see one another in terms of black and white, the more alike they really *make* one another. Every slightest move, every single reaction becomes more and more immediately self-defeating. The more these characters deny the reciprocity among them, the more they bring it about, each denial being immediately reciprocated.

At the moment when difference should be most formidable, it begins to elude not one protagonist but the four of them all at once. Characters dissolve and personalities disintegrate. Glaring contradictions multiply, no firm judgment will hold. Each protagonist becomes a masked monster in the eyes of the other three, hiding his true being behind deceptive and shifting appearances. Each points at the hypocrite and the cheat in the others, partly in order not to feel that the ground is also slipping from under him. Helena, for example, accuses Hermia of being untrue to her real self: 'Fie, fie! You counterfeit, you puppet, you!' (III, ii, 288). Hermia misunderstands and thinks Helena is making fun of her shortness:

Puppet? Why so? Aye, that way goes the game.
Now I perceive that she hath made compare
Between our statures; she hath urged her height,
And with her personage, her tall personage,
Her height, forsooth, she hath prevailed with him.
And are you grown so high in his esteem
Because I am so dwarfish and so low?
How low am I, thou painted maypole? Speak!
How low am I? I am not yet so low
But that my nails can reach unto thine eyes. [III, ii, 289–298]

C.L. Barber correctly observes that the four young people vainly try to interpret their conflicts through something manageably related to their individual identities, but they never achieve their purpose:

Only accidental differences can be exhibited. Helena tall, Hermia short. Although the men think that 'reason says' now Helena is 'the worthier maid,' personalities have nothing to do with the case. . . . The life in the lovers' part is not to be caught in individual speeches, but by regarding the whole movement of the farce, which swings and spins each in turn through a common pattern, an evolution that seems to have an impersonal power of its own.*

The time comes when the antagonists literally no longer know who they are: 'Am I not Hermia? Are you not Lysander?' (III, ii, 273).

Here it is no exaggeration or undue modernization to speak of a 'crisis of identity.' To Shakespeare, however, the crisis is primarily one of differentiation. The four characters lose a self-identity which they and the philosophers would like to turn into an absolute and which becomes relative for that very reason: it is made to depend on the otherness of a model. When Barber points out that Shakespeare fully intends for his characters, in the course of the play, to lose whatever distinctiveness they had or appeared to have at the beginning (which wasn't much anyway), he runs counter to a long

---

* *Shakespeare's Festive Comedy* (Cleveland, OH: Meridian, 1963), 128.

tradition of criticism, the whole tradition of 'realism' and of 'psychology.' Many critics do not find it conceivable that a writer like Shakespeare might be more interested in the undoing and dissolving of 'characters' than in their creation, viewing as they do the latter task as the one assigned to all artists of all eternity. Only the most honest will face squarely their own malaise and formulate the obvious consequences of their own inadequate principles: they blame Shakespeare for 'insufficient characterization.'

The question is truly fundamental. The whole orientation of criticism depends on it. It is usually the wrong solution that is adopted, all the more blindly because it remains implicit. I personally believe that the conflictual undifferentiation of the four lovers is the basic Shakespearean relationship in both his tragedies and his comedies.* It is the relationship of the four *doubles* in *The Comedy of Errors*; it is the relationship of the Montagues and the Capulets, of course, but also of Caesar, Brutus, and his co-conspirators, of Shylock and Bassanio, of all the great tragic and comic characters. There is no great theater without a gripping awareness that, far from sharpening our differences, as we like to believe, our violence obliterates them, dissolving them into that reciprocity of vengeance which becomes its own self-inflicted punishment. Shakespeare is fully aware, at the same time, that no theater audience can assume the full force of this revelation. Its impact must and will necessarily be blunted. Some violence will be made 'good' and the rest 'bad' at the expense of some sacrificial victim, with or without the complicity of the writer. There is no doubt that, in many instances, Shakespeare is a willing accomplice; but his is never an absolute betrayal of his own vision, because the differences he provides are always at the same time undermined and treated as quasi-allegories. An excessive appetite for 'characterization' and catharsis will take nothing of this into account: it will systematically choose as most Shakespearean what really is least so, at least in the form in which it is chosen. It will thus provide not only our realistic stodginess but

* See my *Violence and the Sacred*, trans. Patrick Gregory (Baltimore: Johns Hopkins University Press, 1977), 43–9.

also our romantic self-righteousness with the only type of nourishment they can absorb.

It is in a comedy like *A Midsummer Night's Dream*, if we only agree to read through the transparence of the 'airy nothing,' that the truth will stare us most openly in the face. Far from lacking substance and profundity, as even George Orwell inexplicably maintained, this play provides a quintessence of the Shakespearean spirit.

Am I not 'going too far' when I assimilate the midsummer night to the tragic crisis; am I not running the risk of betraying the real Shakespeare? The language of differences and undifferentiation is not Shakespeare's own, after all. This is true if we take the matter quite literally; but it is also true that Shakespeare, in some of his writing, comes close to using that same language. A case in point is the famous speech of Ulysses in *Troilus and Cressida*: it describes that very same crisis but does so in purely theoretical language and on as vast a scale as the most ambitious tragedies, as the crisis of an entire culture. The speech is built around one single word, *degree*, which would certainly be condemned as too 'abstract,' too 'philosophical,' if it were applied to Shakespeare by anyone but Shakespeare himself. And obviously Shakespeare applies it to himself as well as to the Greeks: it is the social framework of tragedy which is at stake.*

. . . O, when degree is shaked,
Which is the ladder of all high designs,
The enterprise is sick. How could communities,
Degrees in schools and brotherhoods in cities,
Peaceful commerce from dividable shores,
The primogenitive and due of birth,
Prerogative of age, crowns, scepters, laurels,
But by degree stand in authentic place?
Take but degree away, untune that string,
And hark what discord follows. Each thing meets
In mere oppugnancy. The bounded waters
Should lift their bosoms higher than the shores

* Ibid., 49–51.

And make a sop of all this solid globe;
Strength should be lord of imbecility,
And the rude son should strike his father dead;
Force should be right, or, rather, right and wrong,
Between whose endless jar justice resides,
Should lose their names, and so should justice too.
Then everything includes itself in power,
Power into will, will into appetite,
And appetite, an universal wolf,
So doubly seconded with will and power,
Must make perforce an universal prey
And last eat up himself. [I, iii, 101–124]

The word *degree*, from the Latin *gradus* (step, degree, measure of distance), means exactly what is meant here by difference. Culture is conceived not as a mere collection of unrelated objects, but as a totality, or, if we prefer, a structure, a system of people and institutions always related to one another in such a way that a single differentiating principle is at work. This social transcendence does not exist as an object, of course. That is why, as soon as an individual member, overcome by *hubris*, tries to usurp Degree, he finds imitators; more and more people are affected by the contagion of mimetic rivalry, and Degree collapses, being nothing more than the mysterious absence of such rivalry in a functional society. The crisis is described as the 'shaking,' the 'vizarding,' or the taking away of Degree; all cultural specificities vanish, all identities disintegrate. Conflict is everywhere, and everywhere meaningless: *Each thing meets in mere oppugnancy*. We must note this use of the word 'thing,' the least determined, perhaps, in the English language. The meaningless conflict is that of the *doubles*. Unable to find a way out, men err and clash stupidly, full of hatred but deprived of real purpose; they resemble objects loose on the deck of a ship tossed about in a storm, destroying one another as they collide endlessly and mindlessly.

In light of the above remarks, a precise analysis of the midsummer crisis becomes possible. The four protagonists do not see one another as *doubles*; they misunderstand their relationship as one of extreme if unstable differentiation. A point must finally be reached where all of these illusory differences oscillate so rapidly that the contrasting specificities they define are no longer perceived separately; they begin to impinge on one another, they appear to merge. Beyond a certain threshold, in other words, the dizziness mentioned earlier will make normal perception impossible; hallucination must prevail, of a type that can be ascertained with some precision, being not purely capricious and random but predetermined by the nature of the crisis.

When polarities such as the ones described earlier between the 'beast' and the 'angel' oscillate so fast that they become one, the elements involved remain too incompatible for a harmonious 'synthesis,' and they will simply be juxtaposed or superimposed on each other. A composite picture should emerge which will include fragments of the former 'opposites' in a disorderly mosaic. Instead of a god and a beast facing each other as two independent and irreducible entities, we are going to have a mixture and a confusion of the two, a god that is a beast or a beast that is a god. When the polarities revolve fast enough, all antithetic images must be viewed simultaneously, through a kind of cinematic effect that will produce the illusion of a more or less single being in the form or rather the formlessness of 'some monstrous shape.'

What *A Midsummer Night's Dream* suggests, in other words, is that the mythical monster, as a conjunction of elements which normally specify different beings, automatically results from the more and more rapid turnover of animal and metaphysical images, a turnover which depends on the constantly self-reinforcing process of mimetic desire. We are not simply invited to witness the dramatic but insignificant birth of bizarre mythical creatures; rather we are confronted with a truly fascinating and important view of mythical genesis.

In a centaur, elements specific to man and to horse are inexplicably conjoined, just as elements specific to man and ass are conjoined in the monstrous metamorphosis of Bottom. Since there is no limit to differences that can be jumbled together, since the picture will necessarily remain blurred, the diversity of monsters will appear properly limitless and the infinite seems to be at hand. Insofar as separate entities can be distinguished within the monstrous whole, there will be individual monsters; but they will have no stability: they will constantly appear to merge and marry one another. The birth of monsters, their scandalous commingling with human beings, and the wedding of the one with the other, all these mythical phenomena are part of one and the same experience. The wedding of Titania with the ass-headed Bottom, under the influence of that same 'love juice' that makes the lovers crazy, can take place only because the difference between the natural and the supernatural is gone; haughty Titania finds to her dismay that the barrier between her and ordinary mortals is down:

Tell me how it came this night
That I sleeping there was found
With these mortals on the ground. [IV, i, 103–105]

The conjunction of man, god, and beast takes place at the climax of the crisis and is the result of a process which began with the play itself. It is the ultimate metamorphosis, the supreme *translation*.

In that process the animal images play a pivotal role. I noted earlier that their perfect integration into the disquieting symphony conducted by Shakespeare was not at all incompatible with their identification as literary reminiscences. We must now go further. To say that Shakespeare himself wants them to play in his own work is no longer enough. It is evident that these animal images are especially appropriate to that role and that Shakespeare has selected them for that reason. Most of them come from Ovid's *Metamorphoses*. They are directly implicated in an earlier genesis of myth, still quite mythical, and far removed from the obviously psychosocial interpretation implicitly proposed by Shakespeare. It is no exaggeration to assert that *A Midsummer Night's Dream*, because it is a powerful reinterpretation of Ovid, also provides, at least in outline, Shakespeare's own genetic theory of myth. It is a mistake, therefore, to view the animal images as if they were suspended in midair between the matter-of-fact interplay of desires on the one hand and purely fantastic shapes on the other. They are the connecting link between the two. Thus we can no longer see the play as a collage of heterogeneous elements, as another monstrosity; it is a continuous development, a series of logically related steps that will account even for the monsters in its own midst if they are only followed to the end, if enough trust is placed in the consistency of the author.

At the climax of the crisis, Demetrius and Lysander are about to kill each other, but Puck, on Oberon's orders, substitutes himself for the *doubles* and puts the four lovers to sleep. When they wake up the next morning, they find themselves reconciled, neatly arranged this time in well-assorted couples. Good weather is back, everything is in order once more. Degree is restored. Theseus appears on the scene. He and his future wife hear an account of the midsummer night, and it is for the duke to pronounce the final word, to draw the official conclusion of the whole episode in response to a slightly anxious question asked by Hippolyta. Then comes the most famous passage of the entire play. Theseus dismisses the entire midsummer night as the inconsequential fruit of a gratuitous and disembodied imagination. He seems to believe that the real question is whether or not to believe in the fairies. Hippolyta's later words will reveal that her concern is of an entirely different sort; but, like all rationalists of a certain type, Theseus has a marvelous capacity for simplifying the issues and displacing a debate towards his favorite stomping ground. Much of what he says is true, of course; but it is beside the point. To believe or not to believe, that is *not* the question; and, by trumpeting his famous skepticism, Theseus dispenses himself from looking at the remarkable pattern of the midsummer night and the disturbing clues it may contain concerning the nature of all social beliefs, including his own. Who knows if the crisis and its cathartic resolution are responsible only for the monsters of the night? Who knows if the peace and order of the morning after, if even the majestic confidence of the unchallenged ruler are not equally in their debt? Theseus' casual dismissal of myth is itself mythical in the sense that it will not ask such questions. There is irony in the choice of a great mythical figure to embody this rationalistic dismissal. Here Theseus acts as the high priest of a benign casting-out of all the disturbing phenomena under the triple heading of poetry, lunacy, and love. This neat operation frees respectable men of all responsibility for whatever tricks, past, present, and future, their own desires and mimetic violence might play on them, thus perfectly duplicating the primary genesis of myth, the one that I have just noted.

HIPPOLYTA:
'Tis strange, my Theseus, that these lovers speak of.

THESEUS:
More strange than true. I never may believe
These antique fables nor these fairy toys.
Lovers and madmen have such seething brains,
Such shaping fantasies, that apprehend
More than cool reason ever comprehend.
The lunatic, the lover, and the poet
Are of imagination all compact.
One sees more devils than vast Hell can hold,
That is the madman. The lover, all as frantic,
Sees Helen's beauty in a brow of Egypt.
The poet's eye, in a fine frenzy rolling,
Doth glance from heaven to Earth, from Earth to heaven,
And as imagination bodies forth
The forms of things unknown, the poet's pen
Turns them to shapes, and gives to airy nothing
A local habitation and a name.
Such tricks hath strong imagination
That, if it would but apprehend some joy,
It comprehends some bringer of that joy;
Or in the night, imagining some fear,
How easy is a bush supposed a bear!

This positivism *avant la lettre* seems to contradict much of what I have said so far. Evidence so laboriously assembled seems scattered once more. Where are the half-concealed yet blatant disclosures, the allusive ambiguities artfully disposed by the author (or so I supposed) for our enlightenment? Long before I came to it, I am sure, many skeptical readers had the passage in mind, and they will rightly want to know how it fits into my reading. Here it is, finally, an obvious ally of the traditional readings that quite naturally regard it as the unshakable rock upon which they are founded. As such, it must constitute a formidable stumbling block for my own intricate revisionism.

This lead is provided by Shakespeare himself, and the present status of the passage as a piece of anthology, a *lieu commun* of modern estheticism, testifies to the willingness of posterity to take up that lead. The reading provided by Theseus is certainly the most pleasant, the one which conforms to the wishes of the heart and to the tendency of the human mind not to be disturbed. We must note, besides, that the text is centrally located, placed in the mouth of the most distinguished character, couched in sonorous and memorable phrases, well fit to adorn academic dissertations on the so-called 'imaginative faculty.'

This speech has been so successful, indeed, that no one ever pays any attention to the five quiet lines that follow. Hippolyta's response does not have the same resounding eloquence, but the dissatisfaction she expresses with the slightly pompous and irrelevant *post-mortem* of Theseus *was written by Shakespeare himself.* It cannot fail to be of immense significance:

But all the story of the night told over,
And all their minds transfigured so together,
More witnesseth than fancy's images,
And grows to something of great constancy,
But, howsoever, strange and admirable. [V, i, 23–27]

Hippolyta clearly perceives Theseus's failure to come up with the holistic interpretation that is necessary. He and his innumerable followers deal with the play as if it were a collection of separate cock-and-bull stories. To them imagination is a purely individual activity, unrelated to the interplay of the four lovers. They themselves are the true inheritors of myth when they confidently believe in their simplistic objectivity. They see myth as something they have already left behind with the greatest of ease, as an object of passing amusement, perhaps, when the occasion arises to watch some light entertainment such as *A Midsummer Night's Dream*.

There is no doubt that we are dealing with two critical attitudes and that Shakespeare himself vindicates the one that has always been less popular. When I suggest that *A Midsummer Night's Dream*, behind all the frills, is a serious genetic theory of myth, I am only translating the five lines of Hippolyta into contemporary parlance. It is not I but Shakespeare who writes that the midsummer night is more than a few graceful arabesques about English folklore and Elizabethan lovers. It is not I but Shakespeare who draws our attention to *all their minds transfigured so together* and to the final result as *something of great constancy*, in other words, a common structure of mythical meaning.

I have suggested that *A Midsummer Night's Dream* might well be two plays in one. This hypothesis is now strengthened. At this point, the two plays are coming to life as individuals; they are speaking to us and to each other, one through Theseus, the other through Hippolyta. The exchange between the bridegroom and his acutely perceptive but eternally overshadowed bride amounts to the first critical discussion of the play. Representing as he does blissful ignorance and the decorum of Degree enthroned, Theseus must hold the stage longer, speaking with a brilliance and finality that confirms the dramatic preeminence of the surface play, a preeminence that is maintained throughout. Since he gives a voice to all those – the immense majority – who want nothing more in such an affair than 'airy nothings,' Theseus must be as deaf and blind to his bride's arguments as Shakespeare's audiences as critics seem to have been ever since. The debate seems one-sided in the duke's favor, but how could we fail, at this juncture, to realize that the real last word belongs to Hippolyta, both literally and figuratively? In the context of the evidence gathered earlier, how could we doubt that Hippolyta's words are the decisive ones, that they represent Shakespeare's own view of how the play really hangs together? If we really understand that context, we cannot be surprised that Shakespeare makes his correction of Theseus as discreet and unobtrusive as it is illuminating, visible only to the same thoughtful attention already needed to appreciate such pregnant ambiguities as 'to choose love by another's eyes' and other similar gems of exquisitely direct, yet almost imperceptible revelation.

Hippolyta is gently tugging at Theseus' sleeve, but Theseus hears nothing. Hippolyta has been tugging at that sleeve for close to four hundred years now, with no consequence whatever, her words forever buried under the impressive scaffoldings of Degree once more triumphant in the guise of rationalism, eternally silenced by that need for reassurance which is answered first by belief in myths, then by a certain kind of disbelief. Shakespeare seems to give his blessing to both, ironically confounded in the person of Theseus. He places in the hands of his pious and admiring betrayers the instruments best designed to blunt the otherwise intolerably sharp edge of their favorite bard's genius.

Collective Violence and Sacrifice in Shakespeare's *Julius Caesar*

The theater deals with human conflict. Curiously, dramatic criticism discusses the subject very little. Can we automatically assume that Shakespeare shares the commonsense view according to which conflict is based on differences? Can we assume that tragic conflict is due to the different opinions or values of the various protagonists? This is never true in Shakespeare. Of two persons who do not get along, we say: *they have their differences*. In Shakespeare the reverse is true: the characters disagree because they agree too much.

Let me explain this paradox. Why does Brutus hate Caesar? Most people will answer that they stand on opposite sides in a meaningful political struggle. This is true in the sense that Brutus is a sincere Republican and that Caesar's popularity makes him a real threat to the Republic, but the reason for Brutus's hatred of Caesar lies elsewhere.

To understand this hatred we must start from its opposite which is the love of Brutus for Caesar. Yes, Brutus loves Caesar dearly. He says so and we can believe him; Brutus never lies.

To Brutus, Caesar is what we call today a role model and much more; he is an incomparable guide, an unsurpassable teacher. To a Roman with political ambition, and Brutus's ambition is great, being patterned on Caesar's, Caesar is the unbeatable champion and therefore an insurmountable obstacle. No one can hope to equal him and become another Caesar, and this is what Brutus really wants to be. Far from excluding hatred, Brutus's love for Caesar necessarily leads to it. Caesar is Brutus's rival because he is his model and vice versa. The more Brutus loves Caesar, the more he hates him, and vice versa. This ambivalence must not be defined in Freudian but mimetic terms.

I call the desire of Brutus mimetic or mediated desire. Everything Brutus wants to have and to be, he owes to Caesar; far from having differences with Caesar he has none and that is why he hates him.

He is like a lover who sees the woman he loves in the arms of another man. The woman here is Rome herself. And Brutus loves that woman because Caesar loves her. My erotic comparison is not psychoanalytical; it is inspired by Shakespeare's comedies which are as full of mimetic desire as the tragedies.

Mimetic desire is the mutual borrowing of desire by two friends who become antagonists as a result. When mimetic rivalry becomes intense, tragic conflict results. Intense conflict and intense friendship are almost identical in Shakespeare. This paradox is a source of linguistic effects that should not be dismissed as pure rhetoric. They are highly meaningful. *Beloved enemy* is no rhetorical expression; it is exactly what Caesar is to Brutus.

When mimetic rivalry escalates beyond a certain point, the rivals engage in endless conflict which undifferentiates them more and more; they all become *doubles* of one another. During the civil war, Brutus sounds increasingly authoritarian and majestic, just like Caesar. In order to be Caesar, Brutus acts more and more like Caesar. After the murder, in his speech to the Romans, Brutus imitates the terse prose style of Caesar. The shout that rises from the crowd: 'Let him be Caesar,' is enormously meaningful. Sincere Republican though he is, Brutus unconsciously turns into a second Caesar and this must be interpreted less in terms of individual psychology than as an effect of the worsening mimetic crisis. Caesar is a threat and, in order to restore the Republic, he must be eliminated; but, whoever eliminates him, *ipso facto*, becomes another Caesar, which is what Brutus secretly desires, anyway, as do the people themselves. The destruction of the Republic is this very process; no single man is responsible for it; everybody is.

The political genius of Rome is the ability of its Republican institutions to accommodate the kind of rivalry that exists between Brutus and Caesar. This is true but only up to a point. The Republic is a *cursus honorum*, and as long as rival ambitions keep each other in check, liberty survives. Rival ambitions can become so intense, however, that they no longer tolerate one another. Instead of competing within the limits of the law, the rival leaders turn violent and treat each other as enemies. They all accuse each other of destroying Republican institutions and this false excuse quickly becomes the truth of the situation. All of them together are destroying the Republic.

We cannot say that these leaders have their differences; they want the same thing; they all copy each other; they all behave in the same way; what Shakespeare portrays is no conflict of differences, but a plague of undifferentiation.

The very first lines of the play suggest that the populace itself partakes of this leveling process. The common people show up on the Forum without the insignia of their profession, reflecting the undifferentiation at the top. The Roman Republic is unraveling from top to bottom:

Hence! home, you idle creatures, get you home!
Is this a holiday? What! know you not,
Being mechanical, you ought not to walk
Upon a labouring day without the sign
Of your profession?

These Romans are not soldiers but their regular organization resembles the military and their departure from tradition recalls the confusion of ranks in the Greek army, such as Ulysses describes in *Troilus and Cressida*, the 'choking' or 'neglection' of Degree. The word Degree means the differential principle thanks to which the cultural and social order is what it is. In the eyes of Shakespeare, the end of the Roman Republic is a historical example of such a crisis.

I think that Shakespeare conceives that crisis exactly as all traditional societies do; his genius does not contradict and yet transcends traditional wisdom. The reason that the mimetic crisis exacerbates more and more is the peculiar logic that it obeys, the logic abundantly exemplified in Julius Caesar, the logic of mimetic rivalry and mimetic contagion. The more mimetic desire there is, the more it generates, and the more attractive it becomes as a mimetic model.

A conspiracy is a mimetic association of murderers; it comes into being at an advanced but not yet the most advanced stage of a mimetic crisis. Shakespeare dedicates his first two acts to the genesis of the conspiracy against Caesar, and he treats the subject in full conformity with the logic of mimetic desire.

The instigator of the conspiracy is Cassius, and his maneuvers are dramatized at length. Once the conspiracy has become a reality, Brutus agrees to lead it, but its real father is Cassius who is the dominant figure at the beginning. Cassius plays the same role as Pandarus, the erotic go-between, at the beginning of *Troilus and Cressida*; he works very hard at instilling in his associates his own desire to kill Caesar.

Cassius's mimetic incitement is very similar to that in many comedies, except for the fact that the people he manipulates are mimetically seduced in choosing not the same erotic object as their mediator but the same victim, a common target of assassination.

The conspiracy originates in the envious soul of Cassius. Envy and mimetic desire are one and the same. Caesar portrays the man as a self-tortured intellectual unable to enjoy sensuous pleasures. Unlike his modern posterity, this early prototype of ressentiment – Nietzsche's word for mimetic envy – has not yet lost all capacity for bold action but he excels only in the clandestine and terroristic type exemplified by the conspiracy.

Cassius reveals his envy in everything he says. Unable to compete with Caesar on Caesar's ground, he claims superiority in small matters such as a swimming contest that he once had with the great man. Had it not been for himself, Cassius, his rival, who helped him across the Tiber, Caesar would have drowned. Cassius refuses to worship a god who owes him his very life.

Cassius's invidious comparisons, his slanted anecdotes and his perpetual flattery of Brutus are worthy of Pandarus and, therefore, they also recall Ulysses, the political counterpart of Cressida:

Brutus and Caesar, what should be in that 'Caesar'?
Why should that name be sounded more than yours?
Write them together, yours is as fair a name;
Sound them, it doth become the mouth as well;
Weigh them, it is as heavy; conjure with 'em,
'Brutus' will start a spirit as soon as 'Caesar'.

Now in the names of all the gods at once,
Upon what meat doth this our Caesar feed
That he is grown so great? [I, ii, 142–150]

A little later, Cassius resorts to the language of Ulysses with Achilles in *Troilus and Cressida*, also for the purpose of stirring up the spirit of mimetic rivalry in a man obsessed by a successful rival. The two plays are very close to each other from the standpoint of their mimetic operation.

The second man recruited for the conspiracy is Casca; he is superstitious in the extreme. He describes a violent but banal equinoctial storm exclusively in terms of supernatural signs and portents. Shakespeare does not believe in astrology and, in order to refute this nonsense authoritatively, he resorts to no less a man than Cicero, who contradicts Casca's interpretation. This is the philosopher's only intervention in the play.

The mimetic seducer, Cassius, is no more superstitious than Cicero; his famous saying on the subject shows it:

The fault, dear Brutus, is not in our stars,
But in ourselves, that we are underlings. [I, ii, 140–141]

Cassius does not believe in astrology but, for the purpose of seducing Casca into the conspiracy, he can speak the language of astrology. Instead of deriding his interlocutor's irrationality, he tries to channel it in the direction of Caesar. What he condemns in Casca is his failure to blame Caesar for the terrifying storm:

Now could I, Casca, name thee to a man
Most like this dreadful night,
That thunders, lightens, opens graves and roars
As doth the lion in the Capitol –
A man no mightier than thyself, or me,
In personal action, yet prodigious grown,
And fearful, as these strange eruptions are. [I, i, 57–76]

Cassius never mentions Caesar by name because he wants Casca to name him first; this credulous man will believe that he discovered Caesar's evil influence all by himself. Casca finally comes up with the right name:

Tis Caesar that you mean; is it not, Cassius?

Cassius literally hypnotizes Casca into believing that Caesar is responsible for the bad weather. If someone must be *most like this dreadful night*, why not Caesar, the most powerful man in Rome? Seeing that Cassius seems angry rather than afraid, Casca feels somewhat reassured and, in his eagerness for more reassurance, he makes the other man's anger his own; he eagerly espouses Cassius's quarrel against Caesar.

Casca's decision to join the murderers is more disturbing than Brutus's because, unlike Brutus, the man is obsequious with Caesar and totally unconcerned with abuses of power and other political niceties. He is petty and envious but not talented enough to feel jealous of such a towering figure as Caesar. If Cassius had directed his mimetic urge toward someone else, Casca would have chosen someone else. His participation in the conspiracy has nothing to do with whatever Caesar is or might become; it rests entirely on his own mimetic suggestibility, stimulated by fear. Caesar is being turned into what we call a scapegoat and Shakespeare insists on all the scapegoat signs that designate him to the crowd, his lameness, his epileptic fear and even a bad ear, an incipient deafness that Shakespeare seems to have invented all by himself. The other physical infirmities are in Plutarch and Shakespeare emphasizes them because he understands their importance in the overall scheme of victimization.

After Brutus and Casca, we witness the recruiting of Ligarius, a third citizen, into the conspiracy. The man is so susceptible to mimetic pressure, so ready for conspiratorial mischief that, although very ill, as soon as he understands that the gathering around Brutus must have some violent purpose, he throws his bandages away and follows the leader.

Ligarius does not know the name of his future victim and he does not even want to know. Brutus gives no indication that he finds this behavior shocking; his equanimity is as disturbing as Ligarius' irresponsibility. This virtuous Republican sees nothing wrong, it seems, in a Roman citizen blindly surrendering his freedom of choice into the hands of another:

LIGARIUS: Set on your foot,
And with a heart new fir'd I follow you
To do I know not what; but it sufficeth
That Brutus leads me on.

BRUTUS: Follow me then. [II, i, 331–334]

The times are nasty and normally law-abiding Romans are more and more easily swayed in favor of murder, less and less selective regarding the choice of their victims. Being part of the crisis, the genesis of the conspiracy is itself a dynamic process, a segment of an escalation in which the murder of Caesar comes first, then the murder of Cinna and finally the ever intensified violence that leads to Philippi. Instead of putting an end to the crisis, the murder of Caesar accelerates it.

Let us make the mimetic significance of what we read quite explicit. The intensification and diffusion of mimetic rivalry has turned all citizens into hostile carbon copies of each other, mimetic *doubles*. At first these *doubles* are still paired in conformity with what they have in common; they have been fighting for the same objects and, in this sense, they truly 'belong' to one another. This is the case of Brutus and Caesar. Conflicts are still 'rational' to the extent at least that each double is truly entitled to call his antagonist 'his own.'

This element of rationality is still present in the case of Brutus. It seems that Brutus would not have to be recruited at all, since he really hates Caesar, but he is a law-abiding citizen and, were it not for the mimetic incitement of Cassius, his hatred, intense as it is, would never become homicidal.

When the crisis gets worse, this last element of rationality disappears. When mimetic effects constantly intensify, the disputed objects disappear or become irrelevant. The mimetic influx must find some other outlet and it affects the choice of the only entities left inside the system: the doubles themselves. Mimetic contamination determines more and more the choice of antagonists.

At this advanced stage of the mimetic crisis, many people can exchange their own *doubles*, their own mimetic rivals for the *double* of someone else. This is what Casca does. The someone else is a mediator of hatred and no longer a mediator of desire, Cassius. This is a new stage in the process of violent undifferentiation. The more 'perfect' the *doubles* are as *doubles*, the easier it becomes to *substitute* one for another.

With each of the three Roman citizens successively recruited for the conspiracy, this kind of substitution becomes easier and we go down one more notch in regard to these individuals' ability to think by themselves, to use their reason and to behave in a responsible way.

It is less a matter of individual psychology than the rapid march of mimetic desire itself. As the conspiracy becomes larger, the job of attracting new members becomes easier. The combined mimetic influence of those already attracted makes the chosen target more and more attractive mimetically. As the crisis worsens, the relative importance of *mimesis* versus rationality goes up.

We have reached a point when dual conflicts give way to associations of several people against a single one, usually a highly visible individual, a popular statesman – Julius Caesar, for instance. When a small number of people clandestinely get together for the purpose of doing away with one of their fellow citizens, we call their association a *conspiracy* and so does Shakespeare. Both the process and the word are prominently displayed in *Julius Caesar*.

Whereas the mimesis of desire means disunity among those who cannot possess their common object together, this mimesis of conflict means more solidarity among those who can fight the same enemy together and who promise each other to do so. Nothing unites men like a common enemy but, for the time being, only a few people are thus united, and they are united for the purpose of disturbing the peace of the community as a whole. That is why the conspiratorial stage is even more destructive of the social order than the fragmented enmities that preceded it.

The forming of a conspiracy is a sinister threshold on the road to civil war, significant enough to call for a solemn warning which the author paradoxically places in the mouth of the conspiracy's own reluctant leader, Brutus. There is logic in this paradox, however, since Brutus's purpose is to defend threatened Republican institutions. Brutus himself is aware that his violent medicine could be as bad as the disease and even worse: it could make the recovery of the patient impossible and, indeed, it will. Even though Brutus feels that he must join the conspiracy, this great defender of traditional institutions is horrified by the historical sign that the forming of a conspiracy constitutes:

BRUTUS: O Conspiracy!
Sham'st thou to show thy dang'rous brow by night,
When evils are most free? O then, by day
Where wilt thou find a cavern dark enough
To mask thy monstrous visage? Seek none, Conspiracy!
Hide it in smiles and affability;
For if thou path, thy native semblance on,
Not Erebus itself were dim enough
To hide thee from prevention. [II, i, 77–85]

The conspiracy is said to have a monstrous visage and it certainly does in the usual Shakespearean sense of uniting contradictory features in some kind of artificial mimetic unity, something which happens only at the most advanced stages of the mimetic crisis.

We should not believe that, because he represents the conspiracy harshly, Shakespeare must feel political sympathy for Caesar. At first sight, no doubt, Caesar seems more generous and kind than his opponents. Whereas Brutus hates Caesar as much as he loves him, Caesar's love is free from hatred. But Caesar can afford to be generous; neither Brutus nor any other Roman can be an obstacle to him anymore. This is not enough to demonstrate that Caesar stands above the mimetic law.

On the morning of the murder, Caesar first follows the advice of his wife who is terrified because she has been dreaming of his violent death, and he decides not to go to the Senate; but then Decius reinterprets the dream for him and he goes to the Senate after all. It takes only a few words of ambiguous flattery to change Caesar's mind. He has become a mimetic weathervane.

The more the dictator rises above other men, the more autonomous he subjectively feels and the less he is in reality. At the supreme instant, just before falling under the conspirators' blows, in a strange fit of exaltation, he hubristically compares himself to the North Star, the one motionless light in the firmament. His self-sufficiency is no less deceptive than the erotic 'narcissism' of many characters in the comedies.

The more intense our mimetic pride, the more fragile it becomes, even in a physical sense. Just as the crowd and as the conspirators themselves, Caesar is an example of what happens to men caught in the crisis of Degree. His common sense has left him, just as it will leave Brutus a few moments later. Because of the crisis, the quality of all desires is deteriorating. Instead of feeling neurotically inferior, as his unsuccessful rivals do, Caesar feels neurotically superior. His symptoms look completely different, but solely because of his position inside a fragile mimetic structure; underneath, the disease is the same. If Caesar found himself in the same position relative to some man as Brutus does relative to him, he, too, would join a conspiracy against that man.

Brutus wants the murder to be as discreet, orderly and 'non-violent' as it possibly can be. Unfortunately for the conspiracy, he himself proves incapable of abiding by his own rule. Losing his sang-froid in the hot blood of his victim, Brutus gets carried away in the most dangerous fashion at the most crucial instant, right after the murder. He suggests to the conspirators that they should all bathe their arms in Caesar's blood *up to the elbows* and smear their swords with this blood.

Needless to say, our blood-spattered conspirators do not make a favorable impression, but they make a very strong one and they provide the already unstable populace with a potent mimetic model, a model which many citizens will imitate even and especially if they reject it most violently. The subsequent events tell the whole story. After listening to Brutus, then to Mark Antony, the crowd reacts by collectively putting to death an unfortunate bystander, Cinna, in a grotesque parody of what the conspirators themselves have done. The crowd becomes a mirror in which the murderers contemplate the truth of their action. They wanted to become mimetic models for the people and they are, but not the kind they intended.

When they kill Cinna, the people mimic Caesar's murder but in a spirit of revenge, not of Republican virtue. Mimetic desire is perceptive and it will immediately detect any discrepancy between deeds of its models; it will always pattern itself on and not on what those models do and not what they say.

Cinna is the first totally uninvolved and perfectly victim. He is a poet and he has nothing to do with the conspirator named Cinna; he politely says so to the crowd. His only connection with Caesar's murder is a fortuitous coincidence of names. He even happens to be a friend of Caesar and he mentions the fact, but to no avail; one anonymous shout comes from the mob: 'Tear him to pieces.'

A mob never lacks 'subjective' and 'objective' reasons for tearing its victims to pieces. The more numerous these reasons, the more insignificant they really are. Learning that Cinna is a bachelor, the married men in the mob feel insulted. Others resent the poet in this individual and one more shout is heard: 'Tear him for his bad verse!' Obediently, mimetically, the mob tears the wrong Cinna to pieces.

When it was first organized, the conspiracy against Caesar was still an unusual enterprise that required a rather lengthy genesis; once Caesar is murdered, conspiracies sprout everywhere and their violence is so sudden and haphazard that the word itself, conspiracy, no longer seems right for the spontaneous enormity of the disorder. Violent imitation is responsible for this as for everything else and that is the reason we have a single continuous process instead of the discontinuous synchronic patterns that the structuralists want to discover everywhere, in a misguided denial of history.

The general trend is clear: it takes less and less time for more and more people to polarize against more and more victims, for flimsier and flimsier reasons. A little earlier, Ligarius' indifference to the identity of his victim was still an exceptional phenomenon; after Caesar's murder, this indifference becomes commonplace and the last criteria disappear in the selection of victims. Mimesis learns fast and, after only one single try, it will do routinely and automatically what seemed almost unthinkable a moment before.

The contagion is such that the entire community is finally divided into two vast 'conspiracies' that can only do one thing: go to war with each other; they have the same structure as individual *doubles*; one is led by Brutus and Cassius and the other by Octavius Caesar and Mark Antony. Shakespeare sees this civil conflict not as an ordinary war but as the total unleashing of the mob:

> Domestic fury and fierce civil strife
> Shall cumber all the parts of Italy;
> Blood and destruction shall be so in use,
> And dreadful objects so familiar,
> That mothers shall but smile when they behold
> Their infants quartered with the hands of war;
> All pity chok'd with custom of fell deeds;
> And Caesar's spirit, raging for revenge,
> With Hate by his side, come hot from hell,
> Shall in these confines with a monarch's voice
> Cry 'Havoc!' and let slip the dogs of war,
> That this foul deed shall smell above the earth
> With carrion men, groaning for burial. [III, i, 262–275]

Just as Brutus, in Act II, solemnly proclaimed the advent of the fearful conspiracy, Mark Antony informs us in this soliloquy that an even worse stage of the crisis has arrived; his name for it is *domestic fury* or *fierce civil strife*. As each new stage of the crisis is reached, Shakespeare has someone make a rather formal and impersonal speech about it. These speeches do not really tell us anything about the character who utters them; they are unnecessary to the plot; they are speeches about the various stages in the mimetic crisis.

Domestic fury and *fierce civil strife* culminate in the battle of Philippi, which Shakespeare does not treat as a banal military encounter but as the climactic epiphany of the mimetic crisis, the final explosion of the mob that gathered after the murder of Caesar, when the conspiracy began to metastasize.

As Peter S. Anderson observed, in this battle, no one is really where he should be; everything is dislocated; death is the sole common denominator ('Shakespeare's *Caesar*: The Language of Sacrifice,' *Comparative Drama*, 3, pp. 5–6).

Instead of a few victims killed by still relatively small mobs, thousands of people are killed by thousands of others who are really their brothers and do not have the faintest idea of why they or their victims should die.

At Philippi, total violence is unleashed and it seems the point of no return has been reached. No hope remains and yet, in the very last lines of the play, all of a sudden, peace returns. This is no ordinary victory, no mere overpowering of the weak by the strong. This conclusion is a rebirth of Degree; it concludes the mimetic crisis itself.

The return to peace seems rooted in the suicide of Brutus. How could that be? In two very brief but majestic speeches, the victors, Antony and Octavius Caesar, eulogize Brutus. Mark Antony speaks first:

This was the noblest Roman of them all:
All the conspirators save only he,
Did what they did in envy of great Caesar;
His life was gentle, and the elements
So mix'd in him that Nature might stand up
And say to all the world: 'This was a man!' [V, v, 68–73]

This famous tribute is not quite truthful; Brutus was free only from the basest kind of envy. This truth is sacrificed to the new spirit now blowing, a spirit of reconciliation.

Sensing a political master stroke, Octavius Caesar consecrates the new Brutus by granting him full military honors. By absolving Brutus of envy, Mark Antony and Octavius Caesar sanctify his political motives. Only the loving side of his ambivalence toward Caesar remains visible; we remember the words of Brutus after he killed Caesar: 'I slew my best lover'; we remember the words before he killed himself:

Caesar, now be still,
I kill'd not thee with half so good a will. [V, v, 50–51]

It seems that both Caesar and Brutus gave their lives for the same cause, in a mysterious consummation that makes *Pax Romana* possible once again.

Up to that point, unanimity had eluded both parties; neither the Republicans nor their opponents could achieve it. Caesar's death was divisive: one part of the people united against Caesar while the other part united against Brutus and around Caesar. If Brutus and Caesar become one in death, then all the people can unite again and around the same double-headed god.

To Brutus, this posthumous apotheosis would seem the ultimate derision, the supreme betrayal. It makes him a junior partner in the enterprise that he was desperately trying to prevent, the creation of a new monarchy. But the real Brutus no longer matters; a mythical figure has replaced him inside a newly emerging structure of meaning. According to this new vision, the Roman emperor is both an absolute monarch and the official protector of the Republic, its only legitimate heir.

Caesar's murder has become the *foundational violence* of the Roman Empire.

What does it mean for violence to be foundational? Mimetic theory has its own interpretation of this and it throws a great deal of light on what Shakespeare is doing. Mimetic theory believes in the reality of the mimetic crises portrayed by Shakespeare, and, from their nature, as well as from a great many other clues, it speculates that these crises, in primitive societies, must be concluded by unanimous mimetic polarizations against single victims or a few victims only; this hypothetical resolution is the original sacrifice and I call it *foundational murder, foundational violence*.

This original sacrifice means that human communities unite *around* some transfigured victim. There is nothing genuinely transcendental or metaphysical about the foundational murder. It is similar to mimetic polarizations of the *conspiracy* type except for one difference, crucial no doubt from a social viewpoint but in itself minor: it is unanimous. Unanimity means that the people suddenly find themselves without enemies and, lacking fuel, the spirit of vengeance becomes extinguished. The unanimity is the automatic end-product of the mimetic escalation itself; it can almost be predicted from the constantly increasing size of the mimetic polarizations that precede it. Shakespeare sees the importance of this question and that is why the rivalry of Brutus and Mark Antony first takes the form of rival speeches in front of the Roman mob. The real battle is a battle for the interpretation of Caesar's murder.

The conclusion is not the only reason for defining substance of sacrifice as I just did. There are many indications in *Julius Caesar* that Shakespeare espoused this idea.

I see a first reason in the references to the collective expulsion of the last king of Rome, Tarquin. Both Cassius and Brutus invoke this event as a precedent for the murder they contemplate; here is what Brutus says in his soliloquy of Act II, i:

Shall Rome stand under one man's awe? What, Rome?
My ancestors did from the streets of Rome
The Tarquin drive when he was call'd a King. [52–54]

Initially, the violence against Tarquin was an illegal act, one more violence in a violent escalation, just like Caesar's murder when it is committed, but Tarquin's expulsion met with the unanimous approval of the people and it put an end to a crisis of Degree; instead of dividing people along factional lines, it united them and new institutions sprang from it. It is the real foundation of the Republic.

Brutus sees the murder of Caesar as a ritual sacrifice ordained by the murder of Tarquin. He says so in his great speech to the conspirators:

Let's be sacrificers but not butchers, Caius,

. . .

Let's kill him boldly but not wrathfully;
Let's carve him as a dish fit for the gods. [II, i, 166–168]

Brutus interprets sacrifice as a reenactment of the foundational violence, the expulsion of Tarquin, with a different victim, Caesar. The sole purpose is to rejuvenate the existing order. This is the definition of sacrifice according to mimetic theory: the reenactment of the foundational violence. The coincidence between mimetic theory and Shakespearean tragedy is perfect.

In connection with this foundational violence, another passage of *Julius Caesar* which I already mentioned is essential, namely, Calphurnia's dream. If we go back to it and its reinterpretation by Decius, we can see immediately that it is more than a prophecy of Caesar's murder, it is a literal definition of its foundational status at the end of the play.

First, let us read Caesar's initial account:

She dreamt to-night she saw my statue,
Which, like a fountain with a hundred spouts,
Did run pure blood; and many lusty Romans
Came smiling and did bathe their hands in it.
And these does she apply for warnings and portents
And evils imminent, and on her knee
Hath begg'd that I will stay at home to-day.

One of the conspirators, Decius Brutus, immediately reinterprets the dream:

DECIUS: This dream is all amiss interpreted,
It was a vision fair and fortunate.
Your statue spouting blood in many pipes,
In which so many smiling Romans bath'd,
Signifies that from you great Rome shall suck
Reviving blood, and that great men shall press

For tinctures, stains, relics, and cognizance.
This by Calphurnia's dream is signified. [II, ii, 76–90]

The author found Calphurnia's dream in Plutarch, as well as her terrified reaction to it, but, as far as I know, Decius' reinterpretation is a pure invention of Shakespeare, and there are very few in this play. From the point of view of our foundational violence, it is the essential text.

The two texts together are a superb definition of the foundational murder, the original sacrifice, a definition that takes its mimetic ambivalence into account. The two interpretations seem to contradict each other, but in reality they are both true. The first corresponds to what Caesar's murder is at first, during the play, a source of extreme disorder, and the second to what this same murder becomes in the conclusion, the source of the new imperial order. Brutus's death triggers this transformation but its role is secondary. It is the first ritual sacrifice of the new order, ordained to a new divinity: Caesar himself. Ironically, Brutus, who wanted to sacrifice Caesar to the Roman Republic, is the one who ends up carved as a dish fit for the gods, and the real god is Caesar. Caesar is a god because his murder is the paramount event, the pivot upon which the violence of the crisis slowly revolved in order to generate a new Roman and universal Degree.

There is a question the critics have always debated about the composition of *Julius Caesar*: why did Shakespeare locate the murder of Caesar in the third act, almost at the precise center of the play, instead of locating it at the conclusion, as a more conventional playwright would have done?

Can a play in which the hero dies in the wrong place be a real tragedy; in other words, can it be satisfactory as entertainment? Is *Julius Caesar* not the juxtaposition of two plays rather than a single one, a first tragedy about Caesar's murder and a second one about the murderers?

The answer is clear; *Julius Caesar* is centered on neither Caesar nor his murderers; it is not even about Roman history but about collective violence itself. The real subject is the violent crowd. *Julius Caesar* is the play in which the violent essence of the theater and of culture itself are revealed. Shakespeare is the first tragic poet and thinker who focuses relentlessly on the foundational murder.

Shakespeare is not interested primarily in Caesar, or in Brutus, or even in Roman history. What fascinates him is the exemplary nature of the events he portrays; he is obviously aware that the only reason why collective violence is essential to tragedy is that it has been and remains essential to human culture as such. He is asking himself why the same murder that cannot reconcile the people at one moment will do the trick a little later, how the murder of Caesar can be a source of disorder first, and then a source of order, how the sacrificial miscarriage of Brutus can become the basis for a new sacrificial order.

To shift the murder from the conclusion to the center of this play means more or less what it means for an astronomer to focus his telescope on the enormously large but infinitely distant object he is studying. Shakespeare goes straight to what has always been the hidden substance of all tragedy and he confronts it explicitly.

Tragedy is a by-product of sacrifice, it is sacrifice without the immolation of the victim, an attenuated form of ritual sacrifice, just as ritual sacrifice itself is a first attenuation of the original murder. Like the great tragic poets of Greece but much more radically, Shakespeare turns sacrifice against itself, against its own sacrificial and cathartic function, and he uses it for a revelation of the foundational murder.

Julius Caesar was written in such a way, however, that it can be read and performed sacrificially and cathartically. Traditional interpretations and stage performances almost invariably turn the play into some kind of monument to the glory of both the Republic and the Empire, of ancient Rome as a whole. Shakespeare wrote the play at two levels: the traditional one which is sacrificial, and the anti-sacrificial one which I am trying to formulate.

If we consider the amount of collective violence in the play, even in purely quantitative terms, we will see that collective violence and sacrifice are its real subject. Not counting Philippi, three instances of collective violence are either displayed on the stage or prominently mentioned: the murder of Caesar, the lynching of the unfortunate Cinna and the expulsion of Tarquin.

Of the three, Caesar's murder is the most important, of course, and no less than three different interpretations of it play a significant role in the play: first we have the Republican sacrifice of Brutus, before the murder occurs; then we have this same murder as total disorder; and then, finally, this same deed becomes the founding of a new order, the original sacrifice from which great Rome shall suck reviving blood. There is not one thing in this play that does not lead to the murder if it occurs before it, and that does not proceed from it if it occurs after it. The murder is the hub around which everything revolves. Who said that this play lacks unity?

The dramatic process I have described contradicts all political interpretations of *Julius Caesar*. Political questions are all of the same differential type: which party does Shakespeare favor in the civil war, the Republicans or the monarchists? Which leader does he like best, Caesar or Brutus? Which social class does he esteem, which does he despise, the aristocrats or the commoners? Shakespeare feels human sympathy for all his characters and great antipathy for the mimetic process that turns them all into equivalent *doubles*.

Political answers are one of the ways in which our insatiable appetite for differences satisfies itself. All differentialism, pre-structuralist, structuralist, or post-structuralist, is equally unable to grasp the most fundamental aspect of Shakespearean dramaturgy: conflictual undifferentiation. We can see this in the fact that the most opposite political views can be defended with equal plausibility and implausibility. The case for a Shakespeare sympathetic to the Republic and hostile to Caesar is just as convincing, or unconvincing, as the reverse political view.

Undecidability is the rule in Shakespeare as in all great mimetic writers, but it does not stem from some transcendental property of *écriture*, or from the 'inexhaustible richness' of great art; it is great art, no doubt, but carefully nurtured by the writer himself, who deals with human situations mimetically.

One of the errors generated by the twentieth-century love affair with politics is the widespread belief that the mob-like propensities of the crowd in *Julius Caesar* must reflect contempt for the common man, a distressingly 'conservative' bias on the part of Shakespeare himself.

His pleasantries about the foul stinking breath of the multitude seem deplorable to our democratic prudishness, but this sentiment had not yet been invented circa 1600. The mob-like propensities of the plebeians are even less significant because all social classes are similarly affected, not only in *Julius Caesar*, but in the other Roman plays and in all crises of Degree, really. Ligarius and Casca, two aristocrats, are no less prone to irrational violence than the idle workers in the first lines of the play.

The crisis turns not only the lower classes into a mob but the aristocrats as well, via the conspiracy, or via their degrading idolatry of Caesar. Our preoccupation with class struggle distorts our appreciation not only of Shakespeare but of tragic literature in general. Our virtuous defenders of the proletariat see only the symptoms that affect their protégés.

Marxism confuses tragic undifferentiation with a vain striving for political neutrality. If Shakespeare does not lean in one direction, he must necessarily lean in the other, even if he pretends that he does not. So goes the reasoning. According to this view, politics is so intrinsically absorbing, even the politics of fifteen hundred years ago, that not even Shakespeare can be even-handed in his treatment of it; his apparent impartiality is only a devious way of playing politics.

Shakespeare does not try to be 'impartial.' We must not see the practical equivalence of all parties in conflict as a hard-won victory of 'detachment' over 'prejudice,' as the heroic triumph of 'objectivity' over 'subjectivity,' or as some other feat of epistemological asceticism that historians of all stripes should either emulate or denounce as mystification.

Mimetic reciprocity is the structure of human relations for Shakespeare, and his dramatization of it is no painstaking obligation, but his intellectual and esthetic delight. In his approach to a great historical quarrel, the objects in dispute, momentous as they seem to us, interest him much less than mimetic rivalry and its undifferentiating effects.

Like 'true love' in the comedies, politics in *Julius Caesar* is always a direct or indirect reflection of what is taking place on some mimetic chessboard. Caesar's politics of imperial reconciliation are a move on this chessboard, and so is Brutus's defense of republicanism. Even the poetry of Shakespeare is inseparable from this undifferentiation, which tends to *confound contraries*, as Shakespeare would say, and to generate countless metaphors and other figures of speech.

I do not want to imply that political questioning is always out of place in Shakespeare. Until the mimetic logic that erases differences is established, it is premature; after this logic is in place, to inquire about the political significance of the logic itself is not only legitimate but imperative.

The perpetual 'plague on both your houses' in Shakespeare must not be void of political significance. When I read *Julius Caesar* I see no Utopian temptation, but I also see an author more nauseated with the aristocratic policies of his time than critics usually believe. I see more satire than most critics perceive. I see an anti-political stance in Shakespeare that suggests a rather sardonic view of history. On political subjects, he reminds me of two French thinkers who are themselves closer to one another than it appears, Montaigne and Pascal. But Shakespeare's mimetic vision, which is artistic form as well as intellectual insight, always takes precedence over other considerations.

Scandal and the Dance: Salome in the Gospel of Mark

Of all the arts, only dance is mentioned in the Gospels, and then in only two of them, Mark and Matthew, which relate the story of the beheading of John the Baptist.

Mark's is the richer text. He tells us that, in the course of a banquet given by Herod, the daughter of Herodias, the tetrarch's wife, 'came in, and danced, and pleased Herod and his guests.' There is nothing further on the dance itself. It is not described in our two Gospels, nor is the dancer's name mentioned. Our direct information is minimal, and yet the dancer and her dance have always fired the erotic and esthetic imagination of the West. Salome danced upon the capitals of Romanesque churches and has kept on dancing ever since. Closer to us in time are Flaubert's 'Herodias,' Mallarmé's 'Herodiade,' Oscar Wilde's 'Salome,' and the 'Salome' of Richard Strauss and of Hugo von Hofmannsthal.

Why this fascination? Mark's narrative (Mark 6:14–29) is not lengthy and deals exclusively with the relations of desire and hatred which separate and join the characters. Herod wanted to take Herodias, the wife of his own brother, as his second wife. John the Baptist condemned this action, and Herodias, with resentment in her heart, demanded his head. Herod did not want to comply and had John imprisoned, not so much to punish him for his insolence, it appears, as to protect him from Herodias, who, however, prevailed, as a result of having her daughter dance in the presence of Herod and his guests.

It all begins as in myth, with a story of rival brothers. Real brothers may be driven to rivalry by their very proximity; they dispute the same paternal heritage, the same crown, the same woman. But this alone does not explain the proliferation of enemy brothers in myth. Do they have the same desires because they resemble one another, or do they resemble one another because they have the same desires? Is it kinship that determines the duplication of desires, or is it the duplication of desires that is expressed in the theme of the rival brothers, often the rival twins? In our text both statements must be true. Herod and his brother constitute both a symbol and a real historical example of the type of desire that dominates our text. Herod really did have a brother, and he really did take his wife Herodias from him. We know from Josephus that the pleasure of supplanting his brother caused Herod serious setbacks. Herod had a first wife whom he had repudiated, and the father of the rejected woman decided to punish his son-in-law's inconstancy by inflicting a bitter defeat on him.

At the very beginning, the hostile brothers indicate the type of relationship that dominates the entire narrative and finally culminates in the murder of John the Baptist. Every detail of this text serves to illustrate some aspect of this desire, and the entire text illustrates all of its stages, each produced by the demented logic of escalation dictated by the immediately preceding stage. Let us begin at the beginning:

For Herod had sent and seized John, and bound him in prison for the sake of Herodias, his brother Philip's wife; because he had married her. For John said to Herod, ' "It is not right for you to have your brother's wife." ' And Herodias had a grudge against him, and wanted to kill him. But she could not, for Herod feared John, knowing that he was a righteous and holy man, and kept him safe. When he heard John, he was much perplexed; and yet he heard him gladly.

The emphasis is not on legality. In the phrase, 'It is not right for you to have your brother's wife,' the Greek verb *exein*, translated by 'to have,' has no legal connotation. To 'have' Herodias, to possess her, is detrimental to Herod, not by virtue of some formal law, but because possession of her can be secured only at the expense of a dispossessed brother. However, this is precisely the reason why Herod desires Herodias. This is what I call mimetic desire: you desire something because someone else does. That person's desire, in turn, is reinforced by your own desire. No sooner is the woman married than she loses all direct influence over her husband. She cannot obtain from him even the head of an insignificant little prophet like John the Baptist. To achieve her ends, Herodias must resort to her daughter, whom she dominates, to reproduce a triangular configuration analogous to the one in which she was the disputed and fascinating object.

Herodias feels herself negated, obliterated by the word of John. And so she is, not as a woman but as an object of mimetic rivalry. The brothers are interested in her only as a function of their rivalry. In shielding the prophet from his wife's vengeance, Herod acts according to the laws of mimetic desire and intensifies Herodias's vengefulness, thus generating more conflict and fulfilling the word of the prophet. Herodias is not primarily a character in a story; she represents the violent next stage in the necessary evolution of mimetic desire.

When I imitate the desire of my brother, I desire that which he desires. We prevent one another from satisfying our common desire. The more the resistance increases on both sides, the more desire is reinforced; the more the model is made the obstacle, the more the obstacle is made the model, so that in the last analysis, desire is attracted only when it is thwarted. It focuses on obstacles only. John the Baptist is first of all the object Herod does not want to yield. As a prophet, on the other hand, he is a tantalizing obstacle, powerless but intractable, resistant to all attempts at corruption, and this fascinates Herodias even more than it does Herod.

The metamorphosis of desire into hatred results from its mimetic nature. The more mimetic it becomes, the more it incites imitation, and the more rapidly it is transmitted from one individual to another. Mark immediately gives an extraordinary illustration of this phenomenon:

For when Herodias's daughter came in and danced, she pleased Herod and his guests; and the king said to the girl, 'Ask me for whatever you wish, and I will grant it.' And he promised, 'Whatever you ask me, I will give you, even half of my kingdom.' And she went out, and said to her mother, 'What shall I ask?' And she said, 'The head of John the baptizer.' And she came in immediately with haste to the king, and asked, saying, 'I want you to give me at once the head of John the Baptist on a platter.'

Something very odd happens here, or rather, does not happen. Salome has no desire to formulate. Young people are supposed to desire a thousand foolish and impossible things, but Salome has nothing to say. Her silence expresses, I think, something essential about the Gospels' conception of desire. Contrary to what Freud believes, to what we all believe, there is no preordained object of desire. Children in particular have to be told what to desire. Unlike the sultry temptress of the nineteenth and twentieth centuries, the Salome of the gospel is really a child. The Greek word for her is not *kore* but *korasion*, which means 'a little girl.'

Children are taught desire through example or speech, or both. Children imitate the desire of prestigious adults. Because Herod offers everything, he suggests nothing. Salome must go out and ask her mother what she ought to desire.

Does the mother really communicate her desire to her daughter? Perhaps Salome is only a passive intermediary, an obedient child who does what she is told to do. The text suggests otherwise. After speaking to her mother, she becomes a different person. Hesitation gives way to eager anticipation: 'And she came in immediately with haste to the king, and asked, saying, "I want you to give me at once the head of John the Baptist on a platter."'

'Immediately,' 'with haste,' 'at once.' In a text with very little descriptive detail, we have three adverbs that signify impatience and feverishness. Salome is worried at the thought that the king might return to his senses after the dance has ended and retract his promise. Her mother's desire has become her own. The fact that Salome's desire is entirely imitative detracts not a whit from its intensity; on the contrary, the imitation is fiercer than the original.

Salome is a child. She has nothing to do with the dance of the seven veils and other orientalia. At first she is a blank sheet of desire, then, in one instant, she shifts to the height of mimetic violence.

It is difficult to imagine a sequence better suited to reveal the mimetic genesis of desire than the passage just quoted: first the girl's silence in response to the overwhelming offer of the king, then the question to the mother, then the mother's response, and finally the girl's espousal of her mother's desire. The child asks the adult, not to fulfill some desire that would be hers, but to provide her with the desire she lacks. To Mark, imitation is the essence of desire. This conception is alien both to our philosophical views of imitation and to our modern theories of desire.

The scene is powerful, but it contradicts superficial realism. However rapid the contagion of desire can be from one individual to another, one can hardly believe that the mother's brief response to her daughter would suffice to kindle desire in the latter. This is too elliptical for Matthew, who deletes the exchange between mother and daughter. He sees only the awkwardness of it, not the genius. He tells simply and reasonably that the daughter is 'instructed' or 'prompted' by her mother. He feels he must interpret Mark. His interpretation is correct, but less vivid, less dramatic than Mark's. We do not see Salome transformed in one instant, mimetically, into a second Herodias.

After absorbing her mother's desire, Salome is one with Herodias. Each woman in turn plays the same role in relation to Herod. Our sacrosanct cult of desire prevents our recognizing this sameness. Desire is supposed to generate differences.

The modern interpreters are just about evenly divided. One half portrays Salome and the other half Herodias as the heroine of the most intense desire. Far from individualizing its victims, as our modern cult of desire demands, mimetic desire makes them interchangeable. If you consider the modern adaptations *in toto*, all of them celebrations of either Salome or Herodias, you will find they unwittingly reassert the truth each one taken separately denies. The mother and the daughter are one and the same. As desire intensifies, it renders its victims increasingly interchangeable.

With the exception of the prophet, there are only mimetic doubles and look-alikes in our text: Herod and his brother, Herod and Herodias, and finally the guests. Herod and Herodias phonetically suggest sameness, and the two names are constantly reiterated in our text, whereas the name of Salome is never pronounced, perhaps because nothing in it echoes the other names and suggests reciprocal mimicry, as in the case of Herod and Herodias.

I have not forgotten the dance, but before coming to it I must consider a notion that pervades our entire text, even though it is not explicitly mentioned: the evangelical notion of 'scandal.' 'Skadzein', in Greek, signifies 'to limp'; *skandalon* designates the obstacle which repels and attracts simultaneously, the stumbling block. As insignificant as the first encounter with the stumbling block may seem, one always returns to it; the initial accident leads us back to it obsessively. Instead of teaching us to avoid it, this strange obstacle causes us to stumble again and again: that is, to limp.

'Scandal' describes the consequences of mimetic desire. The more my model interferes with my desire, the more I interfere with his; the more we both turn each other into fascinating stumbling blocks, the more we 'scandalize' one another. If you examine the various uses of the word scandal in the four Gospels, you will realize that it applies to domains that appear to us independent of each other: obsessive human conflict, many psychopathological symptoms, religious idolatry, mob violence and scapegoating, 'demoniacal' possession, and, of course, mimetic desire. It covers so much ground that we feel it must be a loose and impressionistic concept, whereas in reality it is immensely powerful, although precisely because it is so powerful it is completely misunderstood and neglected: our most trusted intellectual instruments in the sciences of man are unable to grasp it, so this power remains unperceived. The text we are reading unfolds a process of desire, conflict, and collective scapegoating that is one with scandal itself.

To Herodias, John the Baptist is a scandal both as a bone of contention between herself and her husband and as a speaker of an unpalatable truth, the truth of mimetic desire itself: desire has no worse enemy than its own truth. Desire does its best to turn the truth into a scandal. The truth itself becomes scandalous, and this is scandal at its worst. Herod and Herodias keep the truth a prisoner. The same thing happens to Jesus. 'Happy are those,' Jesus says, 'for whom I will not be a cause of scandal' (Matthew 11:6).

Scandal always tends to contaminate everyone still untouched by it, especially those who should remain most alien to it – children, for example. To interpret Salome as I do is to see her as a child-victim of scandal, and to apply to her Mark's words on scandal and childhood: 'Whoever receives one such child in my name receives me. . . . Whoever scandalizes one of these little ones who believe in me, it would be better for him if a great millstone were hung round his neck and he were thrown into the sea' (Mark 9:37, 42). The child inevitably takes the nearest adult as his model. If he encounters only people already scandalized, too busy with their scandalous desire to respond positively, he takes their behavior as a model and turns him- or herself into a mimetic reproduction of it, a grotesque caricature.

To circumvent Herod and to obtain his consent to the death of the prophet, Herodias makes use of her own child. How could she fail to scandalize Salome? To protect herself from scandal, the child embraces it: she embraces her mother's atrocious desire.

Everything that touches upon desire in the Gospels perpetuates the physical connotations of the word *scandal*. The metaphors for guilty and destructive passion are metaphors of paralysis and infirmity: the stone suspended from the neck; hindered movement; being strapped down. Scandal and the dance stand in opposition to one another. Scandal is everything that prevents us from dancing. The grace of the dancer delivers us less from our bodily infirmities, which are insignificant, than from *skandalon* itself. The movements of dance seem to untangle for us the otherwise unyielding knot of our desires. To enjoy the dance is to identify with the dancer; it is to dance with her and no longer to feel our imprisonment in Mallarmé's 'ice' or to be mired in Sartre's 'visqueux.'

This metaphorical opposition between scandal and the dance is evident, but it does not altogether account for our pleasure. The art of the dance simultaneously excites and appeases desire. Dancing is not merely the bodily representation of that freedom to which we aspire; were it only that, its effects would be symbolic in the most shallow and static sense, the sense of traditional esthetic and philosophical theories. This symbolic aspect is undoubtedly present, but there is something beyond; and our text gives us a glimpse, I believe, of that awesome beyond.

Mark has no realistic description in the taste of the nineteenth century; he is not interested in physical detail, like Flaubert; he speaks only of what comes before and after the dance. Nevertheless, Mark is saying more about the dance than modern writers, for all their realism and their symbolism.

The dance accelerates the mimetic process; it brings within Salome's influence all the guests at Herod's banquet and causes all desires to converge upon one and the same object, the head on the platter, the head of John on Salome's platter.

Tradition recognizes Salome as a great artist, and it must have its reasons; a tradition so powerful and durable is not established without a cause. But what is the cause? The dance is never described. The desire of Salome is in no way original, since it is modeled on a previous desire. Even the words belong to Herodias. Salome adds only the idea of the platter. 'I want you,' she says, 'to give me at once the head of John the Baptist on a platter.' Herodias had mentioned the head, but not the platter. The platter constitutes the one object that belongs exclusively to Salome. If there is something in the text that justifies Salome's reputation, it must be this platter. There is nothing else.

The platter, indeed, is the one detail everyone remembers. Everything else is forgettable, but not the platter. At the beginning of the twentieth century, art is almost synonymous with Salome's platter. The idea is scandalous, decadent, so barbarously crude that it is refined; it is the quintessence of *fin de siècle* estheticism.

Being made of metal, like the executioner's sword, the platter stresses the cold cruelty of the two women's desire. But there is something else. Extreme mimetic desire focuses less on some object situated behind the obstacle than on the obstacle itself. Desire feels manipulated and dominated by its model and rival. It wants to dominate and manipulate that same rival; it wants to turn scandal itself into its own thing; it wants the impossible; it wants scandal itself as a property of the dance.

By having John's head brought in on a platter, Salome causes the ultimate nightmare to materialize. The bodies of his victims represent to the murderer the scandal that tears him apart. Because it is more portable and manageable, the severed head provides a better representation, and this same head on a platter a better one still. The platter turns the head into an object offered to all, one of the dishes circulating among the guests at Herod's banquet.

One recognizes here something of the fascination that the head of the antagonist, a member of some neighboring tribe ritually designated by the cultural order as the enemy, exercises on certain primitives. Primitives sometimes subject these heads to a treatment that renders them incorruptible and diminishes their size, transforming them into a type of fetish. This refinement is analogous to Salome's horrible desire.

It is not without cause that the head on the platter crowns and concludes the dance of Salome. The two elements of the narrative explain each other. John, we learn, has become the scandal of Salome; now the dancer and the power of her art succeed in making John's head the scandal of every spectator. This gives pleasure not to Herod alone, but to all of his guests. They all react in the same way, and the king expresses the sentiments of all when he offers Salome half of his kingdom. They are on the verge of being possessed by Salome, on the verge of a collective trance, and in their collective name Herod implores her to make that possession more complete. When you have great possessions you become identical with them, and when you offer them to a dancer, it means you want to be possessed by her.

The platter under John's head symbolizes the dance; it is an artist's idea, as I have suggested, but is it really original? If you look closely, its apparent originality dissolves, giving way once again to mimicry.

When Herodias, in answer to Salome, says, 'the head of John the Baptist,' she probably does not allude to decapitation. In Greek, as in English, to demand someone's head is to demand his death. Period.

The head is a figure of speech that consists in taking the part for the whole. Rhetoricians call this a 'metonymy.' The text had already mentioned Herodias's hatred in a neutral language which suggested no fetishism of her enemy's head: 'And Herodias had a grudge against him, and wanted to kill him.'

Even if Herodias intended to suggest the type of death she wished for the prophet when she mentioned his head, it still might not mean that she wanted to hold that head in her hands, that she desired the physical object. Even in countries where beheading is practiced, to demand someone's head must be interpreted rhetorically, and Salome takes her mother literally. She does not do so intentionally – she has not yet learned to distinguish words from things. She does not recognize the metonymy.

The platter must be less original than it appears. To contemplate the beheading of John the Baptist is one thing; to physically hold his head in one's hands is another. The second eventuality poses a practical problem that Salome solves in the most practical manner. The best place for a freshly severed head is some kind of platter. The head on the platter is not really an esthetic idea; it is not even an idea. It is a commonsense reaction to the misinterpreted command of Herodias. Salome takes her mother's words so literally that she misunderstands the message. She seems perverse and sadistic, and perhaps she is, but it is the same as being merely childish. Anyway, whatever she is psychologically does not really matter. It cannot fail to boil down to some overly literal form of imitation. If you interpret too literally, you will misinterpret through sheer avoidance of interpretation. Excessive concern for accuracy must invariably result in an inaccurate translation. What seems most 'creative' in Salome, most 'innovative,' as we love to say, is the very reverse. It is exclusively mimetic, mechanical, and truly hypnotic in its submission to the model that inspired it.

I am not saying this to depreciate the art of Salome. Contrary to what our exhausted avant-garde believes, all great artistic ideas are of this type – narrowly, myopically imitative. Tradition knew this, and it spoke of art in terms of mimesis, the Greek word for imitation. The modern striving for originality at all costs has reached an impasse. The greatest efforts today lead to insignificant obscenities. To discourage imitation is to drive it underground toward stylistic preciosity and ideological fads. We should not renounce the notion of mimesis but make it broad enough to include desire – or it is desire, perhaps, that should be broadened to include mimesis. By separating mimesis and desire in order to distinguish and protect order from disorder, Plato and his followers mutilated both, and we remain the prisoners of a mutilation that generates all the false dichotomies in our system of knowledge: between the esthetic, for instance, and the ethical or the psychological.

The dance does not abolish but exacerbates desire; it accelerates mimetic contagion and substitutions. We are prevented from dancing by our physical inadequacy, of course, but even more by the dreadful intertwining of our desires. Each of us is a Herodias, afflicted with some importunate prophet. The entanglements of desire are different with each and every one; each and every one has his own model-obstacle system, but the mechanism of scandal is always identical; this identity makes substitutions possible. Like all ritual arts, dance is a mimed drama that turns the participants, and even mere spectators, into a single whole; and the unity of this whole, the participation of all, is strengthened by the designation of a single enemy whose head everybody now demands: the head of John the Baptist.

To say that the dance pleases not only Herod but all his guests is to say that, by the end of the dance, all are possessed by the desire of Salome. In the head of John the Baptist, they identify not her scandal alone, nor scandal in general – that does not exist – but each his own scandal. The collective 'yes!' to the beheading is more than polite acquiescence. Salome's passion has become the passion of all, and they all demand that John's head be produced 'immediately, with haste.' Mimicry once more. The power of the dance resembles that of the shaman who exorcizes the evil demon or the noxious substance that has invaded his patients' bodies. They had been possessed by some tormentor, and the dance liberates them through another possession. The dancer can make the lame and the hunchback dance because her dance exorcizes the demon that was in them. She performs a collective act of revenge. By espousing the violent desire of Salome and her mother, all the participants vicariously satisfy their own desire. It is not Hegelian 'negativity' nor the Freudian unconscious that guarantees the symbolicity of the prophet's head, but the mimetic contagion of collective murder.

The beheading of John the Baptist results from a process of scapegoating that owes its distinctive character to mimetic desire, to the same force, therefore, that caused the earlier cleavages and fragmentations. The narration coincides with a mimetic crisis that concludes and resolves itself with the execution of the prophet. There is an element of randomness in the process, and it is clearly illustrated by the 'What shall I ask?' of Salome. The choice of the victim comes last, after the dance, at the moment when the already mimetic desire of Herodias transmits itself mimetically to her daughter, who, mimetically too, retransmits it to her admirers, and finally to Herod.

Beyond a certain threshold of excitement, almost any human group will focus on almost any victim. Mimetic desire spreads as it exacerbates. Its evolution is a shift from the private to the public sphere, from duality to multiplicity, from the individual to the mob. Like the Passion of Jesus, the passion of John the Baptist illustrates the birth of mimetic desire, its development, and finally its paroxysm and resolution in unanimous scapegoating. Salome's question, 'What shall I ask?' marks the beginning of Salome's desire and also its end, since it refers to a victim and reveals that, at that instant, designated by Herodias or perhaps by anybody else, any victim will do.

Mimetic desires cannot fail to oppose each other as long as they focus upon the same object, upon the same living being whose life they want to spare in order to appropriate that being – as did Herod with John when he locked him in prison: mimetic desires are irreconcilable at first, and they gradually disrupt the entire community. Only when they have reached the stage of fascinated hatred can they be reconciled in the destruction of some common object. The dreadful paradox of these desires is that they can make peace with each other only at the expense of some victim.

Herod's final decision is not the independent act of a sovereign;

it, too, is the fruit of mimetic suggestion. Only he can ratify a death sentence, but, like Pilate's sentence against Jesus a little later, this one is not really the sovereign's sentence. Herod is subjugated by the formidable mimetic pressure that emanates from his guests.

When he learns that the dancer demands the head of John, 'the king was exceedingly sorry, but because of his oaths and his guests, he did not want to break his word to her.' Like Herod, the guests, being pleased, want to please the dancer, and they do not have the same reason as Herod to deny her request. John means nothing to them. At the crucial moment, therefore, the guests provide a decisive supplement of mimetic energy. Mimetic influence depends on the number, the quality, and the intensity of those who exert that influence. Mark carefully points out that the guests are numerous and influential: they comprise the entire elite of the kingdom, 'courtiers and officers and the leading men of Galilee.'

In a mimetic crisis, cultural institutions dissolve and are returned to the mob. This is what happens here to the kingship of Herod, in an attenuated form. The ultimate source of all sovereignty is the mimetic unanimity of the mob. At the height of a mimetic crisis, a single head can suffice to appease the universal perturbation. Concrete objects have disappeared. Nothing is left except for all the desires crisscrossing each other. A single head may suffice, therefore, to appease the universal perturbation. Order is restored.

Widespread scandal precluded the satisfaction of all desires and troubled all relationships, but now scandal, the inert and docile object that circulates on Salome's platter like a thing offered, has become a bond of sociability. It has power to reconcile, both as a terrifying spectacle and as an object of exchange: 'And immediately the king sent a soldier of the guard and gave orders to bring his head. He went and beheaded him in the prison, and brought his head on a platter, and gave it to the girl; and the girl gave it to her mother.'

When I emphasize mimetic desire everywhere, do I not minimize the effective manipulation of people and circumstances by Herodias in her power struggle with her husband? To arrive at her end, Herodias makes use of certain circumstances and customs: 'But an opportunity came when Herod on his birthday gave a banquet for his courtiers and officers and the leading men of Galilee.' Herod's birthday, the assembling of important officials, the banquet, the dance itself: these are, in effect, institutions that Herodias succeeds in utilizing against John. Behind this power is a knowledge which makes it possible, a knowledge of the effectiveness of ritual.

The opportune day, Herod's birthday, is a holiday that returns each year on a fixed date. All important people assemble, festive activities take place. A banquet is held, a dance is performed. These activities are certainly not 'religious,' but they derive from ritual. They resemble the rites of primitive cultures that often culminate in the ritual immolation of an animal or even a human sacrifice. All the data in our text can be read in a ritual and sacrificial key. Herodias succeeds in harnessing against her enemy certain forces that belong to ritual.

The climactic moments in our story can be read in a ritual key. But is this a new direction, different from the one I have taken? I do not think so. I have tried to show, in my work, that ritual is the reenactment of a mimetic crisis that was spontaneously resolved by the unanimous destruction of an arbitrary victim, a victim selected by mimetic desire itself when it tends to polarize on a so-called scapegoat at the height of the mimetic conflict brought about by mimetic desire itself. The whole sequence is religiously reenacted in ritual because the mimetic scapegoat mechanism constitutes an effective resolution of the crisis. That is the reason why primitive people resort to sacrificial ritual when confronted by a real or imaginary threat to the stability of their cultural order. Especially when they feel menaced by real mimetic discord, men resort to the ritual mimicry of that discord, not for its own sake but for the sake of the doubly vicarious sacrificial conclusion that might reconcile them once again and bring back the peace at the expense of a new victim. Ritual introduces nothing really new, nothing absolutely specific into the picture.

Ritual activity is intended as a protection against mimetic conflict primarily, but it acts indirectly and paradoxically. Far from trying to oppose that desire directly, in the sense that taboos and prohibitions do, it encourages, irritates, and accelerates the mimetic interplay with the purpose of channeling it in the direction of the designated victim, the victim sacrificed to the peace and harmony of the entire community.

There is no structural difference between ritual, properly speaking, and the natural, spontaneous course of the mimetic crisis. Thus a ritual dimension can be incorporated into the text of Mark with the greatest of ease. It is already built into it, so to speak. Far from running counter to the general course of events, the maneuver of Herodias, like all successful maneuvers, does nothing but reinforce and exploit that course to the detriment of the prophet.

This does not mean that everything is the same and that I confuse the sinister plot of Herodias with authentic ritual. The latter reenacts a former mimetic crisis and stirs up a partly artificial one, so to speak, in a spirit of religious and social collaboration. The scapegoat mechanism is reactivated in order to reconcile the entire community, rather than aimed against any particular victim. Even in the most savage rituals, the accent is on the positive. This is precisely why the historical evolution of ritual runs invariably toward an attenuation and even an elimination of religious violence.

Institutions like banquets and the dance are examples of this attenuation. Even the most diluted rituals, however, retain an affinity for collective violence. After eating and drinking, a crowd asks for something more, something extraordinary, an exciting spectacle, erotic or violent, or better still, both simultaneously. Herodias knows this: she knows how to make institutions derived from ritual help her murderous scheme. Being more interested in the death of her enemy than in the welfare of the community, she perverts the ritual function. Just as Herod's role runs parallel to that of Pilate in the Passion, hers is somewhat reminiscent of Caiaphas, who also perverts religious power. This perversion amounts to a return of ritual mimesis to its original virulence and violence. Herodias brings sacrifice back to its origin in collective victimization. Like the Passion itself, the story of John reveals that origin. The two gospel narratives are not myths but revelations of the scapegoat mechanism responsible for mythical representation. The prince and principal of this world is Satan, who is an imitator and a murderer from the beginning (John 8:44).

All modes of art are aspects of ritual made relatively autonomous by the 'esthetic' perspective. Dance cannot appear as a specific activity until the corporal and gestural aspects of the mimetic sequence have become distinguished from the aspects that turn into singing, or into the drama. All the traditional arts emerge from ritual. That is why they traditionally consist of a crisis that resolves itself in the contemplation of a victim whose ordeal and death reflect the transcendence of a superhuman order. Art is neither a meditation on death in general nor an 'esthetic experience' that would be truly independent. Philosophers and estheticians miss a point that is powerfully made by our gospel narrative because it is the very opposite of a pious tribute to the dance; it does not misrepresent or prettify the violent aspects of the dance.

There is a popular legend regarding the death of Salome. She was skating on the ice and she lost her balance; her neck hit upon a sharp edge in a sheet of ice, and in the fall, her head was severed from her body.

This legend confirms the association between the dance and sacrificial death in the popular mind. A successful dance puts the mimetic power in the hands of the dancer, who channels it in the direction of her choice, whereas an unsuccessful dance, the loss of balance on the ice, turns the dancer herself into a victim. The artist, the political leader, the master of ritual either stay on top and dominate the mimetic forces they unleash or they fail. They lose control and they become the victims. Salome seems to be alone in that legend, but she is not – the ice is a mirror and an image of the mimetic double.

Being one with the intersubjective process of mimetic desire in its progress toward a sacrificial denouement, our text is one with the dance. Even though he barely mentions it and above all does not attempt to describe it, Mark says a lot, even about dancing itself, because he necessarily espouses the movement of the dance as he unravels his mimetic sequence of mimetic rivalry, conflict, and sacrificial resolution. This sequence cannot fail to resemble some kind of ballet: each dancer in turn occupies the foreground, then rejoins the others in order to play his or her part in the unanimous paroxysm of sacrifice.

In the Western world, the arts of language tend to rebel against their sacrificial origin and function, often with paradoxical results. There is a close but highly complex relationship between this rebellion and the biblical and Christian impregnation of our culture. It is probable, even certain, that some analogous rebellion is taking place in the dance; many choreographers and dancers must consciously reject rather than unconsciously deny the collective and violent roots of their art. This is another story, however, quite different from the story of Salome. Dancers perhaps have the right gestures for it, but I am not sure we have the right language. The old words cannot do, and the new ones are not yet invented.

Peter's Denial and the Question of Mimesis

For the first time in the history of theorizing about literature and art, certain traditional notions have lost their prestige. Mimesis is one. Our modern idea of esthetic creation as mimesis, as a process of imitation, goes back to Aristotle who really borrowed it from Plato, although in Plato esthetic mimesis has negative connotations which we do not really understand.

Until recently mimesis has remained the imperial concept, the number one signifier of Western literary theory. But its signification, the meaning we attach to the term, has undergone strange metamorphoses. In Aristotle, mimesis is essentially dramatic and theatrical; the actor is a mime who imitates an action. During the Renaissance and after, Western writers felt inferior to their Greek and Roman predecessors and they exhorted each other to imitate them. A little later they became less modest and they decided they needed no intermediaries to imitate nature, meaning human nature. The concept of nature was gradually broadened and, in the nineteenth century, it turned into 'the whole of reality' – whatever that means. A vast middle-class audience demanded an art that would mirror its own perception of the world, its preoccupation with material objects, inseparable from the esthetics of realism and naturalism. Writers should aim at 'a faithful representation of reality.'

In the middle of the nineteenth century, the poet Charles Baudelaire and others reacted violently against the idea that the function of art was to imitate reality. They equated this idea with a defense of middle-class provincialism and philistinism. In our time, the rebellion of modernism has become the new orthodoxy. In recent years, the general emphasis on language and literary structuralism has

René Girard

discredited mimetic realism, at least on the European continent. Language is made up of arbitrary signs. There is no common yardstick between words and things, and the idea that literature can imitate reality is entirely mythical. It depends on an act of faith in the universal validity of a certain discourse.

It is true that the esthetics of mimetic realism are often associated with other Western ideas such as faith in science, in social equality, in political democracy, and more generally with faith in historical progress. Realistic literature is a dimension of that most powerful grasp on reality which is the essence of the West and, as the West realized this essence, its literature became more mimetic and realistic. When it fails to do so it neglects its mission; its true nature is perverted. One finds such ideas not merely in the Marxist theoreticians of literature such as Georg Lukács, but in non-Marxist critics as well. In the magnum opus of Eric Auerbach, entitled *Mimesis*, not only is the literature of the Christian and post-Christian West regarded as more mimetic and realistic than any other, but as becoming more so during the course of history. The unity of the works and the unity's dynamics are one with this single *idée-force*.

One interesting aspect of Auerbach is his insistence on the role of the Gospels in this orientation toward mimesis. The word 'mimesis' is Greek but the impetus is Judaic and Christian. In order to demonstrate his point, Auerbach refers at some length to the episode of Peter's denial in the gospel of St Mark. Auerbach vigorously stresses the modernity of the Gospels from the standpoint of mimetic realism and he gives a veritable *explication de texte*, even though the original text of Mark, or even a translation of it, is not provided. This is quite contrary to the practice of Auerbach elsewhere in the book. He would probably have justified this omission on the grounds that the gospel is really a non-literary text, a religious text. From Auerbach's own standpoint, the difference between the two is questionable.

I will now go back to the text of Peter's denial in order to investigate further its relationship to mimesis. After Jesus had been arrested, the disciples fled in all directions, but Peter alone or, according to John, Peter and another disciple, followed at a distance right into the courtyard of the High Priest's palace, and, I quote: 'there he remained, sitting among the attendants, warming himself at a fire.' John says that 'the servants and the police had made a charcoal fire, because it was cold, and were standing round it warming themselves.' And Peter too 'was standing with them, sharing the warmth.'

The text shifts to inside the palace, where a hostile and brutal interrogation of Jesus was taking place. Then we shift back to Peter and, again I quote:

Meanwhile Peter was still in the courtyard downstairs. One of the High Priest's servant girls came by and saw him there warming himself. She looked into his face and said, 'You were there too, with this man from Nazareth, this Jesus.' But he denied it: 'I do not know him,' he said. 'I do not understand what you mean.' Then he went outside into the porch; and the girl saw him there again and began to say to the bystanders, 'He is one of them,' and again he denied it. (Mark)

Again, a little later, the bystanders said to Peter, 'Surely you are one of them. You must be; you are Galilean.' At this he broke out in curses, and with an oath he said: 'I do not know this man you speak of.' Then the cock crowed a second time; and Peter remembered how Jesus had said to him, 'Before the cock crows twice you will disown me three times.' And he burst into tears. (Mark)

Auerbach makes some shrewd comments on that text: 'I do not believe,' he writes, 'that there is a single passage in an antique historian where direct discourse is employed in this fashion in a brief, direct dialogue.' He also observes that 'the dramatic tension of the moment when the actors stand face to face has been given a salience and immediacy compared with which the dialogue of antique tragedy appears highly stylized.' It is quite true, and I am not averse to using such words as 'mimesis' and 'mimetic realism' to describe the feeling of true-to-life description which is created here, but I do not think that Auerbach really succeeds in justifying his use of the term 'mimesis.'

Careful and sensitive as he is as a reader, Auerbach did not perceive something that is highly visible and which should immediately strike every observer: it is the role of mimesis in the text itself, the presence of mimesis as content. Imitation is not a separate theme but it permeates the relationship between all the characters; they all imitate each other. This mimetic dimension of behavior dominates both verbal and non-verbal behavior. Peter's behavior is imitative from the beginning, before a single word is uttered by anyone.

In Mark and John, when Peter entered, the fire was already burning. People were 'standing round warming themselves.' Peter too went to that fire; he followed the general example. This is natural enough on a cold night. Peter was cold, like everybody else, and there was nothing to do but to wait for something to happen. This is true enough, but the Gospels give us very little concrete background, very few visual details, and three out of four mention the fire in the courtyard as well as Peter's presence next to it. They mention this not once but twice. The second mention occurs when the servant girl intervenes. She sees Peter warming himself by the fire with the other people. It is dark and she can recognize him because he has moved close to the fire and his face is lighted by it. But the fire is more than a dramatic prop. The servant seems eager to embarrass Peter, not because he entered the courtyard, but because of his presence close to that fire. In John it is the courtyard, upon the recommendation of another disciple acquainted with the High Priest.

A fire in the night is more than a source of heat and of light. A fire provides a center of attraction; people arrange themselves in a circle around it and they are no longer a mere crowd; they become a community. All the faces and hands are jointly turned toward the fire as in a prayer. An order appears which is a communal order. The identical postures and the identical gestures seem to evoke some kind of deity, some sacred being that would dwell in the fire and for which all hands seem to be reaching, all faces seem to be watching.

There is nothing specifically Christian, there is nothing specifically Jewish about that role of fire; it is more like primitive fire-worship, but nevertheless it is deeply rooted in our psyches; most human beings are sensitive to this and the servant girl must be; that is why she is scandalized to see Peter warm himself by that fire. The only people who really belong there are the people who gravitate to the High Priest and the Temple, those who belong to the inner core of the Jewish religious and national community. The servant maid probably knows little about Jesus except that he has been arrested and is suspected of something like high treason. To have one of his disciples around the fire is like having an unwelcome stranger at a family gathering.

The fire turns a chance encounter into a quasi-ritualistic affair and Peter violates the communal feeling of the group, or perhaps what Heidegger would call its Being-together, its *Mitsein*, which is an important modality of being. In English, togetherness would be a good word for this if the media had not given it a bad name, emptying it entirely of what it is supposed to designate.

This *Mitsein* is the servant girl's own *Mitsein*. She rightfully belongs with these people; but when she gets there, she finds her place occupied by someone who does not belong. She acts like Heidegger's 'shepherd of being,' a role which may not be as meek as the expression suggests. It would be excessive in this case to compare the shepherd of being with the Nazi stormtrooper, but the servant maid reminds us a little of the platonic watchdog, or of the Parisian concierge. In John she is described as precisely that, the guardian of the door, the keeper of the gate.

This *Mitsein* is her *Mitsein*, and she wants to keep it to herself and to the people entitled to it. When she says: 'You are one of them, you belong with Jesus,' she really means, 'You do not belong here, you are not one of us.'

We always hear that Peter acts impulsively, but this really means mimetically. He always moves too fast and too far; but still, why move so close to the center, why did the fire exert such an attraction on him?

The arrest of Jesus has forever destroyed the community of his disciples, or so did the desciples believe, so did Peter himself believe. The disciples have fled. 'I will smite the shepherd and the sheep of his flock shall be scattered abroad.' Peter had abandoned everything to follow Jesus. His Being-together was there and it was lost. This is the reason Peter answered the way he did the first time the servant girl addressed him. The question is always the same: 'Are you one of them, are you with him?' That question has become meaningless. That is why Peter answers, 'I do not know. I do not understand what you mean.' This is not the barefaced lie we imagine. There is no such thing, perhaps, as a really deliberate lie. Peter does not belong anywhere or with anybody. He has lost touch with his own being.

In his state of shock, only elementary impulses are left in him. The night is cold and there is a fire; everybody turns to the fire and so does Peter. Just like everybody else at this juncture, but more than anybody else, Peter is shivering in the cold and groping about in the dark. That explains, perhaps, why he got so close to the edge of the fire, in the most visible spot. His ontological deprivation made the fire even more attractive to him than to the others. To him especially, the fire is more than a source of light and heat. By himself Peter is nothing; there is no life in him. Being means Being-together; the important thing is not the warmth as such, but the fact that it is shared with the others. John emphasizes this sharing: 'And Peter too was standing among them, sharing the warmth.' Luke also gives prominence to the Being-together: 'They lit a fire in the middle of the courtyard and sat around it, and Peter sat among them.'

The servant girl feels that Peter tries to share in something in which he should not share. Peter immediately understands the significance of the fire; he moves away from it but he does not leave the courtyard. He moves to a less conspicuous spot but does not really try to hide. Once aroused, however, the servant girl demands more; she has kept an eye on Peter and a second time she says: 'This fellow is one of them.' In Matthew it is a second servant girl who addresses Peter the second time, but I prefer Mark's version. The same servant girl repeats her own words, except that this time she addresses the crowd rather than Peter; she imitates herself in order to be imitated by the crowd. The first time she shows what everybody else should say to Peter, but nothing happens. The second time she gives an example of how her own example should be followed. And this time she succeeds. The bystanders repeat after her: 'Surely you are one of them. You must be; you are a Galilean.'

The pattern initiated by the servant girl is one of collective pressure against Peter and the bystanders adopt it readily because it corresponds to the normal behavior of a community in the face of an intruder. Either you belong around the fire and you do not belong with Jesus or you belong with Jesus and you do not belong around the fire. No *Mitsein* extends to the whole of mankind or it is no longer a *Mitsein* in the Heideggerian sense. In order to keep a *Mitsein* healthy and shepherd it properly, it is not sufficient to keep together those who belong together – one must also keep out those who do not belong. Heidegger says nothing of this but the gospel text does, and it is not difficult to show that much human behavior proves the gospel right. The Being of a community is one with the exclusiveness of its Being-together. Against an intruder, it is not difficult to mobilize all those who belong together, and this is what the servant has done.

There is no lack of communication between Peter and his antagonists. They all know what is at stake. Peter has been caught stealing into the community of those who warm themselves by the fire. The servant girl loudly proclaims that he belongs with Jesus because she takes it for granted, like most people, that membership in one group is exclusive of membership in the other.

Only one *Mitsein*, one Being-together, is explicitly mentioned, the group of Jesus and his disciples, but two are at stake and the more important of the two at this point, even in the eyes of Peter, is the one that is not mentioned, the one which has the fire as its symbolic center. The people around the fire really say to Peter: 'You pretend to belong with us but you can't because you belong with Jesus and the other Galileans.' The bystanders imitate and repeat exactly what the servant girl has said except for this one addition: 'You are a Galilean.' Matthew is even more explicit: the bystanders say to Peter: 'Your accent gives you away.' The maidservant had said nothing about Peter's accent because Peter had not yet opened his mouth. Like the people of Jerusalem, Peter speaks Aramaic, but with a Galilean accent, a provincial accent. If you do not belong with the people around you, they say that you have an accent; in other words, you speak with a difference, you cannot imitate their speech as perfectly as they imitate each other's speech. Perfect imitation and the togetherness of being go hand in hand.

An outsider will never be acceptable unless and until his imitation becomes perfect. Mimesis is the only key that can open a closed community. A mimetic definition of culture does not result in too much openness; it does not do away with the barrier between insiders and outsiders. Only the most superficial forms of imitation are voluntary. However hard Peter tries, he must always speak like a Galilean. He is an adult and he cannot change the way he speaks. This is the reason the matter of his accent is brought up at this point. The more Peter speaks, the more he betrays his real identity. He betrays himself and, in order to counter this self-betrayal, he is forced more and more into the betrayal of Jesus.

The people around the fire are loyal servants of the Temple. They belong to the inner center of Jewish religious and national life, but they have no education and their contribution is minimal. Their pride of place resembles the snobbery one finds today in the cultural centers of our world – great universities, for instance, or world capitals. The less one can do for the place in which one lives, the more importance one attaches to living there; and rightly so, because it is the place which is doing something for one, and one feels intense disdain for the people who do not belong there. Peter senses this, and his desire to make himself acceptable increases each time he is denounced as an outsider and is rejected as such.

The dialogue between Peter and his persecutors becomes sharper and sharper; it is a form of competitive emulation or mimetic rivalry. The conflictive nature of the relationship does not make it less imitative; it is more imitative than ever. Since Peter cannot lose his Galilean accent, he must emphasize another kind of imitation. Why does he become vociferous in his denial of Jesus? His antagonists know the truth and he knows that they know. He is not trying to make himself believable or to intimidate anybody. By resorting to violence, he is not widening the rift with the people around the fire: he is trying to establish a bridge. His violence is not directed against his listeners. With these people, he knows, the arrest of Jesus is equivalent to a conviction of guilt. His furious refusal to have anything to do with Jesus amounts to a rejection symmetrical to the one of which he himself is the object. Peter is an imitator once more. What these people are doing to him, he is doing, too; but he is doing it to Jesus in the hope that all will be able to unite and be reconciled against Jesus, that the togetherness which is denied to him will generate the common victimization of Jesus. What he really means is: 'We have the same enemy and therefore must be friends.' The Being of a community does not consist merely in loving together but in hating together as well. The only imitation which is not superficial and which is accessible to an outsider like Peter is this togetherness of hatred, mimetic scapegoating. Peter does not really deny his past, but he tries to atone for it and to present himself as a new man.

Peter's denial is part of the Passion of Jesus; it is presented as an episode of this Passion. It is part of a larger process that also depends on mimetic relationships between the various actors. These may mimetically disagree at first, but then are mimetically reconciled against Jesus; the whole process tends, therefore, to a mimetic unanimity which is never achieved in the episode of Peter but which is achieved in the case of the Passion as a whole. The jealousy and fears of the religious authorities, the caprice of the crowd, the political prudence of Pilate when he yields to that caprice, all the various sentiments of the people involved amount to variations of mimetic desire or contagion that finally converge and unite in a unanimous assent to the Crucifixion.

Most anthropologists and historians of religion are convinced that the Gospels are nothing but the accompanying text, or the founding myth, of a new sacrificial cult. All stable forms of association among men are cemented in blood. Either institutionally, in religious communities founded on sacrifice, or spontaneously, men are irresistibly drawn into common victimization in order to preserve or to establish a bond of unity between them.

On this point, the most archaic theologians see eye to eye with the philosophers of the Enlightenment and their heirs, the contemporary social scientists. On this point there is a perfect agreement between the most traditional Christianity and the modern belief that there is nothing truly original in Christianity, that it is a sacrificial religion similar to all others. This unanimity is impressive, but the text we have just read raises the most serious doubts regarding the sacrificial reading of the Gospels. Nineteenth- and twentieth-century anthropologists have done a superb job of showing that the central event in the Gospels, the death and resurrection of Jesus, is really the same or pretty much the same as in most sacrificial myths. They have proved their point convincingly, I believe; but far from excluding an unbridgeable difference between the two, this identity of the central event opens up a possibility which they have missed. The Passion is really a sacrifice, and so is Peter's denial; it is not a fully effective sacrifice but it is an attempted sacrifice. One point, however, has been overlooked, and this point is crucial. Sacrificial cults are interpreted and performed from the standpoint of the sacrificers – in other words, from the standpoint of the actors in the Passion or, in the case of our episode, of the people who rightfully warm themselves by the fire. The primary concern of these cults is the social bond which, in our episode, is suggested by the fire, then reinforced when those who, because they truly belong there, mimetically unite against Peter. In sacrificial cults, fire, indeed, is sacred; there may be no other deity but fire itself or its heavenly counterpart, the sun. The sacrificial victim may be interpreted ultimately as a divine but is viewed primarily as a threatening outsider, a malevolent intruder who should be expelled and destroyed.

The attitude of the people around the fire and the intimations of fire worship are certainly consonant with most religious cults – we cannot be surprised to see Peter slipping back into the immemorial practice of mankind – but this practice is not what the Gospels advocate. The Being-together of Heidegger with its basis in ethnic, linguistic, and cultural characteristics is also alien to the message of the Gospels, as it is essentially pagan.

Peter's denial is an aborted return to something both very banal and very fundamental in human culture. Either institutionally, in religious communities founded on sacrifice, or spontaneously, but always mimetically, men are irresistibly drawn into such forms of victimization in order to establish or to preserve their social bond.

Peter denies his Lord in order not to be derided and persecuted, in order to avoid a fate similar to, if less tragic than, that of Jesus. It is a well-known Christian idea, indeed, that we all inflict more suffering on Jesus in order not to suffer with Him, in order not to be crucified with Him. Peter's denial is a literal illustration of this theme.

Peter's denial makes a good deal of sense in the context of initiation rituals. An initiation often consists of an act of violence by the future initiate. The young man is supposed to prove his worth to the tribe by killing a dangerous animal or even a man, and his victim is perceived as the enemy of the entire group. In the cultures of head hunting, for instance, the victim normally belongs to the alien group from which such victims are regularly drawn; between this group and the group which the sacrificer will now join, thanks to the mediation of this sacrifice, a state of permanent hostility prevails. Initiation into the rival group is exactly the same process, with the two groups inverted.

To deny Jesus in the sense of Peter's denial means to sacrifice him. When Jesus accepts death, therefore, he cannot be performing a sacrifice, at least in the same sense. Jesus accepts death in order never to behave like Peter and the other people around the fire. Jesus dies to put an end to sacrificial behavior; he dies not to strengthen closed communities through sacrifice but to dissolve them through its elimination. When the death of Jesus is presented as sacrifice, its real significance is lost. The sacrificial definition makes it impossible to distinguish Peter's denial and Peter's confession of faith. The definition suppresses all differences between the perspective of the persecutors and the perspective of the victims. Most victims, of course, are only would-be persecutors, like Peter. Jesus, therefore, is a very special victim who refuses not only the vicious circle of mimetic violence but also the breaking of that circle through the mimetic violence of unanimous scapegoating. Regarding the relationship of sacrifice and victimization, social unity and victimization, the Gospels spell out a truth which is nowhere else to be found.

An essential component of that truth, of course, is the mimetic nature of victimization and the mimetic nature of the human relations that lead to victimization. I believe that the text of Peter's denial is highly characteristic in that respect. The amount of redundancy or repetition in it is astonishing. Everybody is doing the same thing, everybody is saying the same thing. Peter is told the same thing three times, the first two times by the servant girl alone, the third time by the people around the fire. Peter, too, imitates himself as well as the others; except for its increasing violence, his denial remains the same every time. And yet this repetition is not mere rhetoric: the text manages to sustain our interest, it teaches us something about the mimetic nature of desire and of human relations, something no other text ever taught. Even though it is very brief, this text reveals three modalities of mimetic interaction that are found throughout the gospel. First, there is a mimesis which is one with the cohesiveness of human culture, or subculture: around the fire, everybody behaves in the same manner, everybody speaks the same words. Second, there is a mimesis of desire that is divisive and destructive of culture because it produces rivalry around an object that two or more desire; partners, co-imitators of each other's desires, who cannot share or do not want to share: the servant girl does not want to share the warmth of the fire with Peter. If one looks carefully at Plato's theories of mimesis one will see that these first two modalities are present in his work, but they are hopelessly confused and, as was shrewdly pointed out by Jacques Derrida, Plato contradicts himself in regard to mimesis. Sometimes he sees it as a factor of social order and sometimes as a factor of disorder, with no criteria of distinction between the two; as a result, Plato's view of mimesis cannot be made systematic and coherent.

The problem is not with the passage from the integrative mimesis to the disintegrative mimesis: the mimesis of social order becomes degraded into the mimesis of desire and rivalry. Many dialogues of Plato, and above all, *The Republic*, illustrate that degradation. The problem lies in the passage from disorder to order. There is nothing in Plato that can explicate genesis of order, the transmutation of mimetic rivalry into the functional culture. There is no intelligible transition between the two; that is why, in Plato, the genesis and perpetuation of the social order is a transcendental and metaphysical mystery, just as obscure as the religious mystery in primitive mythology and ritual. The revelation of the social mechanism that transmutes the bad mimesis into the good mimesis and into order is a purely biblical discovery; it occurs in Chapter 53 of Isaiah and elsewhere in the Bible, but it is most explicit in the Gospels. It is the mimetic mechanism of unanimous victimization; it is the mechanism which Peter tries vainly to reactivate with Jesus as the victim in the text I have just read.

The Gospels are the first texts in which this mechanism is fully revealed as a human and purely mimetic phenomenon rather than as a transcendental mystery. It is true, of course, that transcendence is present in the Gospels, but it does not rest on that mechanism, which is fully demystified in the sense that the representation of the victim as a culprit is deconstructed and the mimetic genesis of this collective representation is revealed.

Auerbach's view that Peter's denial is much more mimetic than all ancient literature is an indirect acknowledgment of the mimetic content I have just described, of the Gospels' gigantic but still misunderstood advance beyond the platonic concept of mimesis. The best estheticians of mimetic realism, like Auerbach, sense this but are unable to explicate what they sense. In their relationship to the gospel they are completely tongue-tied, like the father of John the Baptist; they try to comprehend a view of mimesis enormously superior to that of Plato, from the standpoint of an inferior view, a view that is an impoverishment of the platonic concept. In Plato, the darker and more sinister side of conflictive mimesis is unaccounted for, but it is present, whereas in Plato's successors, beginning with Aristotle, mimesis has been totally divorced from desire and reduced to the sheepish and bland porridge of esthetic imitation.

Totalitarian Trials and the Obliteration of Memory

For scapegoating to be a success, the community must consent unanimously to the guilt of the victims. Even the accused must enthusiastically endorse their own destruction. These ancient strategies, evident in the Book of Job, anticipate modern propaganda.

The scapegoated become 'non-persons' whose names must no longer be mentioned. They continue to be seen as a potential source of contamination for the society.

Two compelling essays from Girard's Job: The Victim of His People *give us new insight into modern show trials and demonstrate how the ancient scapegoating mechanism has reappeared in terrorism and totalitarianism.*

The Totalitarian Trial

Envy and mimetic rivalries are reabsorbed into the phenomenon of the scapegoat mechanism and are transformed into a positive religion – provided, of course, that there is no residual aftermath; or rather, provided that the hostility to the scapegoat is completely unanimous.

If there is just one exception, if even one single voice is raised in disagreement with the unison against the victim, then there is no guarantee of a favorable outcome. The drug loses its effect; the group's unity cracks. If the hatred appears in the least bit lukewarm, doubt may spread, comprimising the cathartic effects on the morale of the community.

Reinforcement of the community is identical with the strengthening of socio-religious transcendence. But such reinforcement demands a flawless scapegoat mechanism, completely unanimous agreement that the victim is guilty.

So long as the victim lives, he is a part of the community; he can therefore participate in the unanimity forming against himself. The need for unanimity is the community's primary concern. There is no reason for him to be an exception. In fact, his assent is the most important of all.

The three friends try to obtain Job's assent to the verdict that condemns him. That is the true purpose of their mission, since the efficacy of the scapegoat mechanism depends on it. This is no abstract discussion of the question of Evil.

The three friends seek to consolidate the 'system of representation' based on the selection of Job as a scapegoat. Admittedly they set about it in the wrong way, but the only other way is not to intervene at all and to allow scapegoat systems of representation to form and disintegrate of their own accord.

The system consists of whitening the community by blackening the scapegoat; to consolidate it, the belief in this mythic blackness must be strengthened. The most effective means, obviously, is the victim's confession, in due and proper form. Job must publicly admit his infamy, proclaiming it loudly and convincingly.

Look at Oedipus at the end of his tragedy. He keeps repeating that he is a horrible impurity, disgusting to both gods and men: what in Greek is called *miasma*. He demands his own expulsion with an enthusiasm that will eventually earn him the community's respect. His docility immediately gains him attenuating circumstances, first with the Thebans who are content to exile him, and then again, in our day, with everyone. Ultimately, the only reason he is allowed to live is his exemplary behavior as a victim, which is quite the opposite of Job's.

The victim is expected to explain to his fellow-citizens all the evil that should in future be attributed to him. This facilitates everyone's adherence to the orthodoxy that is being developed. The strength of this adherence, in primitive societies, makes it possible to tie the final knot and make the scapegoat the principle of social unity, a god who is both harmful and beneficial.

On Job's level, the knot has already come loose. For some time the scapegoating process has no longer produced this kind of divinity, but the sacrificial crisis only renders more necessary the victim's enthusiastic and spontaneous adherence to the mimetic frenzy that dishonors and destroys him.

Every time a 'wicked man' presents himself, the community brings out the same unchanging ritual machine, but Job's insubordination upsets the scenario: the producers, obviously, did not anticipate this form of resistance.

The intervention of the fourth inquisitor, Elihu, helps us to understand the truly unheard-of quality of the event: a victim who stands up to an entire community. The scandal is so great that an indignant reader, I suppose, tried to suppress it by inventing the character of Elihu. The inability of the first three 'friends' to reduce Job to silence has put this eager supporter of the God of vengeance into a terrible rage.

Essentially, Elihu is so in agreement with the first three lynchers that he cannot imagine any other reason for their failure than their incompetence. His resentment against them, as well as against Job, is a symptom of the exacerbation of the sacrificial crisis. Like all superficial reformers, he uses his own youth as his chief argument, the proof of his superiority. When the operation of the 'ancient trail trodden by the wicked' fails, there are always men like Elihu who complete its disruption by trying to make it work again.

A comparison between the Dialogues and Sophocles' *Antigone* will help us understand what is at stake in the debate. Everything in that tragedy hinges on a scapegoat operation that is a little too visible to succeed in playing its role; the problem, as always in such cases, rests on the lack of unanimity in the community's adherence.

Only the necessity for unanimity can explain the importance of Antigone's rebellion in Creon's eyes. Neither the young woman's personality nor her relationship with Polynices gives weight to her disobedience, but rather the break in unanimity. By showing that

René Girard

Polynices is no different from Eteocles, his fraternal enemy; by demanding funerals for both of them, Antigone prevents the sacrificial resolution Creon wanted. She prevents the hollowing out of a mythical difference.

There is not the slightest difference between the two brothers who died as they lived, in the hostile symmetry of doubles. They are as alike as the two drops of water in *Menaechmus*. They are the same twins of violence. If the Thebans were to understand that their scapegoat, Polynices, had been chosen arbitrarily, if they were truly to recognize him as a *scapegoat*, the scapegoating would not 'take'; the victim would not appear to be responsible for the discord that destroys the community. The community would not be rid of its evil.

Thus is tragic discord perpetuated: this is, in fact, what happens in *Antigone*; the failure of the scapegoating process constitutes the tragic action. In the absence of a victim who is unanimously considered to be guilty, a sufficiently disguised scapegoat, tragedy rebounds and new doubles confront each other: Antigone and Creon, the armies of Eteocles and Polynices.

What is at stake is the same as for Job, except in his case Antigone and Job are one and the same person. The scapegoat himself denounces the arbitrary expulsion. Job is the Antigone of his own cause. He is expected to acknowledge the justice of his own martyrdom, and he refuses.

The three 'friends' demonstrate the same wary obstinacy with Job as King Creon does with Antigone. Violence is within their capability, but they cannot use it openly. It is important to obtain the victim's free consent to his punishment.

The inquisitors begin to soften their tone and resort to strategy. They alternate threats of assassination with vague promises of reinstatement. It is to this, I think, that we owe – through the intermediary of the prologue, naturally – the particularly fallacious interpretation of the three friends as comforters. The relative moderation of the three owes nothing to pity. The friends never forget that their goal is to break Job's resistance, without any apparent constraint.

If Job's consent appeared to be obtained by force, it would lose all its value in the eyes of the community. This strategy foreshadows modern propaganda.

Since they are not successful in officiating at a sacrifice whose majesty is undisturbed, the group, first consisting of three, and then of four, friends begins to resemble more and more a circle of police around a suspect. They are not quite executioners, but any form of intimidation or psychological pressure is acceptable to them in order to obtain the 'spontaneous confession' so precious to dictatorial societies. The failure of the process of sacralization weakens the truly sacred connotations. Thus everything I have said about a religious regime can and should be applied to other regimes as well – if not, properly speaking, to a judiciary regime, then to police states and totalitarian governments.

There are remarkable analogies between that universe and ours. Something in Job reminds us of a certain decline in modern justice. Everywhere ideology decomposes the legal system, legal parodies multiply and prompt behavior patterns like those of the three inquisitors at Job's bedside.

In societies that have so far been spared this disturbing evolution it is difficult to explain the importance totalitarian regimes attach to the semblance of justice, just as it is difficult to explain the relentless efforts of the friends to make Job confess. Comparison of the two mysteries helps to explain them both.

In both cases, the proof and guarantees needed by judicial systems which respect human rights are lacking. This is what the persecutors are after, in the form of the sincere agreement of the accused in their own condemnation without proof, in their annihilation 'without trial,' as Elihu proudly states. This agreement must replace the proof.

A perfect agreement between the perspective of executioners and that of the victims must be secured. The existence of a single truth is at stake, a truth that is properly transcendent and would be binding for all men without exception, even those crushed in the triumph of its procession. It must be shown that this truth is so constraining that it eventually wins over even those who, having failed to appreciate it, must suffer the consequences. They must recognize that they have sinned and that all their suffering is justified.

The need for a consenting victim characterizes modern totalitarianism as well as certain religious or para-religious forms of the primitive world. The victims of human sacrifice are always completely convinced of its necessity. It is this persecutor's point of view that modern neo-primitivism fails to criticize.

Totalitarian ideologies destroy belief in an impartial and sovereign justice, foreign to the conflicts of the earthly city. Regimes that triumph on the ruins of a systematically flouted code of justice can no longer avail themselves of it in time of need. They have destroyed the law's effective transcendence in relation to the individuals that make up society.

When this transcendence no longer exists to secure the sovereignty and continuity of judicial institutions; when there is no principle invulnerable to rival ambitions, to the vicissitudes of history, and to the corruption or mediocrity of its representatives, something immeasurable has been lost. Either there is no longer any common truth or, to impose one, one must live it to the end and, if necessary, die for it just as one is ready to kill for it. One must become it, be its *incarnation*.

In totalitarian systems, the rulers tend towards this status of incarnation. They write only infallible books and articulate only inspired words. They are treated as the living truth, the sacred king. We call it the 'cult of personality.'

But when there are several idols, the slightest discord between them affects and compromises a truth that truly exists only in its privileged incarnations. In the conflict of idols we see the division and fragmentation of the sacred; ultimately the whole of society runs the risk of breaking up and decomposing. The physical victor of one faction over his rivals is not sufficient to re-establish the unity of truth.

The conquered must freely recognize their fault. A confession of guilt is needed that is not seen to be extorted by violence. The accursed must give their blessing to the malediction that strikes them. They are not asked to forgive – especially not to forgive, for this would imply that the persecution was not necessarily infallible. What is required is their enthusiastic agreement with the decision to destroy them.

This is precisely what the three friends ask of Job. The losers must recognize that they were always in the wrong and were traitors. They thought they were innocent but must acknowledge that they were from the start guilty of parricide and incest. They deceived the people into acclaiming them when they did not really incarnate the truth.

Once institutional transcendence is destroyed, it can only be precariously and temporarily re-established, by means similar to those of primitive societies also lacking permanent transcendence for the opposite reasons: they have not yet created it. Modern totalitarian societies have finally destroyed that transcendence; primitive societies have not succeeded in producing it.

In both cases there is only one recourse: the scapegoat mechanism. Before totalitarianism, modern societies had not managed to eliminate scapegoats but they had both forced the worst of their violence outside themselves and reduced the violence left within their boundaries. This modern progress has been compromised in our time by the growing virulence of international conflicts and the powerful return of the scapegoating process in both terrorism and totalitarianism.

The three friends are no more interested in truth than are Soviet persecutors. They are there to persuade Job to recognize in public that he is guilty. It does not matter of what he is guilty, provided that he confesses it in front of everyone. In the last analysis, the unfortunate man is asked to confess that he has been struck by an infallible god rather than by fallible men. He is asked to confirm the sacred union of the unanimous lynching.

Translated by Yvonne Freccero

Retribution

There are other characteristics shared by both totalitarian trials and the process by which Job is made a victim. One of the most striking of these is the erasure of memory, the desire to eliminate not only the scapegoat but everything that might remind us of him – including his name, which must no longer be mentioned.

In the world of religion, this sort of conduct is justified by the pollution spread by the scapegoat. It is considered so insidious and formidable that the slightest emanation, even a faint recollection such as merely recalling his name, might cause contamination. The victim is so impure that his path must be covered with sulphur and disinfectants, and the last traces of his presence on earth must be destroyed.

His memory fades from the land,
　his name is forgotten in his homeland.
Driven from light into darkness,
　he is an exile from the earth,
without issue or posterity among his own people,
　none to live on where he has lived.
His tragic end appals the west,
　and fills the east with terror.
A fate like his awaits every sinful house,
　the home of every man who knows not God. (Job 18:17–21)

There is nothing more ritualistic and traditional than this abolition of memory, the radical annihilation of the pseudo-guilty. In our era this demand for extreme destruction reappears in laicized form. Certain religious proceedings even remind us of prophylactic measures taken against epidemics and, even today, medicine is often involved in this type of business. A whole primitive apparatus makes its reappearance in modern totalitarianism.

The radical elimination of the 'guilty' reminds us of the manipulation of history in the totalitarian world. In the days of Stalinism, the disgraced leader became a nonperson and his name disappeared from the encyclopedias and official annals.

There are no commemorative plaques along the 'ancient trail'. All that remains is the memory of the trial itself in the form of a vague threat hanging over all citizens which, in the case of Job, becomes more definite. Everyone who displays 'wickedness' in the eyes of those who manipulate public opinion is in danger of taking a little trip along this trail. In Job's case, the definition of 'wickedness' is his refusal to give in, his independence of judgment, his determination not to yield to the terrifying mimesis of the herd.

The cult of personality and parodies of legal process are not merely a question of unfortunate but excusable 'deviations'. Rather they suggest a relapse into social forms based directly on the scapegoating process. Because of ideological complicity many people are led to minimize what is happening, and that too is part of what is happening. They are persuaded that the 'deviations' will end once and for all on the day when the 'good' seize power and chase the 'evil' away for ever – in short, on the day when the 'good' alone will be in charge of the purifying expulsion.

This relapse into a type of social form that has unquestionably controlled most of human history is totally lacking in 'authenticity', and we do not know whether we should consider it less dangerous or, on the contrary, even more dangerous because of this. Whatever men do in future they cannot forget the scapegoat dimension of the Judeo-Christian revelation. The reactiviation of the scapegoat mechanism is always clumsy and suffers from its obvious falsehood.

The conscious element of manipulation is stronger in totalitarian worlds that were formerly Christianized than in those that were never aware of the truth of the scapegoat. Our contemporary world revives primitive violence without rediscovering the absence of knowledge that endowed former societies with a relative innocence and prevented them from being unliveable.

When modern societies which have increasingly distanced themselves from primitive religion over the centuries without ever making a complete break yield to totalitarian temptations, they again come close not to primitive religion but to its disintegration. Possibly they surrender increasingly to these temptations for reasons that are inaccessible to narrowly political and even sociological patterns of thought.

It is no accident that the texts most capable of enlightening us on what is happening are the great texts that belong to the tragic and prophetic universe, the works most inspired by the sacrificial decadence of the ancient world. People are fond of saying that there is no need to 'make a tragedy of things', but perhaps we are caught up in the tragic in its strongest sense.

This is why the Book of Job strikes such a contemporary chord. As our understanding of the victim's function in the primitive world grows, we shall be more able to penetrate the nature of human relationships in the totalitarian world. In both cases, the essential is the same unique absence that goes unnoticed because it is the absence of a thing that is not a thing and that many do not see. Its existence and importance are often discovered too late, at the moment when it ceases to be and as a consequence of its absence.

I am speaking of a social transcendence that is so strong and stable that it has no need of a constant recourse to the scapegoats within a threatened group. Most Westerners are too protected by this transcendence to imagine the possibility of losing it and the undeserved privilege they still enjoy.

Any society in which the scapegoat resumes his immemorial role of founder and restorer of transcendence is totalitarian; but biblical and Christian knowledge has brought an awareness of the implications of the scapegoat that makes impossible the revival of the illusion of Job's friends, and of all those who believe they live in a flawless universe. The friends naively describe a universe governed by infallible justice, a universe that is undoubtedly atrociously cruel. Even without a lapse into neo-primitivism, we can admit that the unshakable conviction of those who inhabit such a world implies a kind of innocence and freshness lacking in the stifling totalitarian parodies of the modern world.

The demand for absolute perfection might well provide the

common ground between the society of Job's 'friends' and current totalitarian societies. Faced with imperfections too obvious to be denied and with all that obviously fails to function correctly, the first reaction of totalitarian society is judicial rather than pragmatic. In order to find concrete solutions, the most fruitful state of mind is to think that perhaps no one is 'guilty'. To learn to cure the plague, one must first renounce the oracles of Laius and the hunt for a scapegoat. Totalitarian worlds renounce that renunciation. Unwittingly they reintegrate, in the name of 'progress', the state of mind so well defined by Eliphaz:

Can you recall a guiltless man that perished,
    or have you ever seen good men brought to nothing?
I speak of what I know: those who plough iniquity
    and sow the seeds of grief reap a harvest of the same kind.
A breath from God will bring them to destruction,
    a blast of his anger will wipe them out. (Job 4:7–9)

It is easy to understand why the three friends think as they do. They have always participated with the lynchers, as members of the community, in the episodes Eliphaz is describing. The Righteous are those who have never been lynched and who end up as well off as they began.

Generally speaking, those who are lynched are not around to talk about it: that is precisely what makes the speeches of Job an extraordinary exception and an abomination for an entire universe that can see in his complaints only an unforgivable subversion of the very idea of divine justice.

In the eyes of the friends, so long as there is no Job to trouble the enactment of the scapegoating process, everything is clearly best in the best of worlds. It is other men who are always pursued by divine vengeance; obviously, only the wicked are trampled by the crowd. Under these conditions, is it not natural to think that the world is extremely well made?

Those who are enveloped by the scapegoat mechanism, and completely convinced by it, live in a world that always conforms to the demands of Justice. If, momentarily, this world ceases to be just, sooner or later the scapegoating process will intervene to re-establish its perfection. The friends confirm this in the case of Job, just like the narrator of Psalm 73. Sometimes the celestial armies are a little slow to get going but, once in motion, they are quick to settle the accounts of the wicked. Ultimately, good and evil here below always receive what they deserve from God. Such is the power of the idea of retribution: an essential aspect of every system of mythological representation. A bit of reflection reveals that it is entirely based on the mechanism of a victim.

This is why belief in retribution dominates primitive religion. It is much more than a philosophy or even a theology. By primitive I mean every society that is structured on scapegoat mechanisms that are still intact. Transcendent justice is the same as the scapegoating process described by Job, so long as there is no Job to interfere by describing it. It is therefore as natural as it is supernatural, as transcendent as it is immanent. It is always there, for it is identical to mimetic unanimity, and eventually mimetic unanimity is always re-established in opposition to some victim or other.

On this point as so many others, the revelations of the Book of Job are invaluable. The three friends could not believe as they do in the culpability of Job and all previous scapegoats without believing equally in an absolute Justice that always triumphs in this world. The two are one and the same. All those whom the whole community perceives to be guilty are in fact punished and all those who are punished, or seem to be punished – perhaps quite simply by a mishap – are immediately perceived to be guilty, and also become scapegoats. Justice inevitably triumphs.

The well-oiled scapegoat mechanism generates an absolutely 'perfect' world, since it automatically assures the elimination of everything that passes for imperfect and makes everything that is violently eliminated appear to be imperfect and unworthy of existence.

There is no room in this world for unpunished injustice or unsanctioned evil, any more than there is a place for the just person who is unlucky or the persecuted person who is innocent. This is what Eliphaz says. The circle has no break: the principle of this perfection will never discover what is fallacious about it. The mimesis is too strong. Job can go on yelling to the end of time without making his friends or anyone else understand.

The generative principle cannot be subverted. As soon as anything appears that might uproot it or make it seem illusory – like the voice of Job proclaiming that he is a scapegoat – the mechanism of elimination is set in motion, either in a primitive physical form, as is shown in Job, or in a derived attenuated and intellectualized form of which the thousand ways of disregarding what Job is saying provide excellent examples. The fact that every 'system of representation' closes in on itself is ultimately a result of the scapegoat mechanism.

The tendency to attribute society's imperfections to scapegoats both within and without is certainly universal but, instead of discouraging and denouncing it, totalitarian societies foster and systematize it. They nourish with victims the myth of their own perfection, which they wish to promote.

A Method, a Life, a Man

Michel Treguer: We've put a lot of emphasis on the unconscious nature of mechanisms and phenomena. Which leads me to the following, rather paradoxical, question: in the end, does it help to reveal Revelation, to talk about it explicitly as you're doing?

René Girard: What do you mean by 'does it help'? If religion is the truth, 'it helps' more than we can imagine. If Christianity is false, what we're doing has no value whatsoever.

MT: I'll modify my question. Shakespeare doesn't speak *explicitly* about mimetic desire, he doesn't talk about it in his plays, he allows us to intuit its existence by showing us characters who are tangled in its web.

RG: He indeed does what you're saying, but at the same time he offers commentary and explanations. When I'm working on an author, it's no doubt possible that, in my enthusiasm, I sometimes exaggerate the revelatory value of what he's saying. And yet whenever I open up my Shakespeare, I'm never disappointed. I wrote a book on him in part, it's true, because of the content of his plays, which is extraordinary, but even more so, perhaps, because of the dozens of expressions that he plants in strategic places and that define the mimetic process from start to finish. In the comedies, it's of course mimetic desire that is featured, but in the tragedies, above all *Julius Caesar*, it's the scapegoat mechanism and sacrifice.

The night before his assassination, for example, Caesar has a bad dream: the Romans run toward him joyously to bathe their hands in his blood. Foreseeing the danger, his wife persuades Caesar not to go to the senate. All of that is already in Plutarch, whom Shakespeare follows very closely. But, at this particular moment, our author adds something all his own, and it's a second interpretation of the dream. One of the conspirators comes looking for Caesar, and, in order to entice his victim to the senate where his murderers are lying in wait, he reinterprets the dream in a way that shouldn't reassure a man who is worried for his life but that flatters Caesar's gigantic ambitions. He predicts the future transfiguration of his collective murder, the transfiguration that will make him into the tutelary god of the Empire, the founding scapegoat of the political regime that will emerge after the Republic. 'From you great Rome/Shall suck reviving blood' (*Julius Caesar*, II, ii, 87–88). You have to admit that, for someone who's interested in the idea of a founding murder, that's worth taking note of! Of course, to truly appreciate it, you have to read Shakespeare in his native tongue, which is inimitable. He's not only the Corneille and Racine of English literature, but also its Montaigne, with everything that comparison implies in terms of a linguistic flavor that has since been lost. Don't even get me started on Shakespeare.

MT: Why didn't Christ write?

RG: Christ didn't write, but he is identical with his word. He is the Verb, the true *Logos*. He dies for the reasons that cause him to speak. He speaks for the reasons that cause him to die. The specifically Christian revelation is clarified only after the fact, in the Spirit's descent, which is the fruit of Christ's *sacrifice*. The germ of Christianity resides in the fact that a perfect imitator of God cannot fail to be killed by other human beings, because he lives and talks just as God would speak and live if He were himself on this earth. That man is therefore one with God, he is God. Thanks to him God is now present among us. Everything that Christ conquered by escaping the world and its violence without taking part in it, He offers to all human beings who are willing to let themselves be raised up by grace. Christ's act re-establishes the connection between God and human beings that had been damaged by original sin.

Above, I used the word *sacrifice* to mean the giving of oneself even unto death. This is not at all what sacrifice means in archaic religions. In fact, it's a complete reversal. In the past, I was too exclusively insistent on the difference between the two. I wanted to show that those who accuse Christianity of ultimately being just like human sacrifice, cannibalism, and so on, are wrong.

I put too much emphasis on that difference, and not enough on the ultimate symbolic unity of sacrifice, which, if one examines all of the term's meanings, sums up humanity's entire religious history. Christians are right to use the word 'sacrifice' for Christ: they grasp that unity intuitively and, in any event, those who aren't ready to understand certain things will never be convinced by logical and anthropological arguments.

MT: Well, at this religious level, it looks like I'm going to have trouble pursuing my line of questioning about writing. It still seems odd that someone who obviously wanted to leave an eternal message wouldn't choose to set it down in writing himself, once and for all, nipping any and all possible future distortions in the bud. Unless, of course, he foresaw a danger. You're familiar with the text from Plato's *Phaedrus* in which Plato (in writing!) has Socrates (who also didn't write anything) badmouth writing: 'Writing, which cannot itself respond, as a master could, to the pupil's questions,' and so forth. I would even add that History has taught us that the fixedness of writing can be a handicap: it also perpetuates errors, and above all it makes it possible for demagogues to alter a text's meaning while appearing to respect it word for word. The history of both Christianity and socialism is full of such misappropriations.

RG: You just answered your own question. One can't prevent all future distortions by putting down in writing a message that's simply 'true,' exempt from any sort of ambiguity. Writing and speech issue from our sacrificial origins and are thus fundamentally insufficient. Only the death of Christ is perfect, and all the writings that reproduce it suffer from an essential and necessary imperfection. It's this insufficiency of all transmission, of all communication, that justifies the existence of multiple written accounts, of not one but four canonical Gospels, each different from the others, whose drafters, moreover, are always emphasizing their lack of comprehension. Christianity is not a 'religion of the book' the way Islam and Judaism are.

MT: Not only doesn't Christ write, but he seems mistrustful of any sort of logical demonstration, of the essay, if you will. He prefers to speak in parables, he tells stories.

RG: Yes, but the Gospels themselves say that the parables are aimed at the crowd rather than directly at the disciples. They can be characterized by the fact that they reinstate a god of violence and vengeance, who is in fact refuted by the Gospels, for the benefit of listeners who wouldn't be able to conceive of him any other way. The Christian God makes his light shine indiscriminately on the just and the unjust. In the parables, that's not how it is. Those who don't obey the rules of the Kingdom often seem to be punished by divine, transcendent violence. In reality, violent actions penalize themselves by eliciting the reprisals that they indeed deserve. Violent people punish one another, like the two wicked sisters in King Lear, the two enemy sisters. The punishment appears transcendent because it spares nobody, but it comes from reciprocity, from mimetic desire, which makes it so that the evil we inflict on others will sooner or later be returned to us, with interest. You don't project that violence onto God unless you fail to see the reciprocity, or unless, for strategic reasons, as in the parables, you put it in parentheses. The Gospels shouldn't be reduced to the parables. There is a lot of direct teaching.

MT: Your extreme rhetorical dexterity sometimes makes me a little uneasy. For example, let me go back to the ambiguous face that the West presents to the third world. Isn't it going a bit too far to assert, as you do, that as soon as a person claims to be a victim, they're behaving in a Western, Christian way? You'll grant me that the West has made real victims who have real reasons for complaining. Their complaints are natural, ordinary. They would have said the same things without Christian revelation. Your observation undermines the legitimacy of their complaints and more or less justifies Western aggression.

RG: Their complaints are objectively just, you're right. In the archaic world, they would have been expressed within the group or among fellow groups who are presumed to be friendly, as is the case in Aeschylus's *The Suppliants* or *The Persians*. After their defeat in the Battle of Salamis, the Persians tell themselves: 'We must have brought this punishment down on ourselves, because of some past misdeed.'

What's extraordinary in our world is that we say to the foreign persecutor: 'You owe me something in your capacity as a persecutor.' The traditional persecutor would have replied: 'Alright, I'm going to persecute you some more. It's clear that I haven't persecuted you enough because you're still capable of complaining.' But today the alleged persecutor recognizes the debt he bears with respect to his victims. That's what's absolutely unique, that now we address the persecutor, saying: 'Acknowledge that you owe me something, because ultimately we believe the same thing, we both consider violence to be unacceptable.'

MT: I'm under the impression that when the Christian West points out victims, you think that's good, but that when victims of the West point out that they're victims, you judge their complaints to be inadmissible, biased.

RG: I certainly don't want to give that impression, and I haven't said anything that truly suggests it. To the contrary, I'm saying that when victims complain, it's legitimate, but only from a Christian perspective. Don't forget that for me, contrary to what Nietzsche thinks, the Christian perspective isn't just wishful thinking: it alone is true, it's the truth.

The mere fact of a dialogue between victims and persecutors is a Christian phenomenon. In a situation where persecution is taken as far as it can go, there is no dialogue between victim and persecutor. In general, history is written by the victors. We're the only society that wants history to be written by the victims. And we don't see the unprecedented nature of the reversal. That reversal makes new historical research necessary: there aren't a lot of traces of the victims, because until now the victors have been the ones doing the talking.

MT: I'm not letting you off that easily: here we are once more, walking the blurry line between universalism and imperialism. There were peoples who were fine the way they were, who kept their little local cultures chugging along. And then the Christians come along with their missionaries, their soldiers, and their crusades. The former obviously have every reason to tell them: 'You're bothering us!' But it's then that René Girard pops out of his box and declares: 'Ah, you see! You're complaining, thus you're already Christians!'

Don't ask me to believe that you can't complain outside of Christianity.

RG: After the Roman conquest of Gaul, Vercingetorix gets brought back to Rome to play a part in Caesar's triumph: he was kept alive for several years exclusively for that purpose. After the parade, he's strangled, not brought to the senate with much pomp and circumstance to negotiate 'an international aid program for underdeveloped Gaul.' Never before in history have people spoken as we speak, nor have they even acted as we act. The sort of shrewd people Pascal calls 'half-clever' see this only as a form of imperialism that's sneakier than in the past, but they can't explain why nobody discovered it until now.

I grant you that the richest countries are far from doing enough, but it's astonishing all the same to note that, only three months after the end of the Cold War, the West was thinking of nothing but aid for Russia. That was a real first in human history.

Given that all the objective conditions of our world are determined by Christianity, we don't have a choice, it's quite obvious. I repeat: we're certainly not doing enough. But this 'not enough' is totally meaningless outside of Christianity, and it's hypocritical to deny it. In any event, the refusal to tell the truth is a part of that same truth, because it's necessarily based on a secularized version of charity: 'the right hand mustn't know what the left one is doing,' and so forth. When you dissect the kind of doublespeak we use today you expose the incessant appeals it makes to Christian theology, even in what we're forced to hide, so as to appear doubly humble. Seen from the other side of the Atlantic all of this is probably clearer than it is in France because, being at the heart of the system, America doesn't have the luxury of a second America waiting there to serve as a temporary scapegoat in time of need. And then, the Americans are less underhand than the French, less practiced at hiding the Christian element in their divisions.

MT: I'd like to come back to what I called your rhetorical 'dexterity.' It's also a result of your immense field of reflection. You have an answer for everything because in your view everything – and its opposite – is explicable, everything can serve as proof. Nothing flusters you. One has the impression that when faced with a fact or a work that you've happened upon, you look for a way of fitting it in, but that you never have occasion to say: 'Damn, it doesn't work!'

For example, you're quite willing to show that there are many obstacles to the process triggered by Revelation, that sacrificial mechanisms are hard to kill off, and that they often even redouble their violence. Thus, when Communism falls, you see that as the proof that the Revelation is under way; but had Communism grown stronger, you could just as easily have seen that as proof that the very same Revelation was generating forms of resistance. Never for an instant would you have considered the possibility that your analysis might be wrong.

RG: If I had found facts that didn't corroborate my thesis, I would have modified the latter a long time ago.

But we should come to an agreement on the nature of the facts that interest me. I'm not talking about current events. I don't pretend to have views that correspond to my fundamental insights on everything, at the drop of a hat. All I can bring to a lot of your questions are 'personal opinions' that could very well change from one moment to the next. I'm probably also sometimes mistaken about what truly is a part of my fundamental insights, and what isn't.

MT: All the same, even if you can explain the vicissitudes of history and the traps of the Antichrist, it seems to me that the vestiges of the sacrificial system and the exaggerations of the Christian attitude, on the one hand, and, on the other, the various kinds of resistance to uniformization should remain objections to your theory, rather than proofs, no?

In fact, if you want to know what I'm really thinking, I'd say that, in the face of a planetary nuclear holocaust, it would be completely meaningless to say: 'Too bad, we could have had paradise!' Such an event would instead be the retrospective proof that all our rhetoric about the golden age to come was just a bunch of nonsense. It would be definitive proof that all our magnificent 'progress' was in truth nothing but a Satanic trap: a march toward death (while sing-ing, if you like)!

RG: You remind me of those people who ask for 'a sign,' and Jesus answers by telling them that the only sign is 'the sign of Jonah,' that is to say the sign of the scapegoat, the sign of the unfortunate wretch thrown to the whales by the sailors who hold him responsible for the storm. What I'm saying is that Christianity reveals its power by interpreting the world in all its ambiguity. It gives us an understand-ing of human cultures that is incomparably better than that offered by the social sciences. But it's neither a utopian recipe nor a skeleton key for deciphering current events.

MT: But, all the same, it's not the same thing to say that Revelation will fulfill itself in the flowering of a new golden age as to say that it will end in a destructive apocalypse, is it?

RG: If by that you mean that I have all the pugnacity of an intellectual of my generation, I willingly concede the point. And my personal flaws, as I've already suggested, make some of what I say sound harsher than I would like, and, in a general way, hinder my effectiveness.

But this world that's always teetering between a new golden age and a destructive apocalypse – you're not going to tell me that I'm the one who invented it, are you? You encounter it every morning in the newspaper and every evening on TV. You're making me out to be more unique than I am. And you see systematic analyses where they don't exist. Once you allow yourself to see the cartoonlike Christian dimension of contemporary history, it's easy to see that it's every-where. Except that, once more, true Christianity has never promised either a golden age or an earthly paradise. Everything I'm saying is ultimately just a watered-down version of that famous quote from Bernanos: 'The modern world is full of Christian ideas gone mad.'

If we try to make religion into just one more means of increasing the comfort of our little lives, well, 'we have a tiger by the tail.' Don't blame me for this necessarily inexact sacrificial metaphor. It's a par-able as defined earlier.

It's the nature of the real, which isn't going to change so as to make things any easier for us, and not religion, that scratches and bites us. Our God isn't a ferocious tiger but a sacrificed lamb. We're the ones who transform him into a tiger through our utter inability to do without sacrificial support.

Christianity is not the religion of the exit from religion, as Marcel Gauchet thinks. I wouldn't wait around for it to set us down gently in the dainty flower beds of a consumer society that's been tended and prettified by 'Christian values.' If I'm right, we're only extricating ourselves from a certain kind of religion so as to enter another, one that's infinitely more demanding because it's deprived of sacrificial crutches. Our celebrated humanism will turn out to have been nothing but a brief intermission between two forms of religion.

MT: We've come back to the mystery of an all-powerful and omniscient God who leaves his creatures free . . . who acts as if he doesn't know where they're headed.

RG: If I'm giving the impression that God is playing cat-and-mouse with us, or if you prefer, tiger-and-mouse, I've explained myself poorly. To try to understand the relationship between the call that comes from God, on the one hand, and on the other, the interplay of mimetic desire and freedom, I'm going to do a little textual analysis. We're going to take one of the best-known gospel narratives, the one about the adulterous woman who is saved from being stoned. It's a slightly mysterious text, because it's not in the oldest manuscripts of John. Many commentators think it recalls Luke's style rather than John's, and that seems pretty accurate to me. 'In any event,' says the Bible of Jerusalem, 'nobody doubts its canonicity.' Here it is:

The scribes and Pharisees brought a woman along who had been caught committing adultery; and making her stand there in the middle they said to Jesus, 'Master, this woman was caught in the very act of committing adultery, and in the Law Moses has ordered us to stone women of this kind. What have you got to say?' They asked him this as a test, looking for an accusation to use against him. But Jesus bent down and started writing on the ground with his finger. As they persisted with their question, he straightened up and said, 'Let the one among you who is guiltless be the first to throw a stone at her.' Then he bent down and continued writing on the ground. When they heard this they went away one by one, beginning with the eldest, until the last one had gone and Jesus was left alone with the woman, who remained in the middle. Jesus again straightened up and said, 'Woman, where are they? Has no one condemned you?' 'No one, sir,' she replied. 'Neither do I condemn you,' said Jesus. 'Go away, and from this moment sin no more.'

Mosaic law prescribes the stoning of those condemned to death. I of course interpret this method of execution as the ritual imitation of a founding murder, that is to say of an initial stoning which, in the distant past, reconciled the community. It's because the community was reconciled that it has made this unanimous violence into a ritual model, a model of unanimity. Everyone must throw stones. This is obviously how the mimetic hypothesis explains the existence of institutionalized stoning such as can be found codified much later in Leviticus.

Stoning was only required for adulterous wives, not for husbands. In the first century of our era, that prescription was challenged. Some found it too harsh. Jesus is faced with a terrible dilemma. He is suspected of having contempt for the Law. If he says no to the stoning, that will appear to confirm those suspicions. If he says yes, he is betraying his own teaching, which is aimed entirely against mimetic contagion, against the violent escalation of which this stoning, if it took place, would be an example, in the same way as the Passion. Jesus is repeatedly under threat of stoning in the scenes that foreshadow and prepare the way for the Passion. The revealer and denouncer of the founding murder cannot fail to intervene in favor of all victims of the process that will finally overcome him.

If the men who question Jesus didn't want to bring about the stoning, they wouldn't display the guilty party 'for all to see,' they wouldn't exhibit her so obligingly. They want the power of scandal that stems from adultery to radiate out onto the crowd and any passers-by. They want to push the mimetic escalation that they have triggered to its fatal conclusion.

To set the stage for his intervention, to make sure it works, Jesus needs to meditate a little, to buy some time, and he writes in the dust with his finger.

Everyone always wonders what he might have written. It's a silly question as far as I'm concerned. We can leave it to those who are infatuated with language and writing. There's no point in going back to the Middle Ages.

Jesus doesn't bend down because he wants to write, he writes because he's bending down. He's bending down so as not to look his challengers in the eye. If Jesus looked back at them, the crowd would feel that it was being challenged in turn, it would think that it was seeing its own defiant look and its own challenge in Jesus's eyes. The face-off would lead straight to violence, which is to say to the death of the victim whom Jesus is trying to save. Jesus avoids giving even the slightest hint of provocation.

And finally he speaks: 'Let the one among you who is guiltless be the first to throw a stone at her!' Why the first stone? Because it's the key. The one who throws it has nobody to imitate. There's nothing easier than imitating an example that's already been provided. Providing that example yourself is something altogether different.

The crowd is mimetically mobilized, but there's one threshold it still has to cross, the threshold of real violence. If someone threw the first stone, there would immediately be a shower of stones.

By attracting attention to the first stone, Jesus's words reinforce the final obstacle to the stoning. He gives the best among those in the crowd the time to hear what he's saying and to examine themselves. If their self-examination is real it cannot fail to uncover the circular relationship between victim and executioner. The scandal that the woman represents in their eyes is already present in those men, and they're projecting it onto her in order to rid themselves of it, which is all the easier in that she is truly guilty.

To stone a victim willingly, you have to believe that you are different from that victim, and I note that mimetic convergence is accompanied by an illusion of divergence. It's this real convergence combined with the illusion of divergence that triggers what Jesus is seeking to prevent, the scapegoat mechanism.

The crowd precedes the individual. Only he who escapes violent unanimity by detaching himself from the crowd truly becomes an individual. Not everyone is capable of such initiative. Those who are capable detach themselves first, and in doing so, prevent the stoning.

There is something authentically individual about this imitation. The proof is that the time it takes varies from individual to individual. The birth of the individual is the birth of individual temporalities. So long as they form a crowd, these men stand together, speak together, and say exactly the same thing, all together. Jesus's words dissolve the crowd. The men go away one by one, according to how long it takes each of them to understand the Revelation.

Because most people spend their lives imitating, they don't know what they're imitating. Even those who are most able to take the initiative almost never do so. It takes an exceptional situation such as an aborted stoning to show what an individual is capable of.

'The eldest' are the first to cede. Perhaps they're not as hot-blooded as their younger counterparts, perhaps the proximity of death makes them less strict with others and more strict with themselves. Anyway, it's not important.

The only important distinction is the one between the first ones and all the others.

Once the eldest have left, the less old and even the youngest leave the crowd, faster and faster, as the models increase in number. Whether we're throwing stones or, to the contrary, not throwing them, *only the beginning has any value. That's where the real difference lies.*

For the first imitators of those who started, it's still possible to speak of a decision, but in a sense that grows ever weaker as the number of those who have made up their minds increases. Once it is imitated, the initial decision quickly becomes pure contagion, a social mechanism.

Alongside the individual temporalities, then, there is still a social temporality in our text, but it is now aping the individual temporalities, it's the temporality of fashions and political and intellectual fads. Time is still punctuated by mimetic mechanisms.

To be the first to leave a crowd, to be the first not to throw stones, is to run the risk of becoming a target for the stone-throwers. The reverse decision would have been easier because it went with the current of the mimetic escalation that had already started. The first stone is less mimetic than the following ones, but it is still carried along by the wave of mimetic desire that generated the crowd.

And the first ones to decide against the stoning? Should we think that at least in their case there isn't any imitation? Certainly not. It's present even in them, because it's Jesus's suggestion that leads these men to act as they do. *The decision against violence would remain impossible, Christianity tells us, without the Divine Spirit that is called the Paraclete,* which is to say, in everyday Greek, 'the defense lawyer,' which is exactly the role that Jesus himself plays here.

And he lets it be understood that he is the first Paraclete, the first defender of victims. Above all through the Passion, which is of course the subtext here.

The mimetic theory places emphasis on the universal tendency to follow, on people's utter inability not to imitate the easiest and most popular examples, because that's what predominates in every society. But it shouldn't be concluded that it denies the existence of individual freedom. By situating true decisions in their real context, which is that of omnipresent mimetic contagion, the theory causes decisions that are not mechanical, yet that are in no way different on a formal level from those that are, to stand out in a way they do not in the work of thinkers who never stop talking about freedom and who, for this very reason, thinking that they're extolling it, devalue it completely. If you glorify decisiveness without seeing what makes it so difficult, you never get out of the emptiest sort of metaphysics.

Even the renunciation of violent mimetic desire cannot spread without being transformed into a social mechanism, into blind imitation. There is a stoning in reverse that is symmetrical to actual stoning and it, too, is violent to some extent. That's what our era's travesties clearly demonstrate.

All the people who would have thrown stones if there had been someone to throw the first one are mimetically induced not to throw any. For most of them, the real reason for nonviolence isn't stern self-examination or renunciation of violence: it's mimetic desire, as usual. There is always mimetic escalation in one direction or another. Rushing pell-mell in the direction already chosen by their models, the 'mimic men' congratulate themselves on their decisive and independent frame of mind.

We mustn't deceive ourselves. Though we live in a society that no longer stones adulterous women, a lot of people haven't really changed. Violence has decreased, and it is better hidden, but it remains structurally identical to what it has always been.

Rather than an authentic exit from mimetic desire there is mimetic submission to a culture that advocates that exit. In any social venture, whatever its nature, the proportion of authentic individualism is necessarily minimal, but not nonexistent.

It must not be forgotten that the mimetic desire that spares victims is infinitely superior, objectively and morally speaking, to the mimetic desire that kills them by stoning. The game of false moral equivalencies should be left to Nietzsche and to decadent aestheticisms of all stripes.

The story of the adulterous woman helps us see that social behaviors that are identical in terms of form and even to some degree in terms of content, because they're all mimetic, can nonetheless be infinitely different. The proportion of mechanicalness and freedom they contain is infinitely variable.

But this inexhaustible diversity does not prove that human behaviors are incomparable or unknowable. Everything we need to know in order to resist automatic social reflexes and runaway mimetic contagion is accessible to our understanding.

MT: Thank you. That was a marvelous demonstration, and very complete – too marvelous, and too complete, indeed, for me to harass you any more in these pages. Just one question. I thought I heard you say that goodness, too, only takes hold through mimetic desire; in other words, that many Christians are only Christian through mimetic desire, so as to be like their neighbors. It seems to me that this is a vision of mankind that's extremely undemocratic.

That's not necessarily a criticism, but I'd like to know what you think. Are there people who are born to take the first step, to lead others?

RG: It's excessive to say that 'goodness *only* takes hold through mimetic desire.' The people who take the first step aren't necessarily the ones that society calls 'leaders.' Taking the first step could consist in agreeing to follow instead of leading.

MT: You said earlier that the gospel writers were just men who at the time didn't understand at all; you said that for us, as for them, subsequent intellectual reflection was necessary to get a grip on, or perhaps to create, the meaning of events. You also spoke of Joyce's Stephen Dedalus who faced hostility from the literary critics. Do you wish your work was more widely accepted? Or would it make you apprehensive to see it understood too fast and too easily?

RG: Whatever he may say, an author is never indifferent to the way he is received. If he's poorly received, he counts on posterity, or on the Apocalypse, for vengeance. You could interpret me this way.

MT: You run the whole gamut of human phenomena – individual behaviors as well as collective myths, history and prehistory, and so on. When faced with such a mass of information, do you ever feel like you're pushing the limits of the human brain?

RG: Once again I think you're looking at the wrong end of things. My knowledge isn't as vast as it seems to you. My intuition comes first, and it leads me toward vivid examples, or burns them into my memory when I happen upon them by chance. You'll tell me that I'm selecting what works best with my hypotheses. And it's obviously true. But that doesn't mean that those hypotheses are false. The examples that are less vivid at first would often be very good once I got to the end of my analysis, but it would take us more time than we're taking now. Analyses that were too long wouldn't be suitable for a conversation like this one. They're not even suitable for scholarly publications, to judge by the lack of understanding that often surrounds my work, even – and perhaps especially – among 'specialists.'

I'm probably partly responsible for this situation. I'm under the impression that I've never been able to lay out my insight in the most logical, most didactic, and most comprehensible order.

MT: But is there such an order? I'd have a tendency to say that you'd be hard pressed to lay out a set of ideas like yours, with so many transversal connections, in linear fashion without doubling back and repeating yourself here and there, and so forth. The global image I have of your theory isn't a line but rather an inextricable ball of twine, similar to the network of neurons in our brains. The latter is sometimes even compared to a hologram: when a wound damages a lobe, the neighboring zones learn to perform the functions that disappeared with it: *because the whole is in each of its parts.* That's why I fear, as I was saying earlier, that solutions that are too elegant and too unique are nothing but traps laid for our vanity by Logic, which I would characterize as the 'Satan' or the 'Antichrist' of the mind.

RG: Your metaphors are excellent, but in spite of everything I haven't given up on finding a better order. The mimetic hypothesis makes me think not so much of a very tangled ball of twine but rather of a road map that has been folded over on itself so many times that it's just a little rectangle. To use it, you have to unfold it, and then fold it up again. Clumsy people like me can never find the original folds, and the map soon tears. It's those tears that make it possible for skeptics to think that the map I carry around in my head isn't all in one piece, that it's just a bunch of fragments that have been assembled and stuck together in an artificial manner to make up the 'Girardian system,' as they call it, which is good for amusing the peanut gallery for a little while, before being placed on the scrap heap, next to Postman Cheval's 'Ideal Palace.'

If I could do just one thing in the time I have left, I would like to learn to unfold and refold my road map in such a way as not to tear it. If I managed to do this, I could then write an apology for Christianity that was accessible to so-called uncultivated people, to those who probably aren't wrong not to have followed any of what's been happening over the last thirty years in the social sciences and philosophy.

MT: While going through the transcripts of our many conversations (which have taken place over ten years), in the course of which I've often repeated the same questions, I sometimes happen upon an illuminating answer, an absolutely dazzling summary – I tell myself that maybe you yourself have forgotten them.

RG: I too sometimes have the feeling of finding something only to forget about it later.

MT: What we're saying now interests me because we have to make do with our bodies, with our human language, and because, a bit earlier, what you were saying about creation being possible 'only from within tradition' left me wanting more somehow. We haven't said anything about the new properly speaking. It's been shown that the neurons that are activated when new ideas emerge are the same as those responsible for triggering dreams.

RG: If that's true, it's incredible!

MT: The means of understanding the sensation we're talking about is precisely to observe that in both cases we're struggling with the same phenomenon of immediate amnesia. An idea occurs to us, and, if we don't write it down, it disappears like a dream when you wake up.

RG: Exactly! I go to have a coffee, and I tell myself: 'I'll write that down when I get back.' And it's already too late.

Lately, I seem to have made some progress in formulating some of my ideas. Everything came to me at once in 1959. I felt that there was a sort of mass that I've penetrated into little by little. Everything was there at the beginning, all together. That's why I don't have any doubts. There's no 'Girardian system.' I'm teasing out a single, extremely dense insight.

MT: You've already told how after a very moderately Christian youth, you came to your current ideas, first via Proust. Personally, I suspect you of concealing an event that you've never spoke about, a mystical awakening, a veritable encounter with God, a 'Road-to-Damascus' experience.

RG: To say that my youth was Christian, even moderately so, would be an exaggeration. My mother, of course, was an excellent Catholic who was at once a firm believer and very open-minded. When I tell that to devotees of psychoanalysis, they give a knowing nod. It reassures them enormously. But there are others who aren't content with a 'return to the womb.' Certain ladies who prod my Oedipus complex find it 'rather tough, even very much so . . .'.* I've already been the target of three or four articles on the subject.† I'm extremely honored, of course.

---

* Translator's Note: 'Duriuscule, pour ne pas dire dur . . .' The line is from Molière's *Imaginary Invalid*, in which Doctor Diafoirus and his son, Thomas, subject Argan, the imaginary invalid of the title, to a comprehensive (and absurd) physical examination.

† Among others, Sarah Kofman in *The Enigma of Women: Women in Freud's Writings* (Ithaca, NY: Cornell University Press, 1985), 59–63; and Toril Moi, 'The Missing Mother: The Oedipal Rivalries of René Girard', in *Diacritics*, Summer 92, 21–31.

I'm not concealing my biography, but I don't want to fall victim to the narcissism to which we're all inclined. You're right, of course, about there being a personal experience behind what I say. It began thirty-five years ago.

In autumn 1958, I was working on my book about the novel, on the twelfth and last chapter that's entitled 'Conclusion.' I was thinking about the analogies between religious experience and the experience of a novelist who discovers that he's been consistently lying, lying for the benefit of his Ego, which in fact is made up of nothing but a thousand lies that have accumulated over a long period, sometimes built up over an entire lifetime.

I ended up understanding that I was going through an experience of the kind that I was describing. The religious symbolism was present in the novelists in embryonic form, but in my case it started to work all by itself and caught fire spontaneously. I could no longer have any illusions about what was happening to me, and I was thrown for a loop, because I was proud of being a skeptic. It was very hard for me to imagine myself going to church, praying, and so on. I was all puffed up, full of what the old catechisms used to call 'human respect.'

Intellectually I was converted, but I remained incapable of making my life agree with what I thought. For a period of a few months, faith was for me a blissful delicacy that heightened my other pleasures, one more treat in a life that, while it was far from being criminal, was, as the English language puts it so well, pure *self-indulgence*.

Curiously, my conversion had made me sensitive to music, and I was listening to a lot of it. What little musical knowledge I have, about opera in particular, dates from that period. Oddly enough, *The Marriage of Figaro* is, for me, the most mystical of all music. That, and Gregorian chant. I also started to like a lot of 'modern' music that I'd never had much appreciation for in the past: Mahler, Stravinsky, the contemporary Russian composers.

During the winter of 1959 I was already teaching at Johns Hopkins, but I was giving a class at Bryn Mawr College, where I had spent four years, and I made the round trip from Baltimore to Philadelphia every week in the squeaky, clattering old railway cars of the

Pennsylvania Railroad. As far as the sights were concerned, I usually just looked out at the scrap iron and the vacant lots in that old industrial region, but my mental state transfigured everything, and, on the way back, the slightest ray from the setting sun produced veritable ecstasies in me. It was in that train one morning that I discovered, right in the middle of my forehead, a little pimple that refused to heal, one of those minor skin cancers that aren't really that dangerous at all; but the doctor I went to see forgot to mention this little detail, as a result, I believe, of the extreme anxiety that seized him when, after having sized me up and listened to me for a few seconds, it hit him that I might at any moment set out across the Atlantic again without having settled the bill. Fortunately, I had medical insurance, and everything that had to be done to rid me of my little pimple forever was duly done.

MT: A *tilaka*, like the Hindus make on their foreheads before going into the temple.

RG: A religious sign. And then, a short time later, some somewhat abnormal symptoms appeared at the very spot where the tiny operation had been performed.

My doctor's peace of mind was slightly disturbed by this, much less, it must be said, than the first time, while I, to the contrary, was much more upset. It was clear to me that my cancer was moving on to a new stage, and that this time it could only be fatal.

My dermatologist was severe, and, ever since that period, he stands in my eyes for everything that's intimidating and even fatal about the American medical system, which may well be the best in the world, but which is also remorseless, not only from a financial point of view but also because of its extreme reluctance to reassure the clientele, so as to avoid nourishing false hopes. That doctor reminds me a bit of those highway robbers who rapidly empty your pockets while constantly making death threats. You shouldn't even think about putting up the slightest resistance. And a few moments later, you find yourself lying on the pavement, completely healed.

In my case, the anguish lasted a little longer. It began in the week of Shrovetide. Before the liturgical reforms of the last council, the Sunday of Shrovetide inaugurated a period of two weeks devoted to preparing for the forty days of Lent, during which the faithful, in imitation of Jesus and the forty days he spent fasting in the desert, are supposed to do penance *in cinere et cilicio*, 'in ashes and *sackcloth*.'

I prepared for that Lent as never before, I assure you, and Lent itself was excellent, too, because my worries increased to the point of keeping me awake at night, until the day when they were banished as suddenly as they had begun by a last visit to my medical oracle. Having performed all of the necessary tests, the good fellow declared me healed, exactly on Holy Wednesday, which is to say the day in holy week that comes before the Passion properly speaking and Easter Sunday, which is the official conclusion of all penance.

I've never known a holiday to compare to that day of deliverance. I thought I was dead, and, all at once, I was resurrected. And what was most amazing for me about the whole thing was that my intellectual and spiritual conviction, my true conversion, had occurred before my great Lenten scare.

If it had occurred afterwards, I would never have truly believed. My natural skepticism would have convinced me that my faith was a result of the scare I had received. As for the scare, it could not be due only to faith. My dark night of the soul lasted exactly as long as the period prescribed by the Church for the penance of sinners, with three days – the most important of all – mercifully subtracted, no doubt so that I could calmly and quietly reconcile myself with the Church before the Easter holiday.

God had called me to order with a jot of humor that was really just what my mediocre case deserved. In the days that followed Easter, which the liturgy reserves for the baptism of catechumens, I had my two sons baptized, and I arranged for a Catholic wedding ceremony. I'm convinced that God sends human beings a lot of signs that have no objective existence whatsoever for the wise and the learned. The ones those signs don't concern regard them as imaginary, but those for whom they are intended can't be mistaken, because they're living the experience from within. I understood at once that, if I escaped it, the memory of the ordeal would sustain me for the rest of my days, and that's exactly what happened.

From the beginning, my Christianity was bathed in an

atmosphere of liturgical tradition. There are some conventionally anti-Christian people who want nothing but the best for me and who try at all costs, so as to defend my reputation in intellectual circles, to make me out to be a dyed-in-the-wool heretic, a ferocious enemy of 'historical Christianity,' ready to plant bombs in all the baptismal fonts.

By saying that the Church remained sacrificial for a long time, did I really deliver a ritual kick after the example of all the asses who are savagely bent on hounding our Holy Mother at present? It must be admitted that I probably displayed some mimetic demagogy in the way I expressed myself.

I would have done better to situate my remarks in the context of our entire religious history. But I didn't want to repeat the error of the Pharisees that I was talking about earlier, the ones who say: 'If we had lived in the days of our fathers, we wouldn't have taken part alongside them in the founding murder.' The last thing I want to do is to condemn the faithfulness, obedience, patience, and modesty of ordinary Christians or the virtues of the generations that came before us. We're terribly lacking in those virtues. I'm too much a man of my era to possess them myself, but I revere them. Indeed, nothing seems more conformist or more servile to me these days than the hackneyed mythology of 'revolt.'

Remnants of avant-gardist jargon are sprinkled through my books, but my true Christian readers weren't led astray: Father Schwager, Father Lohfink, von Balthazar in his late period, Father Corbin, Father Alison, and many others.

MT: A last question. You're the only person or at least one of the only people to say the things you say, and you also entitled one of your first books *Things Hidden since the Foundation of the World*. Are you a prophet?

RG: Absolutely not. I'm just a sort of exegete. All prophecy stops with gospel Revelation. Jesus's phrase, 'I will reveal things hidden since the foundation of the world,' is in the future tense because it's a citation from the Old Testament that he applies to Christian Revelation. One day, after the publication of the book that bears this fearsome title, some Italian friends showed me an article from the

Corriere della Sera in which Madame Françoise Giroud explained to the Milanese that in Paris there was a new megalomaniac on the loose who was even more hilarious than the rest of his tribe: he claimed to reveal, all by himself – hold on to your hats – 'things hidden since the foundation of the world.'

Every day I see people who think I made the title up on my own, and they judge me just about as much as Madame Giroud did. Of the first articles written about my religious ideas, a good half, I think, were of this type, though they were usually less amusing than the article by Madame Giroud, whose prose really isn't half bad, especially in Italian.

MT: But why did René Girard come along now? Why not in the year 1000, or in the year 1500?

RG: Now you're going overboard. Three quarters of what I say is in Saint Augustine.

MT: Sometimes I tell myself that, to the contrary, all you're doing is sticking as closely as possible to the project and commentaries of the apostles. For example, a little bit earlier,* you cited the prophet Joel, and I've noticed since that it's merely a citation from Peter at the beginning of Acts. But I think you're even closer to Paul – with a more modern vocabulary and the knowledge of what's happened over the last two thousand years.

RG: The citation from Joel is behind all the texts we're talking about, which always associate it with the Holy Spirit. Here it is, in the New Jerusalem Bible version:

After this I shall pour out my spirit on all humanity. Your sons and daughters shall prophesy, your old people shall dream dreams, and your young people see visions. Even on the slaves, men and women, shall I pour out my spirit in those days.

What I bring to the table, I think, is a reversal of the conclusions of the comparativist movement, which was sparked by the huge amounts of anthropological research conducted in the nineteenth

---

* At the beginning of chapter 8 in the volume *When These Things Begin*.

and early twentieth centuries. It was discovered at that time that violence, which is always collective and always resembles the violence of the Passion, is already there, everywhere, at the heart of primitive religion. This idea is correct, in my view it may even be the essential discovery of modern ethnology, which, since then, hasn't discovered much of anything.

Ethnologists jumped on this information, which they saw as irrefutable proof that Christianity is just another religion. As for the Christians, they sought to parry the blow by showing that Christianity is original after all, original in the romantic and modern sense, 'esthetically new.' They didn't understand that, instead of fleeing the parallel between Christian and other religions where violence was concerned, they should have thought about it and seen that Christianity interprets that violence in a way that's completely different from primitive religion. Its originality consists in going back to the origin and unveiling it.

Paradoxically, the only one to understand this a little was Nietzsche, him again, Nietzsche in his last days of lucidity, with essential things to say about religion, things that Heidegger never wanted to hear. Let's let him speak:

Dionysus versus the *'Crucified'*: there you have the antithesis. It is *not a difference in regard to their martyrdom – it is a difference in the meaning of it.*

Life itself, its eternal fruitfulness and recurrence, creates torment, destruction, the will to annihilation.

In the other case, suffering – the *'Crucified'* as the innocent one – counts as an objection to this life, as a formula for its condemnation.*

It can be said without paradox, or almost, that this text is the greatest theological text of the nineteenth century. It is mistaken only about the innocence of Jesus, which isn't an argument against

* *The Will to Power*, trans. Walter Kaufmann and R.J. Hollingdale, 542–3. René Girard's italics.

life, a mere 'calumny' of other religions – the expression is found in a nearby text – but the naked truth: in other words, it's the lie of all essentially mythical religions that the gospel Passion unveils by turning it inside-out like a glove. The Gospels denounce the idea that not only the victims of Dionysus but also Oedipus and all the other mythical heroes are guilty of the most varied plagues and calamities, which their expulsion 'heals'; it denounces the violence of religions founded on arbitrary victims. And it's that unveiling that has been shaking the foundations of our society ever since.

Nietzsche's only error, a properly *Luciferian* error (in the sense of 'bringer of light'), was to have chosen violence against the innocent truth of the victim, a truth that Nietzsche himself was the only one to glimpse, in contrast with the blind positivism of all the atheist ethnologists and the Christians themselves. To understand that the twentieth century and its genocides, far from killing Christianity, make its truth all the more dazzling, you just have to read Nietzsche from the proper angle and to situate all the disasters caused by our Dionysian and sacrificial choices along the axis of his writings, the first of those disasters being the madness that was getting ready to swoop down on the thinker himself – a madness every bit as significant as the political and historical insanity that followed.

Translated by Trevor Cribben Merrill

Violence and Religion: Cause or Effect?

The question of violence and religion arouses a great deal of justified interest today. It is a difficult and complex question. If we simply ask 'is this or that religion violent or peaceful?' we do not take into account the fact that violence comes from us human beings. We all believe this regardless of whether or not we believe in God. The question of religious violence, therefore, is first and foremost a human question, a social and anthropological question, and not a directly religious question.

I am going to focus on the role of violence in archaic religions and in the biblical religions. Which religions should be called archaic or primitive? My short answer is that all religions are archaic that are now dying or already dead. This definition includes all the religions of the small non-literate cultures that still existed one, two, three, or four centuries ago. It also includes the religions of the ancient world and all the prehistoric religions about which we know nothing. There probably were religions long before the painted caves of Cro-Magnon man in Southwestern France, 30,000 and 40,000 years ago.

Among modern humanists, there has been a long tradition of interpreting religion as some sort of narrative, in which its practitioners were supposed to believe. In the nineteenth century, for instance, the French philosopher Auguste Comte regarded all religions as failed attempts to account for 'the mysteries of the universe.' The postmodern theory of religion is not very different. Theorists call religions 'grand narratives,' which they regard as entirely fictional, as they do almost all texts.

The archaic religions are completely indifferent to the mysteries of the universe. The only narratives they have are not 'grand' but small, strictly limited to the local genesis of the cults to which they belong. To Darwinian biologists and sociobiologists the fact that religion may be as old as humankind itself suggests that it must have some more vital function than satisfying our idle curiosity about the mysteries of the universe. If it did not, it would have disappeared long ago.

In my opinion, the relationship between violence and religion is so entangled that it should not be mentioned unless one considers the problem in its entirety. I am going to summarize my views on the subject. To do so in the limited space of this essay, however, I must streamline my observations so much that some points may seem arbitrary.

Intraspecies violence already exists among animals, notably in sexual rivalries, but it remains moderate. The victor spares the vanquished, and this is how the relations that play the main role in animal life are established. They are relations of dominance. Human beings are more violent than animals since they often kill each other. We blame this state of affairs on aggression. The problem with this notion is its one-sidedness. It aggressively divides mankind between the aggressors and the aggressed, and we include ourselves in the second category. But most human conflicts are two-sided, reciprocal.

We are competitive rather than aggressive. In addition to the appetites we share with animals, we have a more problematic yearning that lacks any instinctual object: desire. We literally do not know what to desire and, in order to find out, we watch the people we admire: we imitate their desires. Both models and imitators of the same desire inevitably desire the same object and become rivals. Their rival desires literally feed on one another: the imitator becomes the model of his model, and the model the imitator of his imitator. Unlike animal rivalries, these imitative or mimetic rivalries can become so intense and contagious that not only do they lead to murder but they also spread, mimetically, to entire communities. They probably would have annihilated our species if something had not prevented this outcome. What was it?

The foundational myths of archaic religions suggest an answer. They describe the birth of the religion to which they belong. They all begin with a mimetic crisis and conclude with the same type of drama: a single victim is killed by the entire community and is finally divinized. In the Oedipus myth, for instance, the citizens of Thebes firmly believe that this hero not only killed his father and married his mother but also brought a plague epidemic to the city of Thebes. Because of this, they believe that he certainly deserves to be punished. Myths present their single victims as guilty and the mobs who do the killing as innocent.

The Twentieth-Century Rejection of Realism

As I have already observed, during much of the twentieth century, it has been fashionable to believe that myths and other religious texts are purely fictional. If all religious texts are imaginary, the differences between them originate in the private imaginings of a few individual authors and do not have anthropological and social significance. I believe, however, that all the recurrent features in the texts of archaic myths militate against the fictional theory. To begin with there is nothing poetic or playful about these texts. They sound much more like echoes of mob violence reported by the mobs themselves. Four categories of clues, in my view, support this hypothesis:

1) In many myths, the people seem terrified by their prospective victim, concerned solely with protecting themselves from this frightful monster. In reality, the victim seems to be in the situation of the persecuted narrator in the biblical psalms, surrounded by menacing crowds and completely helpless. In the end, the single victim always dies and the people are unharmed.

2) Many of the crimes attributed to the single victims are obvious stereotypes that reappear in myth after myth, such as rape, infanticide, bestiality, and the like. The parricide and incest of Oedipus belong to this group. Far from being the unique insight imagined by Freud,

they are banal accusations of the type still bandied around nowadays by mobs on the rampage. Highly revealing as well are such magical accusations as the evil eye, the supposed power to kill with a single glance. These are opportunistic accusations routinely resorted to by mobs to justify killing whomever they feel like killing.

3) Another highly revealing clue is the physical impairment of many victims: some limp; others are one-eyed, hunchback, or crippled. These handicaps suggest how mobs really select their victims. Animal predators select visibly abnormal prey because they are easier to spot and to catch. Something similar happens, it seems, in the human world: visibly 'damaged' individuals attract the attention of mobs.

4) Another telltale sign, I think, is the remarkably large number of mythical heroes defined as 'foreign.' In isolated and ignorant communities, cultural differences are disturbing. A visiting stranger may start a panic and be attacked simply because his speech and mannerisms differ slightly from the local standards. I do not claim that myths are accurate accounts of the mob phenomena, but rather that the phenomena are real while the accounts are systematically inaccurate, always distorted in the manner that is to be expected from a bunch of unrepentant killers reporting their own actions. That is the reason why the victims are always portrayed as guilty and the mobs never make the slightest mistake. They always kill a *bona fide* troublemaker. It was not the discovery of some authentic criminal, as claimed by myths, that reconciled these archaic communities; it was the illusion of such a discovery. The communities mimetically transferred all their hostilities to the single victim and became reconciled on the basis of the resulting illusion.

How can the same imitation, the same mimetic contagion that previously caused the mimetic rivalries and therefore the violent disintegration of the community suddenly turn into a force for the reintegration, the reconciliation of the community?

As mimetic rivalries intensify, during mimetic crises, they gradually erase all existing cultural differences and turn the best-ordered communities into undifferentiated mobs. Beyond a certain intensity, the objects of desire are consumed, destroyed, or forgotten. The mimetic frenzy refocuses on the antagonists themselves. The same human beings who, a little before, could not stop fighting because they shared the same desires, now share the same antagonists and the same hatred. Paradoxically, when mutual love is absent, the only sentiment that can reconcile human beings is its opposite, a common hatred.

The contagious mimesis polarizes against fewer and fewer antagonists until finally, for some of the insignificant reasons I mentioned earlier, or for no reason at all, the crowd becomes polarized against one last individual. At that point, no one has an enemy left in the community except for that common target and as soon as it is destroyed, violence must come to an end. In Greek, the word for this seemingly miraculous operation is catharsis, which signifies the purification or cleansing of all the violence inside the community. The unanimous mimetic contagion transforms the disastrous violence of all against all into the healing violence of all against one. The community is reconciled at the cost of one victim only.

Ritual Sacrifice

When thus reconciled, archaic communities felt that they had experienced a miracle and were greatly relieved, of course, but not for long. Human nature was unchanged and, sooner or later, the mimetic rivalries had to reappear. The frightened communities tried to limit these rivalries by a system of prohibitions that kept the people most likely to engage in them away from one another. They also tried to preordain rigidly the distribution of the potentially most divisive 'goods,' especially women.

Frequently, these precautions failed, it seems, and when they did, the terrified communities remembered that their previous mimetic crisis was ended by the killing of a victim. They now wondered if the killing of more victims might not repeat the earlier miracle. The result was the invention of the most important religious institution of humankind, ritual sacrifice. All archaic cultures solemnly immolate victims in the hope of preventing mimetic conflicts.

In many archaic cultures, notably in Africa, the important rituals began with some deliberate disruption of the community: the various subgroups taunted and insulted one another; they even came to blows. The idea behind these 'mock crises,' as the anthropologists call them, was to ensure the success of the ritual sacrifice through an exact reproduction of the entire original sequence, including an abbreviated version of the mimetic rivalries. The goal was to facilitate the triggering of the victimizing mechanism, and the 'mock crisis' probably helped.

Let me sum up the 'mimetic theory' of religion and culture: when future human beings became too mimetic to live as animals do, their dominance patterns collapsed and the resulting crises triggered the mimetic victimization mechanism around which the first systems of prohibitions and sacrificial rites coalesced. These were the first religions and the initial form of human culture. Religion enabled humanity to turn to positive use its mimetic power, which is not all violence only but is also our great capacity for learning, our superior intelligence.

If my analysis is sound, far from being the cause of our violence, archaic religions are, or rather were, first a consequence of that violence and, secondly, our primary protection against it. During the longest part of our history or pre-history, they enabled human communities to survive their own violence. Archaic religions are essentially combinations of prohibitions and sacrifices. Prohibitions forbade violence directly, but they often failed and, when they did, archaic communities fell back upon their second line of defense, sacrifice. The paradox of archaic religion is that, in order to prevent violence, it resorted to substitute violence. Jean-Pierre Dupuy has observed that sacrifice, understood broadly, contains violence in both senses of the word. It contains violence as an army contains the attacks of its enemies, and sacrifice also contains violence in the sense of being inhabited by it, of making violence its main resource against violence itself.

During the greater part of human history, the single victim mechanism generated many religions, no doubt, that operated efficiently because the faithful never became aware of their generative principle. They were deluded into believing that their gods, rather than the community itself, had to be appeased with victims. It was the community's own anger that threatened its survival, but no one realized it. The victimization mechanism that produced archaic religions was so unanimous that the first demonized, then divinized victim seemed responsible both for the mimetic crises and their happy conclusion. Those who surrendered to the spirit of the mob saw their own unanimity not as the mimetic contagion that it really was, but as the certain proof of their correct interpretation of the single victim drama.

The Biblical 'Difference'

The Hebrew Bible and the Christian Gospels are the only religious texts that contain reversals of this mythical scheme. The mobs in the Jewish and Christian scriptures think and behave exactly like the mobs in archaic myths. The difference is not in the events but in their interpretation. In myths, the victims have really committed the crimes of which their persecutors accuse them. In the Jewish and Christian scriptures, mobs are blamed for persecuting innocent victims.

In the prophetic texts of the Hebrew Bible, the perspective of the mob is condemned and reversed. For example, Joseph's brothers turn into a kind of ugly mob in their behavior towards him. Job's entire community acts with the solidarity of a mob. In many psalms, the narrator watches helplessly as mobs surround him for the purpose, it seems, of killing him. Many of the prophets were persecuted and even killed by hostile mobs. The most spectacular example is the killing of the Suffering Servant (Isaiah 52–53), whom the Gospels compare with Jesus. The prophetic literature is a long march away from this violent social phenomenon that seems to have played an enormous role in human cultures before and even after the arrival of judicial systems.

The Gospels contain the same overall sequence as myths. Once again, there is a great crisis at the beginning, the crisis of the small Jewish state under Roman occupation, and it culminates in the drama of a single victim, Jesus, who is collectively killed and later divinized by the Christians. But the difference is that the Gospels reverse the verdict of the crowd in myths: the victim is innocent, and the mob is guilty. Especially striking in the Gospels is the fact that the two perspectives – the mob's and the victim's – are displayed side by side. Almost everybody agrees with the local mob. The dissenters are very few, but precarious as their perspective seems at first, it ultimately triumphs for one essential reason, in my view: it happens to be true.

I use the word 'truth' here in an anthropological and social context, not in a religious context. All rational human beings would agree, no doubt, that mobs are notoriously unreliable as judges of right and wrong, especially when it comes to their own victims. It was not the discovery of some authentic criminal, as claimed by myths, that reconciled these archaic communities, but the illusion of such a discovery. The communities mimetically transferred all their hostilities to the single victim and became reconciled on the basis of the resulting illusion.

Since the victim is innocent, what is the force that unites, each time, a large group of violent men against an irrelevant victim? The answer is once again imitation, mimetic contagion.

Whereas myths submit to the mimetic contagion against the single victim, the biblical interpreters resist that same contagion and rehabilitate the victim who is indeed innocent. The biblical resistance to the mimetic contagion reveals the essential deceptiveness of archaic religions, the spirit of the mob that dominates them. This unique power to demystify the unanimous violence is applicable not merely to the specific victims represented in these texts – Joseph, Job, the Suffering Servant, or Jesus – but, potentially, to all similar victims of collective victimization wherever they happen to occur. To demystify a myth, all we need to do is to slip, for example, the account of the Crucifixion beneath its text and compare the one with the other.

The (synoptic) Gospels make it obvious that all witnesses of the Crucifixion behave mimetically. Peter's denial is a spectacular example: as soon as he finds himself surrounded by people hostile to Jesus, he imitates their hostility. His triple denial is a mimetic phenomenon. Pilate is poles apart from Peter and yet, in the end, he behaves just like the apostle. Even though he would personally prefer to save Jesus, he surrenders to the mob; he imitates the mob and orders the Crucifixion. The two thieves crucified with Jesus (only one in Luke) are another, even more caricatured example of crowd imitation. Instead of sympathizing with the man whose dreadful fate they share, they insult Jesus in imitation of the crowd, in a last, desperate effort to rejoin the crowd, to deny their own crucifixion.

The modern world does not perceive this biblical demystification. Just the opposite. Biblical texts are often believed to be equivalent to myths because they do, indeed, resemble myths. In reality, far from ensuring the sameness of all the religious doctrines rooted in all these texts, the presence everywhere of a victimization mechanism opens up the possibility of an enormously significant difference. The tendency to define all texts as mythical is due to the inability of most modern researchers to go beyond the themes and motifs of these texts and to see that the surrender or resistance to the mimetic contagion is the most important factor in the type of text ultimately produced. A text can conceal the deceptiveness of the victimization mechanism and be itself deceptive, or it can reveal that same deceptiveness and, together with it, the injustice of the mob and the undeserved suffering of the victim. The first way is the way of mythology, and the second is the way of biblical texts and, most explicitly, of the Gospels.

The picture of the human world conveyed by myths is rosier than the biblical picture precisely because it reflects the persecutors' deceptive perspective, rather than the more truthful victims' perspective. The only philosopher who realized that this preference for mythology was equivalent, in fact, with siding with the persecutors was Friedrich Nietzsche. But, far from inciting him to shift to the side of the victims, this discovery reinforced his bias in favor of unjust violence and, at least indirectly, his writing on the subject encouraged some of the worst abominations of the twentieth century.

The prophetic literature of the Hebrew Bible and the Gospels stands in absolute opposition to the mythical and sacrificial mentality of archaic religion. Many statements and formulae confirm this opposition. Hosea attributes the following words to Yahweh: 'I desire mercy and not sacrifice' (Hosea 6:6). Jesus advises his listeners to become reconciled with their brothers before they bring their sacrificial offerings to the altar. He warns them, in other words, that they should not count on sacrifices any more as an artificial means of getting along with their neighbors. The truth of sacrifice, which is about to be revealed in the Crucifixion, will destroy once and for all, in the long run, the effectiveness of all sacrifices. As it becomes impossible to elude violence with ritual, a face-to-face reconciliation becomes the only means to avoid the destructive unleashing of mimetic violence.

The Modern Evolution Away from Violence

The non-violent side of the biblical inspiration can be seen quite directly in the long-range historical evolution of our Western societies. In some important respects, ever since the high Middle Ages, our historical world has been moving in the direction of less and less violence. Our world has abolished serfdom and slavery. Our penal legislation has become more humane, the status of women has been raised, and we protect children and the aged. We have invented such things as the hospital, free medical care, and various forms of social protection for the weak and the handicapped. However feeble these mitigations of violence may seem compared with our aspirations, they are without precedent in all of human history.

Our world has become progressively more aware of arbitrary victimization, and our social, political, and legal institutions are making greater and greater efforts to avoid it. The preoccupation with victims often becomes, in the contemporary world, the object of a novel kind of mimetic rivalry that encourages exploitative distortions and turns the whole thing into a caricature. In spite of these faddish aspects, the modern concern for victims, which has been in the making for many centuries, is a major historical development. We are constantly accusing ourselves of persecuting victims not only at the present time but also in the past of our nations, our religious traditions, and our ethnic traditions. We are rewriting history from the standpoint of victims. We often manage, I repeat, to turn this remarkable concern into more mimetic rivalry, and we spend a good deal of time throwing old corpses at each other's heads, in a renewed attempt to justify ourselves at the expense of our neighbors, but these regrettable aspects should not obscure the larger significance of these phenomena.

While our world is less violent than any previous world, I do not have to remind you that this is only one aspect of the world in which we live. The other aspect is the very reverse: a tremendous increase in violence and in the threats of violence. The two opposite trends have been developing simultaneously for quite a few centuries, no doubt, and the gulf between them is forever widening. Our world both saves more victims than any previous world and kills more victims than any previous world. The twentieth century not only had the greatest wars in human history, but it was the century of death camps, genocides, and nuclear weapons. And every day, it seems, new and even worse threats confront us, such as the possibility that our most monstrous weapons will fall into the hands of terrorists ready to die in order to kill the greatest possible number of innocent people.

How can these two aspects characterize our world simultaneously? Is it not a terrible indictment of the biblical tradition that it has proved unable to make peace among us? Is it not true therefore that even the most peaceful-sounding religions do cause violence after all? Many people answer with a resounding 'yes' without taking into account or even suspecting what we discovered earlier regarding sacrifice and the sacrificial values that still permeate our society.

The violence that is slowly undermined by the biblical demystification of sacrifice is sacrificial violence, in other words, the violence that 'contains' violence and has long kept the worst forms of violence in check and, to a certain extent, still does. We are always in debt to sacrificial violence, therefore, and when we get rid of it in a great burst of self-righteous indignation against hypocrisy, it may be a worse violence that, unwittingly, we help unleash.

Because of the sacrificial background, one must refrain from evaluating the influence of the biblical religions and of other religions from the standpoint of a simple opposition between violence and non-violence. The elimination of sacrificial violence is not simply 'good' or 'bad'; it is an ambiguous and ambivalent progress in the struggle against violence, which may include regressive aspects if the human beings whom this violence restrained in the past become more violent as a result of this development. The peace that has been available to us until recently often rests on a sacrificial violence, which is no longer present in the form of blood sacrifice, of course, in this country, but in institutions such as the police, the American army, the superior American power, and the respect it still inspires throughout the world.

When one eliminates the violence of sacrifice, or even weakens it, one cannot avoid weakening the peaceful effects of this violence just as much as the violent aspects. The rejection of sacrificial violence is certainly something good in principle, the result of a righteous battle against the hypocrisy of religious, social, and political institutions always suffused with sacrificial values. But the more we succeed in this undertaking, the more we destroy traditional institutions and the more we weaken the stability of our own world. The more we promote individual freedom, the more all individuals should feel that they have to prevent violence themselves by non-violent means; we must avoid without outside help the disorders that sacrificial cultures prevented through legal violence.

The disappearance of sacrificial limitations and religious prohibitions facilitates the unleashing of mimetic rivalries not only at their most creative, in scientific competition for instance, but also at their most destructive, in the suicidal forms of terrorism that turn the marvels of modern technology into indiscriminately murderous weapons.

Conclusion

Even if my observations are too sketchy to convince you that the mimetic theory of religion is the breakthrough I believe it is, you will agree, I hope, that even the most obviously 'untrue' religions are worthy of our respect. Archaic religions are not simply false explications of the universe. They always had more urgent business to attend to than satisfying the curiosity of idle men. They have always been in charge of keeping the peace. Even if they had to resort to violent means to reach their goal, these means were not really their own invention; they were provided more or less ready-made by the spontaneous course of human relations. We cannot condemn these religions as something alien to our modern humanity. Even as we try to do better than the old religions did, we understand that the task is infinitely more difficult than it was thought a hundred years ago. The violence we would love to transfer to religion is really our own, and we must confront it directly. To turn religions into the scapegoats of our own violence can only backfire in the end.

Belonging

'Belonging' means the fact of belonging to something or someone. A serf belongs to an estate. A slave belongs to his master. In our democratic universe, no one belongs to a lord and master anymore, at least in principle. Nowadays, people only belong to communities of free individuals who are equal under the law – again, in principle.

We all belong to the human race. Nearly all of you here belong to the nation of Italy, to Sicily, to the city of Messina, to such and such a milieu, to such and such a family. Most of you now even have a new level of supranational belonging: your passports are no longer merely Italian but European.

While some relationships of belonging are mainly spatial in nature, they necessarily have a temporal dimension, and vice versa. We all belong to a particular generation. If relationships of belonging are located in space and time, this is because the same is true of people. Some relationships of belonging are purely cultural, such as belonging to a religion, a social or professional group, an ideology, or a political party. Others are predominantly natural relationships of belonging, but which have been 'culturalized': for example, each of us belongs to a particular blood group.

In times past, relationships of belonging were organized hierarchically. In the modern world, they are increasingly variable and unstable. We are now conglomerates of such relationships, though with vestiges of hierarchy.

There are strong and weak relationships of belonging, and their distribution varies from individual to individual, from country to country, and from one era to the next. I'm told that in Italy, the sense of national belonging is weaker than in the United States or

France, but regional and family relationships of belonging are more meaningful.

There are voluntary and involuntary relationships of belonging. There are honorary ones, such as belonging to an academy, and dishonorable ones such as belonging to a group of habitual offenders. There are relationships of belonging that are purely administrative and bureaucratic, and others that, on the contrary, are private and even concealed – for example, secret passions to which an individual belongs body and soul without anyone else knowing. There are also relationships of belonging that no one has any problem recognizing apart from the one who belongs: if I belong to the category of conceited people, I am the only one not to notice.

Our social identity is an intertwining and intermingling of relationships of belonging so numerous and diverse that together they constitute something unique: an individual being that we are the only one to possess. Although our relationships of belonging are never individual in the strict sense, they are so many and varied that, for each individual, they make up a combination distinct from all comparable combinations, a singular identity, a bit like our genetic makeup.

It seems to me that it is in this individualizing multiplicity of relationships of belonging that we need to look for the two meanings – not only different but diametrically opposed – of the word *identity*. To have an identity is to be unique; and yet, outside of that use, the term means the opposite of unique, denoting rather that which is identical – in other words, the complete absence of any uniquely identifying difference.

In short, by dint of belonging to everyone, we end up belonging to no one but ourselves. Our own identity is merely the intersection of all that makes us identical to countless others. This explains the paradox of identity, but in such a way that it is no surprise that so many nowadays are afflicted with what they call 'identity issues.' The very expression highlights and explains their confusion. Such people feel the same as anyone and everyone. What the modern world offers us by way of difference cannot satisfy our desire for uniqueness.

In the highly socialized traditional world, we already define ourselves – exclusively, even – by our relationships of belonging. But since we don't distinguish ourselves from those relationships – since we're joined to them – we're not aware that they're nothing more than a string of 'identities'; or, if we are aware, it doesn't bother us because we feel different from everyone else. We're not yet likely to mistake ourselves for someone else any more than we're likely to lose an identity card that we don't yet have.

In our world, relationships of belonging are becoming looser and looser. As they pull away from us they become visible, and we have the impression that it is we who are pulling away from them. So we frequently judge them burdensome or, conversely, we dread losing them altogether. This is why there has arisen nowadays a problem that was unknown in times past, the problem that concerns us here: the problem of belonging. It cuts across the problems of identity and difference.

Christians used to believe – and still do – in the existence of the individual *person*, inseparable from her relationships of belonging but neither lost in the mass of those relationships nor, even more so, melded with any single one of them such as, for example, her race. During the Romantic period and in the modern era, many thinkers responded to the weakening of relationships of belonging by inventing a pure and empty subject, both impersonal and supremely individual, and which, far from making us into a simple intersection of relationships of belonging, would deify us with the help of neither God nor anyone else. All of this collapsed in very short order.

We live in a world in which the weakening and widening of relationships of belonging goes hand-in-hand with the globalization of all aspects of life – economic, financial, political, and even cultural. However, as such relationships become more and more all-encompassing and less and less restrictive, they also become less and less protective and less able to provide a sense of security.

This weakening is not always easy to spot, since it's often due to a shift in relationships of belonging. For a long time, for example, local relationships of belonging weakened in favor of regional ones, then regional ones declined in favor of national ones, until finally, today, we've moved on to the supranational level.

Many are those who believe the opposite of what I've just been saying: namely that, far from weakening, ancient, ethnic, and, in particular, religious relationships of belonging live on and are getting stronger, as demonstrated by the virulence of conflicts that define themselves as clashes of ethnic, religious, and cultural belonging. I am of the opinion that they are mistaken, and I'm going to try to demonstrate why.

Our earliest relationships of belonging are fundamental for everything we call learning or education. The family provides the individual with his first models: it's by imitating his mother and father that a child learns the basic actions of life. Then come schools, which also provide models without which children would never become adults capable of 'functioning' effectively in society. The professional world is another source of learning. Our earliest relationships of belonging secure our social integration.

Although positive and essential, most relationships of belonging – even the most humble – involve some form of exclusion, rejection, and, consequently, violence. To exist, they have to exclude some people, and even if this exclusion is not achieved through physical violence, it employs means that are inevitably perceived as violent by those who are its victims. The more desirable the relationship of belonging is or appears to be, the more bitterly the violence of exclusion is experienced by the excluded. Also, as a rule, the harder such a relationship is to acquire, the more desirable it appears to be.

The further back in history we go, the more closely certain relationships of belonging are bound up with violence: there was a time when belonging to the most desirable class, the nobility, essentially relied on force of arms. As time passed, the role of physical violence diminished, but wherever relationships of belonging were or appeared to be advantageous, they were subject to competition that led to all kinds of fighting, maneuvering, and scheming – in other words, less brutal but more insidious forms of violence.

One only has to look, for example, at education systems. Even the most democratic of such systems have to include an element of selection if they are to be at all effective. In a world that has become hypersensitive to rivalries, entrance exams, end-of-year exams, anything that is intended to select the most able students is experienced by those who are rejected as an act of unbearable violence. One cannot but acknowledge that even and especially those methods that are clearly the most merit-based are objectively cruel.

Sociologists rarely pay as much attention to the dual nature of relationships of belonging as the subject deserves – or if they do, they treat it simplistically as a political, social, or racial injustice that could easily be rectified by establishing a more egalitarian regime. In doing so, they fail to see that, for reasons of general interest, our societies cannot give up selecting the most competent.

While the violence of exclusion is nowadays very visible and hotly debated, contrary to what we tend to think, it is not the only violence associated with relationships of belonging. Neither is it the most widespread or the worst. There is another form of violence of which we are largely unaware and that can be said to exist inside relationships of belonging. By bringing individuals closer to each other, and by encouraging them to pursue the same goals, all manner of associations – professional, educational, recreational, sporting, and so on – give rise to agreement between those they unite by inspiring in them the same desires. In so doing, they also give rise to a certain type of conflict.

If we desire the same things, we feel close to one another, and this closeness, which constitutes agreement on the spiritual level, can become disagreement on the concrete level. Indeed, there are two possibilities: either the object that two or more of us desire can be shared and we agree to share it, in which case there is no conflict; or the object is one that we cannot or will not share, in which case conflict is inevitable.

I call this conflict *mimetic rivalry*. It presupposes common relationships of belonging that, by the very fact of bringing us together and setting us in opposition to one another, not only foster this type of conflict but also provide it with a battleground in which to rage. Mimetic theory affirms that people's desires are not really rooted in either desired objects or the subjects who desire those objects, but rather in a third party: the model or mediator of our desires. As long as the imitator and his or her model have relatively few relationships of belonging in common, they are not threatened by mimetic rivalry. They are like two stars that, while they may dream about each other, remain light years apart. If, on the other hand, imitator and model have many relationships of belonging in common, they are exposed to the temptations of rivalry. We are always close to our rivals, and the more we compete with them, the more we resemble them, and the more our two identities become one and the same. If models only inspired in their imitators a desire for objects that they then agreed to share with them, violent rivalry would be avoided. What makes such rivalry inevitable is the thirst for exclusive possession, which most often characterizes the imitator's desire precisely because it already characterizes the desire of his or her model.

Voltaire's *Candide* contains a thousand examples of mimetic desire with disastrous consequences. The young hero's private tutor, the philosopher Pangloss, teaches his naive student the optimistic system of his idol, the great Leibniz. Pangloss will unknowingly also serve as a model for a less philosophical activity: passionate love. Indeed, as the tale opens, the beautiful Cunégonde – like Candide, a student of Pangloss – stumbles across the master making love to a castle servant under a bush. Inspired by this scene, the young lady plucks up the courage to declare her love to Candide, who responds enthusiastically to her ardor. But the two lovers are in turn caught unawares by the baron, who would like to provide his daughter with a more aristocratic husband than the unfortunate Candide, whom he unceremoniously boots out.

When a faithful disciple catches his revered master caressing a pretty girl, it is not hard to see how he desires to do the same. And, in his desire to be even more faithful, he ends up being completely unfaithful: he tries to steal his model's partner. This is when the most dreadful conflicts erupt.

While mimetic rivalry can be sexual, contrary to what Freud and his disciples would have us believe, it can also be professional, intellectual, spiritual, aesthetic, sporting, philatelic . . . in short, it can exist in all kinds of forms. As Shakespeare tells us in *Hamlet*, men can fight to the death over an eggshell. The playwright takes up the same image again in *Coriolanus* because he is obsessed by the futility of mimetic rivalry. Perhaps it was this Shakespearean eggshell that gave the satirist Jonathan Swift – another great revealer of mimetic rivalry – the original idea for his inexpiable war of the eggs, between those who break them at the larger end and those who prefer to start at the smaller end.

In short, far from guaranteeing peace, even the most insignificant relationships of belonging arouse not only the external violence of exclusion but also the internal violence of rivalry between individuals who, all desiring the same thing, however absurd, become obstacles to one another and can no longer stop quarreling.

Our capacity for mimetic absorption is not confined to those behaviors that our models wish us to imitate. The violent side of relationships of belonging is the flip side of their positive function. Relationships of belonging thus contain a seed of self-destruction – the basis of their own collapse – which is explained by the mimetic nature of human desire and the resulting rivalry.

It seems to me that a good example of this is the terrible combat between Yvain and Gauvain at the climax of the romance *Yvain* by Chrétien de Troyes. The reasons why these two men are the best friends in the world are the very same reasons that incite them to be secretly jealous of one another, and thus to fight like no two knights have ever fought. Since they both present themselves anonymously and armored from head to toe, in theory they fight without recognizing each other. However, we can assume that, in reality, their excellence is such that they cannot but recognize one another by strength of arms. Each of them possesses the utmost qualities of the perfect knight, and each fears being outdone in a field in which he wants to believe he is without peer.

As we read this romance, we sense that the world of knights – and this is perhaps also true of all cultural worlds – is doomed to self-destruct. Similarly, in some democratic regimes, mimetic rivalries can become so acute that they paralyze public life. Both Italy and France are all too familiar with rivalrous blockages that prevent all decision-making.

The genius of our economic liberalism lies in the fact that it gives free rein to mimetic rivalries in the pursuit of wealth, thus allowing such rivalries to channel themselves in productive directions that are beneficial for society. However, one might wonder whether this system is not also threatened by the effects of overly frenetic competition.

Far from putting an end to rivalries, the weakening of relationships of belonging in our egalitarian world merely exasperates them at all levels of society by arousing ever more symmetrical violence between rivals. The model becomes the imitator of his imitator, and the imitator becomes the model of his model. When this type of relationship mimetically spreads everywhere, it turns into a diabolical machine that ends up blowing up the very framework that makes it possible: the system of relationships of belonging, i.e., culture itself.

Mimetic rivalries give rise to conflictual crises of such intensity that they ought to blow everything up – and there are undoubtedly situations where everything does blow up. But there are also situations, especially in archaic societies, where through their continual exasperation, mimetic crises themselves become their own remedy, so to speak, by triggering the so-called scapegoat mechanism.

In their mimetic escalation, the rivals end up forgetting about the objects they were arguing over and focusing instead on the argument itself; the mimetic to-and-fro tends to polarize no longer around the objects but directly around the antagonists. Since this mimesis is cumulative, there necessarily comes a point when the entire community polarizes around a single individual against whom the lost unity is reformed, thus reconciling the community with itself. This scapegoat mechanism, or single victim mechanism, owes its effectiveness to the unanimous transfer of all the hatred aroused by rivalries onto a victim whose expulsion and/or death necessarily restores peace, since the community believes itself to be rid of all its obsessions, and is thus actually rid of them.

This results in an abrupt end to violence that, not knowing how else to explain it, the community attributes to the victim himself, who, through his own death, will henceforth appear to be an all-powerful force for good while continuing to appear to be an all-powerful force for evil in his capacity as a scapegoat. This dual omnipotence, both good and evil, is the invention of the archaic sacred. When it operates at full capacity, the scapegoat mechanism ensures the genesis of archaic religion. Around the sacralized scapegoat gathers a group that has shared the moving experience of the crisis and its reconciling conclusion. This group endeavors to perpetuate and strengthen its own harmony by evacuating any mimetic discord that continues to arise through new victims who take the place of the original victim. This is what we know as blood sacrifice, which is always a more or less faithful copy of the liberating mechanism.

Each time mimetic rivalries appear to be reigniting, or even when other kinds of catastrophe threaten, communities endeavor to ward them off by once again triggering, through replacement victims, the mechanism that got them out of trouble the first time: the scapegoat mechanism. This mechanism is thus transformed into a ritual technique through the practice – universal until today – of blood sacrifice. Through sacrifice, religion creates culture. It seeks to prevent or cure unfettered violence by administering sacrificial violence.

In my opinion, all social relationships of belonging originate in ritual and sacrifice. Indeed, that is why, in archaic societies, such relationships depend on what are known as *rites of initiation* or *rites of passage*. Candidates are put through trials that recreate the original mimetic crisis and its resolution in victimhood. In prevailing over such trials, the candidates demonstrate that they will be able to overcome the crises that await them and are worthy of belonging to the culture that initiates them. Primitive societies are characterized by the multiplicity and rigidity of ritual and religious relationships of belonging (e.g., matrimonial groups). This multiplicity is intended to prevent desires from converging on the same objects, as a safeguard against mimetic rivalry. What I am saying, in short, is that relationships of belonging always re-emerge from the crises that threaten to destroy them, through scapegoats against whom and then around whom communities beget or renovate their religious and ritualistic systems. As they weaken, our systems of belonging are moving further and further away from this model of radical crisis and violent regeneration.

All that I have just said is directly valid only for archaic societies. In historical and modern societies, an opposing influence is at work: that of Judaism and Christianity, which explains the constant weakening of relationships of belonging.

Christianity condemns sacrificial violence as I have just defined it, since it condemns the death of Christ. The Gospels make manifest cultural violence by presenting the death of Jesus as a mob phenomenon caused by a mimetic frenzy. They tell a truth about human culture that all mythical religion conceals. Christ proposes that humans abandon scapegoating by resisting mimetic reprisals, giving up the spirit of vengeance and replacing sacrifice with the rules of the kingdom of God – i.e., by voluntarily seeking to escape from mimetic rivalry and its consequences. The realistic and mimetic description of the Passion stops the victimizing mechanisms working by revealing their absurdity. Christ is divinized not as a guilty and saving scapegoat, like the pagan gods, but for opposite reasons: because he reveals and upsets the violent mechanisms that moderate mimetic crises.

Christianity weakens all relationships of belonging by revealing that their origin is in no way authentically sacred. It is thus Christianity that weakens the principle of victimhood; and, today, it is not Christianity itself that is weakening: it is the sacred violence with which Christianity is confused.

The weakening of relationships of belonging is an essentially positive phenomenon because it lowers barriers between human beings. It works against exclusion, against the making of scapegoats. But it also has adverse and violent effects: by removing ritualistic mechanisms and the barrier of prohibitions, it further reduces resistance to mimetic rivalry. In the contemporary world, these positive and negative aspects combine in such a complex way that, while the weakening of relationships of belonging paves the way for increasing global unification, such unification entails an increase in rivalry. No longer separated from one another by insurmountable barriers, groups and individuals frenetically imitate one another and acute conflicts – whether national, ethnic, economic, social, religious, etc. – are on the rise.

Since such conflicts are always justified on the basis of some traditional, ethnic, religious, or national belonging, people think relationships of belonging are more alive and virulent than ever. In most cases, however, this is not the least bit true. This is also why, in self-justifying rhetoric, relationships of belonging easily replace one another: they are rarely anything more than excuses. While no one knows definitively whether the Bosnian war broke out for reasons of ethnic, national, or religious belonging, everyone believes that one of these relationships of belonging was the true reason for the conflict; consequently, traditional relationships of belonging appear stronger than ever. On the contrary, it seems to me that their weakening, and the resulting and ever worsening non-differentiation after forty years of Communism, is more important than what remains of their reality.

All conflicts are conflicts between enemy brothers. The only wars are civil wars, between groups whose relationships of belonging are no longer binding enough to truly separate them, and which are henceforth too visible – too ingrained in human thinking – to enable them to unite.

To understand that the conflict between relationships of belonging can be worsened by the weakening of such relationships, there is no need to turn to either sociologists or political analysts. Our human and social sciences, overly fascinated by the natural sciences, treat human intelligence as though it were primarily oriented toward objects – as though our relationships with others were no more than incidental or secondary. The social sciences see relationships of belonging as objects just like any other, while in fact they are arrangements of mimetic relationships founded on forms of initiation, exclusion, and ostracism that derive from primitive scapegoating and ritual sacrifice.

To understand relationships of belonging and what is happening to them in today's world, then, we need to turn not to the social sciences, which understand nothing of conflictual mimesis, but to the true specialists in human relations, those who stage and portray them: in other words, playwrights and novelists – but only the best ones. The dialectics of weak relationships of belonging that seek to become stronger in and through conflict are marvelously described by Marcel Proust in the social interactions of *À la recherche du temps perdu*. At first sight, one might think that the village of Combray and the Parisian salons in which the novelist moves provide too limited a terrain to illuminate the conflicts of the contemporary world. Actually, this is not so: Combray is an admirable scale model of the mimetic relationships sketched out by the novelist.

Combray is a 'small enclosed world.' Its children live in the shadow of their parents and familial divinities, in the same confident intimacy as a traditional village living in the shadow of its church tower. The unit of Combray is spiritual as well as territorial: it represents a vision shared by all the members of the family and even of the village. And, of course, Combray operates by means of scapegoating: by rejecting and eliminating that which it cannot assimilate – everything that might contradict its view of things. There are striking analogies between Combray and the 'society salons.' The *salon Verdurin* was not just a meeting place: it was a way of seeing, feeling, and judging. The *salon* itself was also a 'closed culture.' It rejected anything that threatened its spiritual unity. It perpetuated itself through expulsion and scapegoating.

The spiritual unity of the *salon* had something strained and strict that Combray did not have. From Combray to the *salon Verdurin*, it seems that the structure of the 'small enclosed world' remained: the most apparent traits merely intensified and hardened. The *salon* caricatures Combray's organic unity in the same way that a mummified face caricatures and accentuates the features of a living face. The components of the overall package are the same, but differently ordered. In Combray, the negation and refusal of the outside world is always subordinate to the affirmation of one's own genuinely lived values. Conversely, Parisian snobbery produces the opposite phenomenon. Rites of union between close friends are camouflaged rites of separation. Ceremonies are no longer observed for the purpose of fostering unity or being oneself, but rather to distinguish oneself from those who do not observe them – the other *salons*. Rival salons, in theory hated, are the real gods.

Almost identical relationships of belonging encompass two completely different realities. The more real a group's organic unity, the less that group needs to resort to violence to oppose other groups of the same type, and the more authentically foreign violence is to it.

Combray is always described to us as a patriarchal regime that we cannot pin down as either authoritarian or liberal, since it operates autonomously. Conversely, the *salon Verdurin* is an obsessive dictatorship that tries to pass itself off as a democracy. Its boss is a totalitarian head of state in the modern sense, who governs by dispensing a judicious combination of demagoguery and ferocity in expelling her scapegoats. When Proust speaks of the feelings of loyalty inspired by Combray, he speaks of *patriotism*; when he turns to the *salon Verdurin*, he speaks of *chauvinism*. The difference between the two terms corresponds to the two different types of relationships of belonging. The second appears stronger, since it is bellicose, arrogant, and conflictual; in reality, however, it is weaker. Patriotism is a collective egoism that is still authentic. It is a sincere worship of heroes and saints – i.e., of models too distant to become rivals. The fervor of this worship is not dependent on rivalries with other parties. Chauvinism, on the other hand, is the fruit of such rivalry. It is a negative feeling rooted in resentment – i.e., in the secret worship of an *Other* that is simultaneously venerated and detested.

The interplay between Combray and the *salons* represents a microcosmic reproduction of the weakening of relationships of belonging in today's world and the resulting paradoxical strengthening of rivalries. Violence is fueled not by the strength of relationships of belonging but by their weakness. It is precisely because they are collapsing that relationships of belonging try to dress themselves up in a strength they no longer have.

It seems to me that history bears out Proust's analysis. The decline of feudalism exacerbated feudal conflicts. After the Reformation, when religious fervor waned, religious wars increased. At the end of the eighteenth century in France, the 'noble reaction,' aroused by the weakening of the nobility, helped trigger the Revolution. The First World War, that paroxysm of national conflicts, announced the decline of nationalism.

Right-wing and left-wing ideologies both make the same mistake: they conceive of relationships of belonging univocally and unilaterally. Formerly, men were traditionally compared with a plant rooted in the soil. Back then, the supreme good – that which must be protected at all costs – was 'rootedness.'

Conversely, revolutionary ideology sees relationships of belonging as an entirely bad thing that must be thrown off at all costs – nothing more than an expression of class prejudice and 'superstition.'

I have tried to sketch out a perspective on relationships of belonging that is a little less univocal and unilateral than ideological oversimplifications would have us believe – less swamped in the naivety of for and against, which makes next to no sense in such an area. However, what I have had to say on this extremely complex issue remains schematic and simplified. Our discussion will be an opportunity to clarify, refine, and critique these various ideas.

Translated by Rob Grayson

On Mel Gibson's The Passion of the Christ

Well before the commercial release of his film, Mel Gibson had organized private showings for important journalists and religious leaders. If he was counting on assuring the goodwill of those he invited, he badly miscalculated; or perhaps he instead manifested a superior Machiavellianism.

The commentaries quickly followed, and far from praising the film or reassuring the public, there were only terrified vituperations and anguished cries of alarm concerning the anti-Semitic violence that might erupt at the cinema exits. Even the *New Yorker*, so proud of the serene humor from which it normally never departs, completely lost its composure, and in all seriousness accused the film of being more like Nazi propaganda than any other cinematic production since World War II.

Nothing justifies these accusations. For Mel Gibson, the death of Christ is a burden born by all humanity, starting with Mel Gibson himself. When his film strays a bit from the Gospel text, which happens only rarely, it is not to demonize the Jews but to emphasize the pity that Jesus inspires in some of them: in Simon of Cyrene for example, whose role is amplified, or in Veronica, the woman who, according to an ancient tradition, offered a cloth to Jesus during the ascent to Golgotha on which the features of his face became imprinted.

The more things calm down, the more it becomes clear in retrospect that the film precipitated a veritable tantrum in the world's most influential media that more or less contaminated the entire atmosphere in its wake. The public had nothing to do with the controversy, since it had not seen the film. It wondered with evident curiosity what was it in this Passion that could create such a panic among those who are normally so difficult to shock. What ensued was easy to predict: instead of the 2,600 screens originally planned, *The Passion of the Christ* opened on more than 4,000 screens on Ash Wednesday – a day evidently chosen for its penitential symbolism.

The charge of anti-Semitism has receded somewhat since the film's release. But the film's detractors have rallied around a second complaint: the excessive violence that they see in it. There is indeed great violence, but it does not exceed, it seems to me, that of many other films that Gibson's critics would not dream of condemning. This Passion has shaken up (no doubt only provisionally) the chessboard of media reactions concerning violence in the movies. All those who are normally accustomed to spectacular violence, or even see in its constant evolution so many victories of freedom over tyranny, find themselves condemning it in Gibson's film with extraordinary vehemence. On the other side, all those who see it as their duty to denounce cinematic violence (without their criticisms ever having the slightest impact) not only tolerate this film, but frequently admire it.

To justify their attitude, the detractors borrow from their adversaries all of the arguments that they denounce as excessive and ridiculous when articulated by the latter. They lament that this Passion will 'desensitize' the young, will make them into violence addicts incapable of appreciating the true refinements of our culture. Mel Gibson is treated as a 'pornographer' of violence, when in reality he is one of the rare filmmakers not to (at least in this film) systematically mix eroticism with violence.

Certain critics push the imitation of their adversaries to the point of mixing religion with their diatribes. They accuse this film of 'impiety'; they go so far as to accuse it – brace yourselves – of being 'blasphemous.'

This Passion has, in short, provoked a surprising reversal of position between adversaries who have for so long used the same arguments against one another. This double abjuration plays itself out with such perfect naturalness that it looks like a classical ballet, all the more elegant because it is not in the least conscious of itself.

What is the invisible but supreme force that manipulates all of these critics without their realizing it? I believe that it is the Passion itself. If one objects that the Passion has been filmed numerous times before without ever provoking either great indignation or great admiration (though today the admiration is more secretive than the criticism), I would reply that never before has the Passion been filmed with Mel Gibson's implacable realism.

It is Hollywood saccharinity that first dominated religious cinema, featuring Jesuses with hair so blond and eyes so blue that they could never be subjected to the abuses of Roman soldiers. In the last few years, there have been Passions more realistic yet even less effective, because they are embellished with phony postmodern audacity, preferably of a sexual nature, that the directors counted on to spice up the Gospels, deemed by them to be insufficiently scandalous. They did not see that in sacrificing to the stereotype of 'revolt' they rendered the Passion insipid and banal.

2

To restore to the Crucifixion its scandalous force, it is enough to film it as is, without adding or subtracting anything. Did Mel Gibson succeed completely in this endeavor? Not entirely, but he got close enough to strike fear into all the conformists.

The principal argument against what I have just said consists in accusing the film of being unfaithful to the spirit of the Gospels. It is true that the Gospels merely enumerate all of the cruelties suffered by Christ without ever describing them in detail, without ever making us see the Passion 'as if we were there.'

This is perfectly true, but to take the sparseness and concision of the Gospel text as an argument against Mel Gibson's realism is an evasion of history. It means not seeing that in the first century A.D.

realistic description in the modern sense could not be employed, for it had not yet been invented. Most probably, the first impulse in the development of Western realism came from the Passion. The writers of the Gospels did not deliberately reject a possibility that did not exist during their era. It is clear that far from fleeing realism, they seek to create it, but the means are lacking. The narratives of the Passion contain more concrete details than all of the learned works of the time. They represent a first step in the direction of the ever-increasing realism that defines the essential dynamism of our culture in its periods of great vitality. The first impulse of realism is the desire to strengthen religious meditation, which is essentially a meditation on the Passion of Christ.

In professing its disdain for realism and for the real itself, modern esthetics has completely distorted the interpretation of Western art. It has invented a separation between esthetics on one side and technology and science on the other, a separation that has only come into being with the advent of modernism (modernism is perhaps only a flattering term for our decadence). The will to be true to reality, to paint things as if one were there, has always triumphed in the past, and it has over the centuries produced the masterpieces that Gibson says have inspired him. I have heard that he himself mentions Caravaggio. In the same vein one could think of certain Romanesque Christs, of the Spanish Crucifixions, of a Jerome Bosch, of all the suffering Christs . . .

Far from disdaining science and technology, the great art of the Renaissance and modernity used all the new inventions in the service of its will to realism. Far from rejecting perspective and *trompe l'oeil*, they welcome these things with passion. We need only think of the dead Christ of Mantegna . . .

To understand what Mel Gibson has tried to do, we must, it seems to me, free ourselves from all of the modernist and 'postmodernist' snobbisms and think of cinema as extending and surpassing the techniques of great literary and pictorial realism. If contemporary techniques reveal themselves as incapable of communicating religious emotion, it is because great artists have yet to transfigure them. The invention of these techniques coincided with the first breakdown of Christian spirituality since the beginning of Christianity.

If the artists of the Renaissance had had cinema, do we really believe that they would have turned up their noses? It is this realist tradition that Mel Gibson is attempting to revive. The venture he has undertaken consists in utilizing to the hilt the incomparable resources of the most realistic technique that has ever existed: the cinema. The risks are proportional to the ambition that characterizes this enterprise, unusual today but frequent in the past.

If one truly wants to film the Passion and the Crucifixion, it is obvious enough that one cannot be satisfied with mentioning Christ's agonies in a few sentences. These sufferings must be represented. In Greek tragedy, direct representation of the hero's death was prohibited; a messenger told the audience what had just transpired. In the cinema it is no longer possible to avoid the essential. To cut short the flagellation or the nailing to the cross, for example, would be to shrink back from the decisive moment. These horrific things must be represented 'as if we were there.' Must we be indignant if the result does not resemble a pre-Raphaelite painting?

Beyond a certain number of lashings, Roman flagellation meant certain death; it was a mode of execution like any other, as lethal as crucifixion. Mel Gibson recalls this in his film. The violence of Christ's flagellation is all the more unbearable in that it is admirably filmed, as indeed is the rest of the work.

Mel Gibson is situated in a certain mystical tradition of the Passion: 'what drop of blood have you shed for me?' etc. These mystics see it as their duty to imagine the sufferings of Christ as accurately as possible, not at all to cultivate a spirit of vengeance against the Jews or the Romans but to meditate on our own guilt.

This is not the only possible attitude concerning the Passion, of course. And there would certainly be a bad as well as a good use of his film, but one cannot condemn the enterprise a priori; one cannot with eyes closed accuse Gibson of making the Passion into something that it is not. In the entire history of Christianity, no one had ever before attempted to represent the Passion as it must have truly happened.

In the theater where I saw the film, the projection was preceded by three or four 'coming attractions' filled with a violence that was plainly inane, sardonic, permeated with sado-masochistic insinuations, bereft of any religious or even any narrative, esthetic, or simply human interest. How can those who daily consume such abominations, who comment upon them, who speak to their friends about them, how can they be shocked by Mel Gibson's film? This is beyond me.

3

We must start by absolving the film of the absurd reproach of 'going too far,' 'of gratuitously exaggerating Christ's sufferings.' How can one exaggerate the sufferings of a man who must suffer, one after the other, the two most excruciating tortures devised by Roman cruelty?

Once the overall legitimacy of the enterprise is recognized, one can regret that Mel Gibson went farther in his violence than the Gospel texts require. He makes the brutalization of Jesus start right after his arrest, which is not in the Gospels. If only to deprive his critics of a specious argument, the director might have been better served, I think, to stick with the essential. The overall effect would be just as powerful, and the film would not leave itself open to the hypocritical reproach of flattering the contemporary taste for violence.

What is the source of this great evocative power that all faithful representations of the Passion produce on most people? I think that there is an anthropological level to the descriptions in the Gospels which is not specifically Jewish, Roman, nor even Christian. It is the collective dimension of the event that makes it into what is essentially a crowd phenomenon.

One of the things that Mel Gibson's Pilate says to the crowd is not contained in the Gospels, but it seems to me to be faithful to its spirit: 'Five days ago you wanted to make this man your king and now you want to kill him.' This is an allusion to the triumphal welcome Jesus received the preceding Sunday, known as Palm Sunday in the liturgical calendar. The crowd that receives Jesus triumphantly is the same crowd that shouts for his death five days later. Mel Gibson is right, I think, to emphasize the crowd's sudden about-face, its cruel inconsistency and surprising volatility. All crowds in the world shift easily from one extreme to the other, from passionate adulation to hatred and the frenetic destruction of the same, single individual. Moreover, there is a great biblical text that resembles the Passion in more ways than is generally thought: the book of Job. After having been the leader of his people for many years, Job is brutally rejected by this same people, who threaten him with death through the intermediary of three representatives, always called (rather grotesquely) 'friends of Job.'

The essence of an excited, terrified crowd is not to calm itself before satisfying its appetite for violence on a victim whose identity most often scarcely matters to it. Pilate is well aware of this, for as an administrator he has experience in crowd control. At first, he proposes to the crowd the crucifixion of Barabbas in place of Jesus. After the failure of this first, well-tried method, to which he obviously resorts too late, Pilate has Jesus whipped in the hope that this will satisfy at a lesser cost, if you will, the appetite for violence that is the essential characteristic of this type of crowd.

If Pilate proceeds in this way, it is not because he is more humane than the Jews, nor is it necessarily on account of his wife. The most likely explanation is that in order to be well considered in Rome, which took pride in bringing the *pax romana* to every region, a Roman civil servant would always prefer a trouble-free, legal execution to an execution imposed by the multitude.

From an anthropological point of view, the Passion has nothing specifically Jewish about it. It is a crowd phenomenon that obeys the same laws as all crowd phenomena. Careful observation will detect equivalent phenomena in the numerous foundational myths that recount the birth of archaic and ancient religions.

Almost all religions are, I believe, rooted in collective violence analogous to that which is described or suggested not only in the Gospels and the book of Job, but also in the songs of the Suffering Servant in second Isaiah, as well as in many Psalms. Pious Christians and Jews have wrongly refused to reflect on these resemblances between their sacred books and myths. An attentive comparison reveals that beyond these resemblances, but also because of them, we can observe a difference, at once subtle and gigantic, between the mythical on one side, and the Judaic and the Christian on the other, which makes the Judeo-Christian incomparable with respect to the most objective truth. Unlike the myths that systematically adopt the point of view of the crowd against the victim, because they are conceived and told by the lynchers, and thus always see the victim as guilty (as in the incredible combination of parricide and incest that Oedipus is accused of, for example), our Scriptures, the great biblical and Christian texts, acquit the victims of the crowd, and this is exactly what the Gospels do in the case of Jesus. This is what Mel Gibson shows.

Whereas myths incessantly repeat the murderous delusions of crowds of persecution (which are always analogous to those of the Passion), because this illusion satisfies the community and furnishes an idol around which it can come together, the greatest biblical texts, culminating in the Gospels, reveal the essentially deceptive and criminal character of crowd phenomena, on which the mythologies of the world are based.

In my view, there are two principal attitudes in human history: there is the mythological, which tries to dissimulate violence, because in the final analysis, it is on unjust violence that human communities are founded. This is what we all do when we give in to our instincts. We try to cover the nudity of human violence with Noah's cloak. And we turn away if necessary, in order not to expose ourselves to the contagious force of violence by looking at it too closely.

This attitude is too universal to be condemned. This is in fact the attitude of the greatest Greek philosophers, in particular Plato, who condemns Homer and all the poets because they take the liberty of describing in their works the violence that the myths attribute to the gods of the city. The great philosopher sees in this brazen revelation a source of disorder, a great danger for the entire society.

4

This is certainly the religious attitude that is the most widely shared, the most normal, the most natural to man. And today it is more universal than ever, for modernized believers, Christians as well as Jews, have at least partially adopted it.

The other attitude is much rarer; it is even unique. It is found only in the great moments of biblical and Christian inspiration. It consists not in chaste dissimulation but, on the contrary, in the revelation of violence in all its injustice and all its delusion, everywhere that it is possible to observe it. This is the attitude of the book of Job, and it is the attitude of the Gospels. It is the bolder of the two attitudes, and in my view, the greater. It is the attitude that has allowed us to discover the innocence of most of the victims that even the most religious people over the course of history have never ceased to persecute and kill. This is the common inspiration of Judaism and Christianity, and it is the key, one must hope, to their future reconciliation. It is about the heroic inclination to put the truth above even the social order. It is to this enterprise, it seems to me, that Mel Gibson's film makes every effort to be faithful.

Translated by Robert Doran

The Mystic of Neuilly

René Girard was elected to the French Academy on 17 March 2005 following the death of Father Ambroise-Marie Carré (1908–2004). At the Academy's Thursday, 15 December 2005, session, Girard delivered the following address beneath 'La Coupole' (dome) of the Institut de France:

For any new academician, speaking beneath *La Coupole* for the first time creates a forbidding dilemma. The feelings he experiences are intense but they are also so banal that he wonders if he would do better to keep them to himself rather than express them. In my case, however, silence would be unjust to the Academy. My debt with respect to it is exceptional. The first of my books that it crowned was the second that I published.*

This initial favor was followed by several others over the course of my career and finally by a magnificent prize from the Gal Foundation.† And the most magnificent prize of all is obviously my election to the Academy.

I can say without exaggeration that for half a century the only French institution that persuaded me that I was not forgotten in France, in my own country, as a researcher and as a thinker, was the French Academy.

Like the career of every academician, mine begins on this very day, with an address whose subject, and to some extent even the

---

* *Violence and the Sacred* (1972) was awarded the Prix Broquette-Gonin in 1973.
† In 2004, Girard received the Grand Prix de Littérature Henri Gal, a €40,000 prize awarded to 'a literary oeuvre of high quality.' In 1996 the Academy had awarded him its Grand Prix de Philosophie.

manner of treating that subject, are dictated to me by a tradition as wise as it is venerable. I will speak in praise of my immediate predecessor, the most recent occupant of the seat to which I have had the honor of being elected by the members of the Academy.

The seat in question is the thirty-seventh, whose second occupant was Bossuet and whose most recent was Reverend Father Ambroise-Marie Carré, one of only two members of the regular clergy ever to have been elected to the Academy. Both were famous orators who preached Lenten sermons at Notre-Dame with immense success. Both were Dominicans. The first, the famous Lacordaire, restored his order in France after the Revolution.

The second was Father Ambroise-Marie Carré. He was such a zealous preacher that he practiced this art even in the theaters, music halls, and cinemas where his friendship with numerous artists gave him easy access. He is also the author of a written oeuvre that took on an increasingly important role in his life as his preaching activities subsided with the passing years.

Father Carré published many edifying works, a good deal of occasional prose, many funeral elegies, and many prefaces, among which an introduction to the *Spiritual Writings* of Cardinal Richelieu deserves special mention.

Even in the most worldly of his works, the four volumes of his diary, Father Carré almost never speaks of the political affairs of his century. From 1940 on he played a glorious role in the resistance to the Nazi occupiers. Several times he was almost arrested. For him, this involvement went without saying and he spoke more readily of the feats of others than of his own.

In the religious field he was almost just as discreet. Well before Vatican II, it is true, he spoke in favor of certain reforms that were later adopted by the Council. Unlike many churchmen, he did not wait for the Church to be weakened to criticize its conservatism and its bureaucracy. As soon as the ecclesiastical institution appeared to him to be threatened, on the other hand, he ceased to make these demands. There was no opportunism in him. He abstained from acting like the ass who kicks the aging lion in Aesop's fable.

During the turbulent years that followed, Father Carré let his sermons and his intense pastoral activity speak for themselves. Such discretion was so rare at the time that it attracted the attention of lucid Catholics who were anxious about the future of their Church.

With time, the whiteness of his robe became emblematic of everything that was squandered amidst the post-conciliar chaos – the sense of sin, irrevocable commitments, the love of Catholic dogma, contempt for vain polemics. To assure themselves that these virtues were not dead, the faithful turned readily to this immaculate block of white marble, like the ancient Hebrews to the bronze serpent.

During the years of upheaval, Father Carré displayed an exemplary dignity. What caused him to turn his back on the post-conciliar unrest was above all, I think, his sense of fidelity. It was also the intensity of his pastoral activities. Throughout his life he devoted a considerable amount of time to the sick and the dying, especially in the community of actors and artists for which he was the first official chaplain. His innumerable friends never stopped asking his advice, and the same was true of many others who scarcely knew him but who instinctively trusted him.

The first cause of his discretion was, I think, a vast quantity of indifference. Not for the individuals concerned but for the hodge-podge of activities in which a whole segment of the clergy became involved during the second half of the twentieth century, with a passion that the passage of time has rendered mysterious. At a time when ambitious souls were spelling the word 'Contestation' with a capital 'C,' the futility of what was meant by this term was always obvious to him.

Yet his discretion did not always prevent Father Carré from drawing his readers' attention to the characteristic expressions of the muddle in the Church, something he did with more humor than bitterness. Several times, for example, he inquired into the expression 'en recherche' ('discerning, seeking') which was often used by priests who were hesitating indefinitely between the Church and the world.

It happened that he alerted his readers to the lapses of taste and even of language that the Church committed in abundance in the wake of the Council. Here, for example, is the entry in his Diary dated 25 May 1996:

'John Paul II says the Rosary in French – this is the title of a cassette recording in which the pope recites the Our Father and the Hail Mary in a clear, strong voice. [. . .] "Forgive us our trespasses as we forgive those who trespass against us." The pope does not retain the current formula: ". . . as we *also* forgive those who trespass against us." That "also" is grating. With joy I am going to omit it in my private prayer from now on.'

In the rage for disruption triggered by the Council, the Church had added the 'also' to a formerly magnificent phrase from the Our Father. A strong odor of 'religious correctness' emanates from the new translation. Its ponderous redundancy weakens what it purports to underline, the reciprocity of forgiveness, which is perfectly expressed in the former translation. To destroy the harmony of a sentence is not a good means of reinforcing its meaning. Father Carré is right: 'That "also" is grating.'

Father Carré was too disciplined to disobey his hierarchical superiors. Since the reform of the Our Father, even in his private prayers, he courageously masticated the required adverb until the blessed day when he heard the pope himself reel off a whole series of Our Fathers unburdened of their 'also.' Is not the pope the supreme authority in matters of liturgy? Is it not his model that a humble priest should follow, at least in his private prayers?

As we already know, the French Church sometimes needs the pope to correct errors of doctrine. What we didn't know and what Father Carré teaches us is that the French Church also needs the pope – a Polish pope though he may be – to correct its errors of language.

Father Carré never pushed this sort of satire too far. He had other concerns. And in his eyes the most important of these was the spiritual drama that accompanied him throughout his whole life.

His confidences on this subject are rare, fragmentary, and not always easy to interpret. Father Carré never put together a complete account of his itinerary. That is what I am going to try to do now.

With regard to the questions that interest us, the most important text is only about twenty pages long. It is found at the beginning of a work entitled *Each Day I Begin*,* published in 1975. It describes a very remarkable experience that goes back, the author thinks, to his fourteenth year, more than half a century before the account that I am now going to read to you.

After some affectionate but brief words about his family, Father Carré announces that childhood memories do not interest him. Therefore he does not intend to speak about his own memories, with the exception of one – a memory so important that he describes it in great detail. Here is that description:

'. . . [This memory] accompanies me as a presence at once sweet and thrilling. It will accompany me to my dying hour. A mere glance is enough to bring it back to life, a glance toward the window of the apartment building in Neuilly where my family lived. How old was I? Fourteen, I believe. One evening, in my little bedroom, I felt with an incredible force, leaving no room for any hesitation, that I was loved by God and that life, [. . .] there before me, was a marvelous gift. Suffocated by happiness, I fell to my knees.'

Even at a half-century's distance, Father Carré cannot evoke that evening without awakening within himself the emotion of the original experience. As a general rule, in what we call 'memory,' the traces of the remembered event are just barely sufficient to prevent forgetting. Here, on the other hand, they are so profound that the word memory seems upon reflection to be inadequate. Immediately after the passage I have just read, Father Carré returns to the Neuilly experience and, without noting his own about-face, defines it as *the opposite of a memory*:

An absolute beginning (or that which is closest to being one): that is how, more than fifty years after the fact, I would characterize the only event that ever gave me certainty about my faith, the event, too, that brought me a joy that no other joy was subsequently able to surpass.

In the following pages, Father Carré evokes his education, his studies as a future priest, but without ever losing sight of the Neuilly

* *Chaque jour je commence* (Paris: Éditions du Cerf, 1975).

experience. He holds it responsible for everything good that happened in his youth. It is that experience, he writes, that enabled him to appreciate the teaching of those illustrious Dominicans, Fathers Chenu and Sertillanges. The positive side of his existence is the luminous tail of the comet that lit up the sky of his childhood one evening:

'I have often evoked [. . .] the miraculous instant in which a life becomes conscious of the reality of God and of its bond with Him, when, under the later mentorship of Father Chenu, I studied the theology of the Greek fathers with great wonder and delight. The incarnation of Christ is for them like a recreation of humanity. Yes, that evening I had been recreated . . .'

Father Carré connects that same experience of 'recreation' with the interest inspired in him forty years later by Father Teilhard de Chardin. The brouhaha surrounding Teilhard's work was often motivated by the desire to use it as a weapon against orthodoxy. Without paying attention to these maneuvers, Father Carré goes straight to what in Teilhard's oeuvre recalls his experience at Neuilly: 'Each individual is created throughout his life – I happened upon this sentence three or four years ago in Washington. The letters of Father Teilhard, which I read eagerly in between giving two Holy Week sermons for the French expatriate community, had a revelatory effect on me. The sense of being far from home and the morning silence offered favorable conditions for interior refreshment, as did that strange state that I have always experienced before preaching, combining anxiety, an almost visceral need to arrive as soon as possible at the place where I will be speaking, and at the same time [. . .] an undeniable febrility . . .'

Father Carré ends up connecting to the Neuilly event everything in his life that he was most passionate about at one time or another, including religious eloquence. For him, he tells us, the art of oratory was a major cause of 'febrility.' The latter term denotes a mental state very far from the 'presence at once sweet and thrilling' that emanates from Neuilly, and yet one that is inseparable from that great experience, rooted in an awkward attempt to capitalize on it, to give it a sequel.

How can what happened in the little room in Neuilly be defined? There is an obvious answer, and some of you have certainly already thought of it: it is a *mystical experience*. Many people are wary of this expression which, according to them, has no precise meaning. And yet the broad outlines of the enigma are fairly clearly drawn, notably in the description given by Father Carré, the very one I have just read to you . . .

The first feature is the passive, involuntary character of the mystical experience. No warning precedes it and it requires no effort. A second aspect is joy, 'that no other joy was subsequently able to surpass.' A third is the impression of eternity that it gives, which is inseparable from its infinite power of renewal, its extraordinary fecundity. The last feature sums up all the others and it is the intuition of a divine presence.

For those who turn away from mystical experience, its 'imprecision' is, I think, only a pretext for avoiding the controversies that the notion inevitably arouses. For staunch nonbelievers, it is necessarily an illusion or a sham. Without excluding these possibilities, believers add another: real, authentic mystical experience. It is then the pearl of great price spoken of in the Gospel, so precious that everything must be sacrificed to its acquisition.

At fourteen years of age, the future Father Carré did not hesitate. He decided to become a missionary in pagan territory, with the martyr's palm branch as his sole aim. The priests at his school, Sainte-Croix de Neuilly, did their best to curb his elation. It was then that the adolescent set his sights on the Dominican order.

If mystical experience is a source of happiness that never subsides, if it transcends time, Father Carré should have enjoyed throughout his life the radiant faith that public opinion attributes to him. An attentive look at his writings does not confirm this assumption. On a fairly frequent basis, Father Carré complains of God's silence, of the despair that this causes him. After Neuilly, 'mystical consolations' – as they are often called – were almost always refused him.

Must we conclude that, in *Each Day I Begin*, Father Carré embellished his memories? I don't think so. He seems to me incapable of a lie or even of exaggeration.

To understand the intense and lasting crisis that followed the fervor of the first years after Neuilly, we should first reflect, I think, on how extraordinarily young Father Carré was when that experience occurred.

All the evidence points to the fact that Father Carré first saw the Neuilly experience as the greatest of his life, an unsurpassable summit. As time passed, however, he became used to his happiness. And little by little he reduced it to a mere point of departure in a dynamic conception of his religious future.

To define the ambition that pulled him beyond Neuilly, Father Carré often speaks of his *vocation to holiness*. For him, as for many aspirants to the mystical life, the word 'holiness' implies not just a single encounter with God but a whole series of encounters, each more intense and more prolonged than the one before. All of these mystical experiences would crown the various stages of life, giving way finally to eternity, the ultimate goal of the process of sanctification. This project, noble as it may be, reduced the experience of Neuilly to the role of a first step – the lowest – on a staircase pointed to the sky . . .

This project reflects a typically Western and modern mystical ambition. It is not exempt from 'febrility' in the sense that Father Carré gives to that term. We Westerners are never content with what Heaven sends us, we all dream of unprecedented conquests and matchless exploits . . .

What young man or young woman in our world, put in a situation analogous to Father Carré's, believing what he believed, would not have reacted in the same way? Like so many other modern aspirants to holiness, Father Carré took for his models those our society admires, men of action, 'doers,' 'entrepreneurs' in the almost American sense of free enterprise.

The very thing that gives the modern world an immense advantage in the practical domain – its activism, its voluntarism, its rivalrous passion – constitutes a disadvantage in the mystical life. We Westerners hardly hesitate to take the initiative in domains that, in principle, are God's alone. We should not be surprised if the results do not always meet our expectations.

As the years went by, Father Carré waited with ever greater impatience for new mystical experiences that never came. In *Each Day I Begin*, a sentence that I have already cited clearly suggests the bitterness of his disappointment. In 1975, Father Carré defined Neuilly as *the only event that ever gave me certainty about my faith*. Which is to say that nothing comparable to Neuilly had come to quench a thirst for the divine made inextinguishable by the very power of the experience that aroused it. Father Carré lived out this situation sometimes as a personal failure, sometimes as a deficiency in God himself.

The effects of this spiritual dryness, which became more aggravated over time, on top of the disasters in the world and the unrest in the Church, undermined Father Carré's confidence in the goodness and sometimes even in the existence of God: 'I cannot speak openly,' he writes, 'because my faith appears so certain, so contagious – so it is said – that I would scandalize my neighbor.' It is not hard to find texts where the doubts of Father Carré are expressed without the slightest equivocation: 'Lord [. . .] if you exist, give me back my certainty. And if you nevertheless leave me in the shadows, grant me the intimate conviction that this time of distress has its usefulness.'

As surprising as they seem in the context of Neuilly, these lamentations are easy to connect, indirectly, to that experience. Among mystics there is nothing more common than crises of so-called dryness or aridity.

The more familiar one becomes with Father Carré, the more one realizes that any sort of philosophical or even theological reflection is for him secondary to the desire for personal contact with God. This desire, which for a long time remained unsatisfied, sometimes transforms itself into a kind of revolt which, however, never tips into the anti-Christian nihilism now common in our era.

Father Carré, it seems to me, must be seen not as just another religious writer nor even as a mystic *thinker* but, more radically, as a mystic in the most concrete sense. The fact of having benefited at the outset from an exceptional experience later made him a mystic who was often frustrated and discouraged.

From the point of view I am adopting here, the value of this hypothesis – because that is what it is – is in the light it sheds on Father Carré's oeuvre. It very directly explains his predilection for the saints who suffered from crises similar to his. Saint Thérèse of Lisieux is the example most frequently invoked: 'It amazes me that so many Christians still do not realize that Thérèse's faith was laborious, shaken by storms. She remained faithful only through heroism. She was afraid of blaspheming in her account of her ordeal, afraid of echoing the voice of shadows that raged for months in her heart. [. . .] But she held firm, out of love for Christ and love for sinners.'

Father Carré was also interested in those in Jesus's inner circle. He ascribes to them a 'difficult' or 'laborious' faith. He often uses these two adjectives to qualify his own faith.

In this context, the Apostle Thomas is of course a classic choice. That of the Virgin Mary, on the other hand, is stunningly audacious. Here is a characteristic text:

[The Virgin Mary] has been my chief support in times of doubt. For faith has always been difficult for me.
We underestimate the shock that Mary received on the day of the Annunciation. [. . .] with those final words, Mary finds herself before the unknown. The time of difficult faith now begins for her.

The extremely early arrival of the Neuilly experience inspired ambiguous reactions in Father Carré, as I have already suggested. The pride of the child prodigy who encountered God at the age of fourteen coexists in him with the humiliation of the idea that nothing as remarkable would ever again interrupt the routine of his religious observances.

For a long time, I think, Father Carré feared coming over as puerile, *immature*, to use the ugly term preferred by contemporary psychologists. He forgot that, in our world, the last remaining mystics are children. He forgot the divine words about childhood in general: 'I give praise to you, Father, Lord of heaven and earth, for although you have hidden these things from the wise and the learned you have revealed them to the childlike' (Matthew 11:25).

To understand this kind of forgetting in a Christian as well-formed as Father Carré, we must take into account the pressure that weighed on him in a world ever more empty of God, a world from which fewer and fewer children manage to escape.

Here is the account of a conversation between Father Carré and some adolescents involved in that modern remake of the war between Lilliput and Blefuscu, a war that never took place. We dissimulate the non-being behind a stereotypical formulation: 'the May '68 riots':

[. . .] I had agreed to be questioned by 70 or 80 law students. Without the slightest ceremony, and with an indiscretion that was par for the course, they subjected me to a merciless grilling. The crucial point was the justification of my faithfulness. To what degree is it programmed by my past? Am I not the prisoner of old habits? Does that first calling (whether it came from the Lord or from my imagination) still have a daily impact on my life or is it simply its feeble, sometimes imperceptible, and in any event quite ludicrous, echo that I hear, even if I don't want to admit it?

Father Carré had obviously committed the imprudence of confiding the great secret of his fourteenth year to these young people who were even more conformist than they were ferocious, in the style dictated by their era. In their eyes there was nothing more scandalous than an old man clinging to an old dream of holiness. This was the era when nothing was as contemptible as constancy and continuity. Only 'epistemological ruptures' were seen as having any value. Father Carré perfectly embodied what those young people thought of as *backward*.

The frail old man pretends to be crushed, annihilated by the spiritual lynching to which he was crazy enough to expose himself. But there is humor, I think, in the panicked fear he claims to have felt.

The *soixante-huitards* thought they could 'deconstruct' their victim from a Maoist point of view. In reality, they silently deconstructed themselves. Father Carré saw very clearly that his persecutors were no more Chinese than he was. Often they came from the wealthy suburb of Neuilly just like him, or from the similarly wealthy 16th arrondissement.

These adolescents unthinkingly ascribed Father Carré's ideas to his religious – which is to say 'bourgeois' – education, forgetting that they themselves were from the same milieu and had received just about the same education at the swankiest schools in Paris and its environs. Their Maoism was simply the temporary and banal byproduct of a cultural decadence both further advanced and less interesting than Father Carré's thirst for mysticism. Far from bestriding the social comedy of their day, the *soixante-huitards* were its most benighted protagonists.

Father Carré intuited without difficulty that after treating themselves to a little cultural revolution, at zero risk to their own precious persons, these papier-mâché revolutionaries would be launched on the brilliant career paths predestined by their bourgeois condition, once the childish games were over and done with. Today a good many of them still sit on the boards of our biggest capitalist and state-run companies. They are preparing to enjoy a comfortable retirement.

Father Carré sees further than those who are grilling him. He owes his lucidity not to his own strength but to the experience that his interlocutors take for the darkest obscurantism. Fundamentally that experience is what always protected him not only from fatuous revolts but also from all the intellectual phantasms that gripped so many of the privileged young and less young people around him – Nietzscheanism, Althusserism, etc.

In the final autobiographical pages of *Each Day I Begin*, Father Carré undertakes a severe but in no way despairing self-critique. He likens himself to the great symbol of religious lukewarmness in John's *Apocalypse*, the Church of Laodicea:

'I know your works,' says the narrator, 'I know that you are neither cold nor hot. I wish you were either cold or hot. So, because you are lukewarm, neither hot nor cold, I will spit you out of my mouth. [. . .] Those whom I love, I reprove and chastise. Be earnest, therefore, and repent!'

Father Carré accuses himself of having lost the fervor of his youth but, just like Laodicea, he never completely lost his faith and he is invited to recover it. His is not truly a lost cause; the conclusion confirms this: 'It's sad, even if it's also admirable, to know only how to hold on!'

What did Father Carré cling to all his life, 'sadly,' no doubt, but 'admirably'? What did he call 'the only event that ever gave me certainty about my faith,' the experience at Neuilly? Instead of behaving like a spoiled child and demanding more and more, as a member of the *soixante-huitard* generation would be apt to do, Father Carré understood that he should have modestly and piously cultivated the grace of his youth. It was not God who plunged him into uncertainty, it was his excessive ambition.

After a half-century of fruitless waiting, Father Carré finally decided to look things in the face: ever since his fourteenth year, the summit of his religious life had always been situated not in the future, in front of him, but behind him, in the Neuilly experience. For the first time, he truly sought to reconnect with the extraordinary event that, sometimes in a negative way, but above all in a positive one, had towered over his whole existence.

Initially without much hope, I think, Father Carré started to stir the embers of a fire that he believed had been extinguished for a half century. And suddenly the miracle of the old days was rekindled. Beneath his eyes the experience of Neuilly was transformed into a sleeping beauty emerging radiantly from a long, dark night. Far from having disappeared forever, the former presence was resuscitated, sweeter and more thrilling than ever.

To conduct this positive re-evaluation of the past, Father Carré looks for and finds witnesses close to him, the novelist Julien Green, for example, whom he cites in *Each Day I Begin* and who provides a sentence of remarkable relevance: 'The memory of a past grace can be a new grace.'

For Julien Green as for Father Carré the word 'grace' denotes a spiritual favor, an assurance that God gives of his love. In short this word is a more discreet synonym for mystical experience.

To understand what motivates the appeal to Julien Green, we must return to the two definitions of Neuilly that we already found in *Each Day I Begin*: the first described this experience as a privileged memory, the second as an absolute beginning.

In light of Julien Green, these two definitions are but one. To recall intensely a mystical experience, even a distant one, is to resuscitate it. It hardly matters how the result is defined . . . The line between a very intense memory and an entirely new experience tends to blur . . .

By citing Julien Green, Father Carré gives thanks for his foundational experience, which he had neglected for too long. He recognizes its fecundity, which for a long time was sterilized by his own 'febrility.' He holds himself responsible for his long stretches of spiritual dryness.

Why demand new graces when memory makes it possible to reanimate the old ones? To better convince himself of this truth, Father Carré wants to hear it proclaimed by someone other than himself. The words of others are more prestigious than our own: they seem closer to the divine. To keep himself on the right path, Father Carré calls upon not only Julien Green but other kindred spirits, including Gabriel Marcel.

It is a return to childhood experience that takes place in the late writings. The most revealing text is also, it seems, the latest of all. It is a new conclusion for the reissue of a book on holiness.* It would appear in January 2004, the month of Father Carré's death. It is an admirable summing up of its author's whole religious life:

'I am beginning my ninety-sixth year. The Lord has showered me in graces. [. . .]: if [. . .] he has kept me for so long in the sweet kingdom of the earth, it's doubtless so that I can carry out [. . .] the ministry of old age, which consists in prayer and intercession.'

Far from defining existence in this lowly world as a valley of tears, Father Carré celebrates 'the sweet kingdom of the earth.' In his periods of 'febrility,' he reproached himself greatly, I think, for his excessive love for the things of this world. Now he forgives himself.

His old age was, I think, the happiest period of his life, along with his childhood. His colleagues at the Academy greatly contributed to

* *Croire avec Vingt Personnages de l'Évangile* (Paris: Éditions du Cerf, 2004)

this late happiness. In his final years, he seized upon every pretext to thank them.

During the summer vacation, Father Carré bemoaned the closure of the Academy. When his assiduous academic work was remarked upon, he responded that it was not the work he missed, nor even the Academy itself – it was the academicians. If they loved him dearly, he felt the same about them. The academicians are such delicious people, he said, that having once frequented them one can no longer do without their friendship.

Only the reader who is ignorant of Father Carré's spiritual vocabulary can imagine that his great mystical experience is absent from the lines I read from his January 2004 text.

Look at the first sentence: 'The Lord has showered me in graces.' The plural should not fool us. This sentence is an allusion to the experience at Neuilly, which is unique as an event but infinite in its consequences and sequels. During the years of dryness, Father Carré thought that he was left all alone. In reality, it was he who turned away from God by trying in his modern voluntarism to come close to Him by his own efforts. He was the one who was truly responsible for the misfortune he thought had struck him. The affirmation that he is 'showered in graces' can only be interpreted as a reference to the old mystical experience infinitely multiplied and more fertile than ever after eighty years of good and loyal service.

It seems to me that the *ultima verba* of Father Carré perfectly sums up the spiritual history that I have myself tried to sketch out. To be convinced of this, let's read all the way to the end the text from which I only cited the first lines. Here is the rest:

Of late I have been rereading notes that I took during my ordination retreat. The necessity for me of holiness appears there with a vigor that strikes me in the literal sense of the word. So much light and such strong certainty made me write: 'If I don't become a saint, it will truly be a betrayal.' I do not repudiate those lines written at the age of twenty-four years . . . But I now have a long experience, the experience of a voyager who, on a tiring road, has less and less confidence in his own strength and knows that to get to the end he must rely on more than his own will. A certain febrility of desire gives way today to the sweetness of hope. Holiness or not? The question is no longer asked in this way. I think only of the tenderness of God.

Each sentence here and almost each word echoes the preceding observations. Father Carré expressly rejects what there was of unacknowledged pride in his project of holiness. When he said: 'If I don't become a saint, it will truly be a betrayal' he set a trap for himself, one that then closed around him. But his final humility liberated him.

The experience at Neuilly was, in short, the occasion not so much of a fall as of a long period of stagnation, not because of some intrinsic perversity but because of the naively egotistical use that Father Carré made of his experience. In the end he understood his error and the text that we have just read is the proof. The 'febrile' use of the mystical experience was almost inevitable given the extreme youth of its beneficiary . . .

Instead of making God into an Everest to scale, Father Carré in his late years sees in Him a refuge. It is not a skeptical humanism that is expressed in the 2004 text but abandonment to divine mercy. Without giving up on his mystical aspirations, Father Carré recognizes that he is unable to fulfill them on his own.

It is not I but Father Carré himself who formulates these critiques. I have adopted the perspective of his last text, which is the most profound, I think, and on which one could comment indefinitely.

Like the dog in the fable, Father Carré first dropped the prey to chase a shadow; fortunately for him, the sweet and thrilling presence was never discouraged. It was always there, silent, at his side. It remained through all the wear and tear, all the tiredness, all the desertions.

Although dissatisfaction and aridity played their role in Father Carré's religious life, we should refrain from seeing him as a failed mystic. He was at first a mystic too quickly blessed. For this very reason he remained for a long time a frustrated mystic, victim of what he called his 'febrility.'

His youthful avidity called for a lesson and it was administered to him. To judge from the remarks that we have just read, the lesson was understood and absorbed with great humility.

In spite of appearances, it would be impossible to imagine a destiny preferable to that one, and for those who are listening to me, myself included, I wish none better.

For someone who never knew Father Carré it is a veritable ordeal to speak of him to so many people here who knew him and who will never stop loving him. I hope that I have not overly disappointed them and my hopes will be fulfilled if I have inspired at least a few of you with the desire to go in exploring the mystical works of Reverend Father Ambroise-Marie Carré.

Translated by Trevor Cribben Merrill

Victims, Violence and Christianity

We imagine that everybody has always been talking about violence, since violence has always been with us, but that is not true. Violence is a new subject. In the past, people complained about insecurity, disorder, disorderly societies, and so forth, but there was no theme of violence as such. One can even question whether ancient languages had a word that really means violence in our sense. To ask 'why is there so much violence around us?' may feel like an eternal question, but in fact it is really a very modern one.

What is Violence?

As a Frenchman, I feel that the question really goes back to Voltaire. In *Candide*, the question is 'why is there so much violence in our world?' and the question has been with us ever since. Voltaire's pessimistic cynicism in *Candide* makes him seem more like a twentieth-century man than an eighteenth-century *philosophe*.

Because nowadays we really believe only in science, we try to study violence scientifically. So, we have countless symposia on violence, mostly on what people call the act of violence. People talk about violence in order neatly to circumscribe the subject and this makes it amenable to scientific investigation. They want to isolate the smallest knowable particle of violence.

By the act of violence they mean mugging in big cities. Of course violence in big cities, anonymous violence that strikes like lightning, more or less at random, is a real problem today. It is a very big problem which I do not want to minimize. But all criminologists will tell you that most violence occurs between people who have been acquainted with each other, often for a very long time.

Violence is a relationship, but in order to study it scientifically most people try to forget this fact. Relationships are messy; they are not clear-cut, you don't know where they begin, where they end, where they might lead you. Then they have a strange way of changing without you being aware of it; a good one turns into a bad one without you even noticing it. This is the difference between human relations and relations between animals. Relations between animals usually begin badly, with some fighting, but then they stabilize, usually once and for all and in an uneven way. There is a dominant partner, and a dominated one, and once established, this pattern will go on forever.

Reciprocity

Human relations are not like that at all, especially in a democratic world. Even when we had hierarchies, we nevertheless had a tremendous amount of reciprocity in human relationships. Reciprocity is one of the fundamental anthropological questions. The maturity of a science can be measured, I feel, by its ability to ask elementary questions. 'What is reciprocity?' is a question too elementary and fundamental for the current state of anthropology.

Reciprocity is always present in human relations, whether they are good or bad. If I hold out my hand to you, you will hold out yours to me and we will shake hands. In other words, you will imitate me. If you hold out your hand and I keep mine behind my back, you will be offended, and you will put yours behind your back as well. In other words, you will still imitate me. Even though the relationship is changing drastically, it remains reciprocal, which means imitative, mimetic. Relations of vengeance, revenge, retaliation are just as reciprocal as relations of perfect love.

But what is very interesting is that this reciprocity is absolutely fundamental. I think that in order to talk about violence rationally we must get away from the pure act of violence, which does not exist. Good criminologists will tell you that the man who mugs you in the street and doesn't know you is a product of human relationships which made him violent, which turned him into the violent individual which he probably was not at a certain time in his life.

There is an additional reason why we try to isolate a clear-cut act of violence, namely from the judicial viewpoint. The judicial viewpoint, of course, tries to establish responsibilities. Its function is to keep the peace and in order to do that it must have very clear-cut guidelines. And the shift from violent to non-violent behavior is absolutely essential. You cannot blame the judiciary for doing that, otherwise they could not keep the peace. In fact, if they try to refine their criteria too much, if they have the question of extenuating or aggravating circumstances becoming too complex, then you reach the mad world of the American judiciary today, where nothing can ever be settled and you have appeals that go on for twenty-five years. In order to function efficiently the judiciary must simplify the problem of violence.

How Relationships Change

If we reject all simplifications we have to take into account this strange fact that violent relations are just as reciprocal as non-violent relations. And we don't always realize how and when the one turns into the other precisely because the reciprocity is always there. You can describe very roughly what goes on when a relationship becomes bad. The first thing to observe is that, in most relationships, we all tend to feel that the initiative belongs to our partner, not to ourselves.

We receive a message and it provides us with a means to evaluate the temperature of the relationship – it may be hot, it may be cold, it may be lukewarm and so forth. Normally we are polite to each other but if we feel someone is not quite as polite as they should be, we will return the message with some added emphasis. We do not think we are changing the relationship. We only want to inform our partner that his or her message has been interpreted in the spirit it was sent. Our partner sees things very differently because he also sees himself as the one at the receiving end of the relationship and he will interpret what we regard as legitimate retaliation as a gesture of unprovoked hostility.

Accordingly he will interpret the small increment of sympathy or antipathy as more significant than we feel it is, and then he will return the message with an added emphasis of his own. It takes very few exchanges of this type for the relationship to escalate to open hostility. Neither partner understands why the relationship has gone sour.

All human relations tend to be very complex and delicate. Therefore, they may deteriorate very fast and no one ever feels responsible for the deterioration. You will never find anyone who will say, 'yes, I provoked that individual' or if it does happen, it will only be after a very difficult conversion. Someone may say 'yes I was a persecutor, yes I misbehaved'. It happened to St Peter after his denial, it happened to Paul on his way to Damascus, but it doesn't happen to most of us. Most of us feel completely innocent in our relations, or if we feel we haven't paid enough attention to people we try to correct the situation but usually too late. Therefore, we are all involved.

If we start looking at things in this manner we will realize that human relations have a history. All human relations are historical in the sense that they cannot stay the same. They evolve, and they always evolve in one way or another. And it is always easier to make them evolve in the wrong direction, because to make them evolve in the better direction requires us to swallow our pride rather than retaliating.

Relations of Desire and Shakespeare

The question is, why are human relations reciprocal in this way? In order to understand that, you must go to relations of desire. We never think of relations of desire as reciprocal but some great writers do, in particular Shakespeare. In Shakespeare I feel that relations of desire are reciprocal from the beginning and the earliest plays are the most enlightening about this. The reason for this, I believe, is that the author has just discovered the paradoxes of imitated and mimetic desire and he delights in exhibiting them.

Take *The Two Gentlemen of Verona*, for example. They have been raised together since infancy. They appreciate the same things, they like the same books, they like the same food, they like the same people and they are very conscious that imitation is the principle of their friendship. If they start liking different things, they feel that something is wrong with their friendship, so they do their best to move back on the same track. Then one fine day one of the two falls in love with a girl and of course the principle of imitation is obeyed and the other friend falls immediately in love with the same girl.

The principle of friendship has suddenly turned into a principle of enmity. Nothing has changed in their relationship. The only thing which has changed is the object which they feel they cannot share. The two friends become enemies when they fall in love with the same girl and each one is going to reproach the other for betraying the friendship. Most critics, seeing this situation, interpret it in terms of a broken friendship, of a great distance suddenly separating the two friends. In reality it is a lack of distance which is responsible for the problem.

The same principle can make the most intimate friendship and the most bitter hostility, and the change is extremely sudden. Shakespeare constantly draws our attention to the paradox of human relations, and suddenly we are confronted by something that is like devilish magic, something about a principle in human relations which is about a principle of hostility which is universally present in humankind.

Therefore, when we ask why there is so much violence in the world, we always ask the question as if we had nothing to do with the violence, because we do not go out and mug people in the streets. But if you start thinking about Valentine and Proteus, the two gentlemen of Verona, then you feel that Shakespeare, who never talks directly about violence, is posing the problem of violence at an infinitely deeper level than we ever do. That is why the problem of violence is always very easy for us, because there is always someone responsible for the violence. But in the case of Valentine and Proteus, who is responsible?

If there is such a thing as original sin, maybe we must look in that direction. It must be something that we do not see as sinful and something that belongs to all of us, because we must say that the two friends are equally innocent. But also we cannot deny that the two friends share some guilt, for otherwise who is guilty for the violence there? Can we blame it on the world?

We often try to blame it on the parents Shakespeare borrows from what is called Italian comedy. He pretends to make the parents responsible, but it is clear that he does not believe it. He is fully aware that the young people themselves are responsible for the problem. This makes the play very paradoxical. You go and watch the play after dinner, and you do not want to be worried, especially by comedy, which is supposed to end nicely, without blood. The happy ending is supplied by something like the magical trick that intervenes to stop the bloodletting, like Puck in *A Midsummer Night's Dream*.

Amity as the Author of our Variance

But the problem is still there in all Shakespeare. It is not just a question of love and erotic matters. Take, for example, *Antony and Cleopatra*. Shakespeare offers a definition through a secondary character. This is before Antony and Octavius become enemies, but that they are going to become enemies is prophesied by Enobarbus, who says: 'you shall find the band that seems to tie their friendship together will be the very strangler of their enmity'.

This sentence poses a problem that psychologists have not yet defined. It has nothing to do with Freud and nothing to do with Jung. It comes relatively late in Shakespeare's career and he is so happy to have discovered the real formula for defining the problem that he repeats it, two lines further on: 'that which is the strength of their amity shall prove the immediate author of their variance'.

If that which is the strength of our amity can prove the immediate author of our variance, what sort of creatures are we? We have to ask questions about ourselves because we are likely to be in such situations. We manage to put the whole blame on our partner and we usually talk of conflict in terms of differences. When people are in conflict, we say they have their differences. When people have their non-difference, it is even worse. They are caught in a vicious circle, imitating each other's desire. So what is going to happen?

When you are the model of my desire, you are the friend I admire and I am going to desire what you desire. And the friend is going to oppose this desire and say 'no'. That 'no' is shattering and is going to increase our desire instead of making it less. As our desires increase we are going to move more forcefully towards the object we both desire and we cannot both have. Therefore, our model is going to have his hostility increased and his desire as well.

In this bad reciprocal game, the model becomes the imitator of his imitator and the imitator becomes the model of his model. This results in a relationship based on total misunderstanding. In reality there is more and more identity between the two characters who are fighting, of which they are unaware. They try to interpret their conflict in terms of differences. But they are rivals – the word 'rivals' refers to people who live on the two sides of the same river and they are fighting all the time. The fights between nations, like the fights between individuals, are fights about borders; they are rivalries about the same object. The main human conflict is not difference of ideology or opinion, or about mugging in the streets, but rivalry. We are constantly faced by rivalry in the modern world. We compete. It is very difficult to retain your friendship with someone you are competing with. Unless you are a very strong person, you will be unable to interpret your relationship in terms of difference. You will never face the identity.

Our rivalry increases because we both collaborate to make it more intense. As I regard the object as more desirable, you are going to regard it as more desirable too. As a matter of fact, the modern world has adopted this as the main mechanism of its economic system, which is the stock market. In the stock market we are buying stocks because other people are buying them and we are buying them as everyone buys them and pushed to extremes this is called a speculative bubble.

Of course, Shakespeare already knew that. In *As You Like It*,

Rosalind is incensed with a couple she overhears in which the girl is playing hard to get and increasing her value by rejecting her suitor. Rosalind advises her to 'sell when you can; you are not for all markets'. You would believe this was written by Lord Keynes, not Shakespeare, but Shakespeare understood the relatedness between romantic and economic games. You can create capital with mimetic rivalry, as long as you do not kill each other, as long as it remains some kind of economic game which can be productive up to a point, but which can also be very destructive psychically and physically and in every way.

In other words, we have a great problem of rivalry in our world, as de Tocqueville understood so well when he visited America. He discovered the democratic system, which as you know is the worst of all systems, except for all others, and the democratic system is the system where it is safer to unleash rivalry up to a point; in other words, where people know where to stop and usually do not kill each other. Rivalry becomes incredibly productive not only in the economy, but in science, in the arts and in all sorts of other fields as well, as long as it does not go too far.

A Contagious Fire

What makes mimetic rivalry terrifying is that it is a contagious fire, that it intensifies as it goes on. If you look at mythology, you will see its stories usually begin with an escalation of violence and with a great crisis. My own interpretation is that at the beginning of myth you really have a mimetic crisis of the type I am describing, but in an archaic community it tends to spread to the whole community. If such crises are mimetically contagious, if they tend to spread infinitely and store up more and more violence, the question about our world is not really why so much violence, but why so little? Why are we not always at each other's throats? That is the political question *par excellence*.

The first person to ask this question in a radical way was another English thinker, Thomas Hobbes. He said that when two people desire the same thing and cannot both have it, they become enemies and that is the beginning of what Hobbes calls 'the war of all against all'. I think that Hobbes is in touch with mythology, in touch with the beginning of human communities and with something very important. But after that he is not up to the challenge.

He is not up to the challenge because when he sees the war of all against all, the universal wolf turning into the universal prey, as Shakespeare said, he said that the moment comes when people start thinking about the situation, and they are reasonable (they are English I suppose), so they sign a social contract. The thing that is amazing about them is that people must sign social contracts and entrust their fate to a tyrant in order to have peace among themselves. You must have a master, Hobbes says, and this master human beings choose together among themselves in a friendly and amicable way. In order to stop their fighting, they must get together and form a government. But they do it at the very moment when they should be incapable of doing it, when the crisis is most intense, when the violence should run to extremes.

Long before the weapons catch up, Hobbes is talking of what the theoreticians of atomic power call mutually assured destruction. Hobbes's question is highly relevant. At the time of the Cuban missile crisis, people were wondering if they would be able to have a social contract, or whether they would trigger the apocalypse, the really violent revelation. They were able to have a social contract and this time it was the Russians who turned the other cheek when they turned back their ships. But I do not think that in human society as a whole this ability to refrain from violence at the most basic stage has ever prevailed – it is a modern situation in which we speak about violence. We speak about violence because it is a scandal to us, because we know it can destroy us at any moment. To think nowadays in global terms is constantly to keep in mind the possibility of the destruction of our world.

Braking Mechanisms

But archaic people did not think that way and I do not think they had a social contract. I think there was a built-in braking mechanism in the mimetic crisis. When you have that it is a modern mimetic violence, there comes a point when you forget about the object and you concentrate on your opponent, and ultimately the mimetic influx converges on specific individuals, and there is a tendency for the system to simplify itself, to have fewer and fewer targets, and more and more people polarizing against them until finally everyone polarizes against a single enemy who seems responsible for the whole crisis.

If everybody believes in his or her guilt, in the guilt of the victim, when that victim is killed, the community will find itself free of violence (even if for only a very short time), because the violence will have been killed with that single individual upon whom the entire problem is projected. This is what we call a scapegoat. We use the word 'scapegoat' when someone pays for everyone else. I really think that archaic gods are scapegoats in that sense. Since they solve the problems of violence they are divinized because they are the ones who solve the problem the community could not solve. Therefore, they are regarded at first as very bad and then as very good. The primitive sacred is both very malevolent and very benevolent, but you never know when it will shift from one to the other.

The Christian Story

From this perspective, you have a problem with Christianity. If you look at the Christian story, you will see it has exactly the same profile as the story I just gave you. You have a crisis at first, that of the little Jewish state, and then you have a polarization against a single individual, Jesus. Then there is the resurrection, and Jesus is with God. At the end of the nineteenth century the anthropologists thought they had discovered the real nature of Christianity. They said it is like any other myth, but they did not really understand the scapegoat system. They failed to understand that the victim was really present, really existed, and was a real savior, in the sense that to kill a victim who embodies the violence of the entire community really liberates the people from that violence. So they had a feeling that the Gospels were the same thing as any myth. But there is a huge difference which we do not see because it seems unimportant.

If you look at a myth, like the Oedipus myth, you find someone who is supposed to have given the plague to his community because he has killed his father and married his mother. What kind of accusation is that? It is obviously a witchcraft accusation. If we read the myth as a medieval document, we would immediately recognize this, and we would not believe in it, because we would be in a Christian world and we would interpret it in Christian terms.

However, the prestige of classical learning leads us to look at the Oedipus myth as some kind of unsolvable mystery, and we speculate endlessly about parricide and incest in each one of us. This is exactly the same thing as believing in the parricide and incest, which is exactly what I think Freudianism does. The difference with the Gospels is that they tell you that this victim is wrongly accused, this victim is innocent, this victim is the victim of a mimetic contagion that has overcome violence.

In other words, the Gospels are a failed myth. They are a failed myth because there is a power behind them that rejects the myth and this power is extremely mysterious, since the disciples at the beginning are willing to fall for the scapegoat's killing. At the beginning of the Passion all the disciples abandon Jesus. They cannot wait for him one hour and the best of them, Peter, betrays Jesus. This does not mean that Peter is especially weak psychologically; it refers to all people; people in situations like that always believe in the guilt of the victim and are unable to resist the pull of a unanimous crowd. And the Gospels are the only text which describes the truth of the scapegoat event. Therefore, they introduce us to a world in which we learn not to believe in scapegoating. That is why we can talk about it today.

A myth is the embodiment of scapegoating, its completion, its perfection. It is written by a crowd which believes it has been saved by its own victim in such a way that that victim is seen as a primitive god.

The Gospels do exactly the opposite. Jesus says, 'I do not bring [the] peace [of the scapegoat], but the sword'. In John's Gospel, every intervention of Jesus is followed by, 'they were divided by his words'. Far from reconciling the community, Jesus does not improve the situation of the world in the way which myth does.

Myth enables people to collaborate on the basis of a misunderstanding, which becomes their myth, their national myth. The Gospels destroy this myth. Having for so long been unaware of this, today we are at a great turning point. We are for the first time able to understand the deconstructive side of Christianity and to understand that, far from being a myth, Christianity is what moves us away from myth, and places us in a world where we no longer have the safeguards of scapegoating.

These latter were called sacrifices. What did people do when they had a problem with violence in the ancient world? People had a myth, people had a scapegoating in their past that they remembered as a divine epiphany. So they chose another victim and they all got together and killed that victim. They said, the god wants us to do this in order to reconcile us once again. So an archaic ritual, a sacrificial rite is really an effort to repeat an act of collective scapegoating, which works because it is misunderstood.

People may say of the Eucharist, 'well, isn't that the same thing'? It is certainly the same symbolism. However, it is not a murderous action and the priest and the victim are one and the victim is aware of what the victim is doing. I think that the theory of redemption should be based on the fact that Jesus is aware that he is revealing the scapegoating that has underlain culture until then and taking humankind into a world where that scapegoating – and it will take centuries – is becoming less and less effective. But we are probably reaching the point where scapegoating has exhausted its possibilities. That is why we live in a world where violence and scapegoating have become spiritual stumbling blocks for us.

We talk about violence, we condemn our Christian predecessors for being prone to it. But we condemn them in the name of what superiority? I think we always condemn the past in the name of knowledge which, even if we are not aware, comes ultimately from the Bible. There is absolutely nowhere else, no other philosophy nor religion from which it could come. In other words the similarity between Christianity and myth which was long avoided by Christians as a dangerous thing, and a threat to Christianity, has to be explored. Now, though, the myths are understood from the perspective of Christianity.

If instead of the Oedipus myth – Oedipus guilty of the plague, of killing his father and mother – you look at the story as a passion play, you will realize that Thebes has capriciously moved against its king because it is tired of him. In the Byzantine world they still performed Sophocles' play *Oedipus the King*, but they performed it as the passion of Oedipus, as the suffering of an innocent victim. Maybe they could not verbalize or conceptualize what they did, but instinctively they felt that Oedipus was a victim of the crowd, a victim of the same type as Jesus, not an ugly goat but a kind of Lamb of God.

Literature and Christianity:
A Personal View

We are supposed to be living in the so-called postmodern era which is also labeled post-Christian.* The modern era was anti-Christian but now we are post-Christian. This label means that Christianity is so outmoded, at long last, so completely passé, that its enemies no longer have to worry. Vigilance is no longer needed. Christianity is on its way to being completely forgotten.

Is this so certain, however? You will observe that, in the expression 'post-Christian,' the more evocative word is the second one: Christian. Our time seems unable to define itself independently of what it regards as hopelessly outmoded. A remarkable thing about us is our excessive use, in the labeling of our intellectual fads and fashions, of that Latin word that cannot be used independently in English, 'post.' There seems to be a great scarcity of labels in our world and the same ones have to be used again and again. 'Post' is the fashionable Latin preposition, or rather 'postposition,' right now and it seems indispensable.

In the old days it was mechanical contraptions that were used again and again. They were repaired and renovated endlessly because they were scarce and expensive. Many people had to buy everything secondhand. They bought used typewriters and used washing machines as well as used cars. Nowadays there is so much technical stuff around that to repair a broken gadget is usually more expensive than to buy a new one. The same is true of intellectual fads and fashions. They are countless. The only things that seem in short supply are labels for these intellectual fads and fashions. We cannot afford to

* Girard's introductory remarks have been condensed.

throw them away anymore; they are scarce; they must be carefully stored away because they have to be used several times.

The period before ours was still able to invent new labels such as impressionism, expressionism, cubism, and surrealism. They all ended in 'ism' of course; they all resembled each other and that was not a good sign. It was a warning that our labeling creativity was under pressure and about to run out. After World War II, indeed, it became impossible to invent a truly successful new label. As a result, now, old labels have to be saved and recycled almost as much as taxicabs in Cairo.

How do we recycle our stock of old labels? So far there have been two principal techniques. The first consists in using the adjective 'new' in front of an old label and the second in using the Latin preposition 'post.' The first technique was used a great deal immediately after World War II. There was a *new criticism* and a *new novel*; there were several *new theaters*. One good thing about 'new' is that it could be translated into French, or borrowed from French and then it became entirely *nouveau*. Thanks to this clever device, the recycling was recycled and its life span considerably increased. It was a great feat of literary engineering. The first great success was *art nouveau*, way back in almost prehistorical times, and then there was a *nouveau roman*, a *nouvelle critique*, and a *nouvelle musique* and so forth until the whole thing became an excessively microwaved *nouvelle cuisine*.

The problem with words such as 'new' and *nouveau* is that they are only adjectives and their very devotion to novelty naively proclaims our dependence upon the past. The past is the substantive part of the recycled label, the hated referent which stubbornly reasserts an independent existence we seem to have lost. In order to solve this problem, we have replaced 'new' by 'post,' and that is why the *postmodern* and *post-Christian* era is upon us. It came along with the poststructuralist era which is also post-metaphysical, post-philosophical, post-everything in sight. Everything is so 'post' that we are rapidly becoming post-post.

One problem with 'post' however, is that it cannot be translated into French. The French word for 'post' is always already 'post.'

Since the word cannot be laundered through any other language, its possibilities are somewhat limited and it is already running out of steam. Another problem with 'post' is that, hard as it tries to detach itself from the past, it cannot succeed any better than 'new' or 'nouveau.' The substantive part of the recycled label is still the old word, the hated referent. In the expression post-Christian, the only real content is Christian.

The session on Christianity and literature should be defined perhaps as the official remnant of Christianity in the post-Christian era of the Modern Language Association. Like all remnants, it could turn out to be a seed. A good biblical metaphor for this session is Noah's Ark. We may be at this interesting juncture when Noah is wondering if the waters are still going up or if they are beginning to recede, and if he will soon be able to let loose the dove.

As far as I am concerned the subject of literature and Christianity is literally the story of my whole intellectual and spiritual existence. Many years ago, I started with literature and myth and then moved to the study of the Bible and Christian Scripture. Great literature literally led me to Christianity. This itinerary is not original. It still happens every day and has been happening since the beginning of Christianity. It happened to Augustine, of course. It happened to many great saints such as Saint Francis of Assisi and Saint Teresa of Ávila who, like Don Quixote, were fascinated by novels of chivalry.

One of the greatest examples of literature leading to Christianity is Dante. The experience is expressed symbolically by the role of Virgil in Dante's *Divine Comedy*. There are many reasons why Dante chose Virgil. In the *Aeneid*, Virgil makes his hero Aeneas visit hell. More important was the fact that in the Middle Ages Virgil was regarded as a prophet of Christ and, most important of all, was the fact that Virgil was greatly appreciated by Dante and had really played a role, I believe, in leading the author to Christianity.

What role? In order to understand, you have to take literally the idea of guiding someone through hell. The world of the *Aeneid* is really a world of hellish violence and, according to Dante, the function of profane literature is to guide us through hell and purgatory. This is what Virgil did for Dante and it was a great help to Dante because hell is not a very nice place to live. It is not even a nice place to visit. If you still have even two cents' worth of common sense when you are in hell, you want to get out, for very selfish reasons.

Common sense and selfishness can be good things up to a point. This fact is acknowledged in the parable of the prodigal son. Why does the prodigal son return to his father? Not because of some great mystical reason, not even because he is sorry. He decides to go back to his father when he realizes that even the lowest servant in his father's house is better off than he is now that he has left that house. He still has enough common sense and selfishness to recognize hell when he finds himself in it and he wants to escape.

In my case it was not Virgil nor even Dante who guided me through hell but the five novelists I discussed in my first book: Cervantes, Stendhal, Flaubert, Dostoevsky, and Proust. The more modern the novel becomes, the more you descend down the circles of a hell which can still be defined in theological terms as it is in Dante, but can also now be defined in nonreligious terms – in terms of what happens to us when our relations with others are dominated exclusively by our desires and theirs, and their relationships dominated by their desires and ours. Because our desires are always mimetic or imitative, even and especially when we dream of being completely autonomous and self-sufficient, they always make us into rivals of our models and then the models of our rivals, thus turning our relations into an inextricable entanglement of identical and antagonistic desires which result in endless frustration.

Frustration is the law of the genre but it can be of two kinds. If we are prevented by our model from acquiring the object we both desire, our desire keeps intensifying painfully as a result of the deprivation. If, on the contrary, we acquire the object we desire, the prestige of our model collapses and our desire weakens and dies as a result of being fulfilled. This is the second kind of frustration and it is worse than the first. When it happens, we look for another model for our desire but the moment may come, after many such experiences, when we are totally disenchanted and cannot find any new model. This is the worst kind of frustration, the one the experts call postmodern and post-Christian, perhaps even post-mimetic desire.

The mortality of desire, its finitude, is the real problem in our world since it destabilizes even the most fundamental institutions, beginning with the family. Our psychological and psychoanalytical theories do not even acknowledge the reality of this problem. Desire according to Freud is immortal, eternal, since human beings desire only substitutes for their parents and cannot cease to desire them. Freud is silent about the death of desire. Only great literature has a lot to say about that subject.

The individualism of our time is really an effort to deny the failure of desire. Those who claim to be governed by the pleasure principle, as a rule, are enslaved to models and rivals, which makes their lives a constant frustration. But they are too vain to acknowledge their own enslavement. Mimetic desire makes us believe we are always on the verge of becoming self-sufficient through our own transformation into someone else. Our would-be transformation into a god, as Shakespeare says, turns us into an ass. In Pascal's terms, it becomes *'Qui veut faire l'ange fait la bête'* – 'Whoever tries to act like an angel turns into a beast.'

Understanding the real failure of desire leads to wisdom and ultimately to religion. Many philosophies and all religions share in that wisdom which modern trendiness denies. Great literature shares in that wisdom because it does not cheat with desire. It shows the necessary failure of undisciplined desire. The greatest literature shows the impossibility of self-fulfillment through desire. Mimetic obsessions are dreadful because they cannot vanquish their own circularity, even when they know about it. They are the mother of all addictions such as drugs, alcohol, obsessive sexuality, etc. One cannot get out of the circle even as its radius becomes smaller and smaller and our world becomes more narrowly obsessive.

Unlike most philosophies which are fundamentally stoic or epicurean, Judaism and Christianity preach no kind of self-fulfillment or self-absorption. Nor do they preach self-annihilation in the manner of Oriental mysticism. Christianity acknowledges the ultimate goodness of imitation as well as the goodness and reality of the human person. It teaches that instead of surrendering to mimetic desire, by following the newest fashion and worshiping the latest idol, we should imitate only Christ or Christ-like noncompetitive models.

If one is badly caught up in this circularity and wants to get out of it, one must undergo an experience of radical change which religious people call a *conversion*. In the classical view of conversion, it is not something of our own doing but the personal intervention of God in our lives. The greatest experience for Christians is the experience of becoming religious under a compulsion that they feel cannot come from themselves but from God alone. What makes conversion fascinating to those who have this experience (but also to those who do not) is the feeling that at no time in the lives of human beings is God closer to us and actually intervening in our lives.

This experience is not necessarily identical with the Christian experience. Many good Christians never experience it, either because, as far back as they can remember, they have always believed, or because even though they became Christians in their adult life, they never experienced anything dramatic enough to be labeled a conversion. The religious experience of these people is not necessarily less profound or even less intense than the experience of those who benefited from a dramatic conversion.

Nevertheless the idea of conversion enjoys great prestige with all people religiously inclined because there is no doubt that the Gospels emphasize conversion. The Pauline idea of the new man, and Paul's theme of salvation through faith can be interpreted in terms of radical conversion. Almost everything in Paul can be so interpreted.

There is a problem with the word we use to describe that experience, the word conversion itself, or the Greek word *metanoia*. According to my dictionaries, the Latin word *conversio* was used for the first time in the Christian sense by Augustine. But Augustine, curiously, did not use it in his *Confessions* which are the story of his own conversion. He used it for the first and last time in *The City of God* (VII, 33) in a phrase which refers to Satan's efforts to prevent us from achieving our conversion to the true God.

The problem with the Latin word *conversio* is that it does not really mean what we all mean by a Christian conversion and what Augustine himself undoubtedly meant. It means turning around in a circle; it refers to a full circular revolution that ultimately brings you back to your point of departure. This is not what a Christian conversion is. A Christian conversion is not circular; it never returns to its point of origin. It is open-ended; it is moving toward a totally unpredictable future. It seems to me that the real Latin significance of the word is characteristically pagan in the sense that it reflects the pagan conception of history and time itself which is circular and repetitive. This conception is always reminiscent of that Eternal Return which can be found in the *Puranas* and elsewhere in the East. Various versions of it are also present in some of the pre-Socratic philosophers in Greece, especially Anaximander, Heraclitus, and Empedocles.

The Latin word *conversio* refers to reversible actions and processes, such as the translation of a text into another language, and also to mythical metamorphoses. When Christians adopt the word, they change its connotation from a circular to a linear phenomenon which is open-ended. It now means a change that takes place once and for all, with no conceivable return to the starting point. Therefore it should be irreversible.

The Greek *metanoia* was first used in Greek-language churches to designate a certain type of penance. It does not designate a circular motion but it is not very good either at signifying Christian conversion. It is too weak a word.

Meta-noeo means to change one's mind about something; to have second thoughts regarding something that seemed settled; to perceive a mistake too late, when it can no longer be changed. It can mean therefore regret, but nothing as strong as Christian repentance when the convert hears the question that Paul heard on the road to Damascus, 'Why do you persecute me?'

The Christian conversion is a transformation that reaches so deep it changes us once and for all and gives us a new being, so to speak. The result is so superior that it is not possible to cancel that change, either by moving back or going around in a circle. To us Westerners moving in a circle is a fate worse than death. It is hell. The idea of conversion is much more than reform, repentance, re-energizing, repair, regeneration, revolution, or any other word beginning with 're' which suggests a return to something that was there before and which therefore limits us to a circular view of life and experience. In the Christian conversion, a positive change is connoted which is not caught inside a circle.

Christians give the notion of conversion a depth and a seriousness that must be recognized in order to appreciate the significance of an important episode in the history of early Christianity, the *Donatist* heresy. The Donatists were fourth-century Christians in North Africa who took Christian conversion so seriously that, after periods of persecution, they refused to reintegrate into the Church those people who had not been heroic enough to accept martyrdom and had recanted. They regarded Christian conversion as something so momentous that it could occur only once in a lifetime. One didn't have a second chance. The Donatists felt that people who did not have enough courage to face the lions in the Roman circus and die gladly for their faith were not good enough to be Christians at all.

These people had such an exalted view of the Christian conversion that the idea of its happening twice was blasphemous. In their eyes, it debased the whole process and made a mockery of the Christian faith. The Donatists were condemned by the Church and were certainly wrong from an evangelical viewpoint. If their absolutist principle had applied to Peter on the night of Jesus' arrest, after his triple denial of Christ, he would not have been reintegrated. He would never have become the leader of the Church. The Donatists were wrong. To condemn their intransigence was certainly the right thing to do for the early Church, but their appeal to such great Christians as Tertullian gives us a clue as to how seriously the notion of conversion was taken in early Christianity.

The aspect of literature that corresponds to that view, to that absolute view of conversion, is the belief which I hold, that the most outstanding forms of literary creation are not, as a rule, the product merely of native talent, the pure gift of literary creation, even though that gift exists. Nor are they the product of an acquired skill or technique even though no writer can be really good unless he has sufficient skill as a writer.

The writers that seem the greatest to me do not consider what we call their genius a natural gift with which they were born. They view it as a belated acquisition, the result of a personal transformation not of their own doing, which resembles a conversion. As far as the relationship of literature and Christianity is concerned, my main interest has been the relatedness of a certain form of creation to this notion of religious and especially Christian conversion.

The novelist who made me interested in this relationship was Marcel Proust. In Proust, of course, the hero and the writer are one but not simultaneously. The hero comes first and then the writer takes over at the end of the novel. Thanks to a break, a rupture which the novelist experiences, the hero becomes the novelist. But it is not the novelist's achievement. He feels he had little to do with the event that turned him into a novelist.

When I was writing about Proust, it was already fashionable to say that Marcel the narrator is a pure invention of the novelist, that the art of a writer has nothing to do with his life. This is not true, of course. The novel, even though it is not Christian at all, is, in its beliefs, morals, and metaphysics, an esthetic and even spiritual autobiography which claims to be rooted in a personal experience, a personal transformation structured exactly like the experience Christians call a conversion.

At the beginning of the last volume, *Time Recaptured*, the hero suffers a great illness and finds himself in a state of profound depression. He no longer hopes that, someday, he will become a great writer. Then, at the moment of complete discouragement, even depression, some trivial incidents happen to him, like walking on the uneven pavement of the Guermantes courtyard and being reminded of the same experience in the past. This kind of remembrance triggers in him an esthetic and spiritual illumination that transforms him completely. This tiny event provides him with his whole subject matter, the dedication needed to write the book and, above all, the right perspective, a perspective totally free for the first time of the compulsion of desire, of the hope of fulfilling himself through desire.

The titles chosen by Proust for the novel as a whole and for the last volume of his novel, which is the first, of course, in the sense that it recounts the creative experience, are highly significant. The whole novel is entitled *À la recherche du temps perdu*, which literally means 'searching for lost time,' for the time the hero has wasted and frittered away until the moment of conversion. The title of the last volume which was truly the first to be conceived and written, at least in its main outline, is *Time Recaptured*. It is the story of that spiritual death and rebirth to which I just alluded. It is really the beginning of the great creative period in Proust's life.

Thus we have two perspectives in Proust and other great novels of novelistic conversion. The *first perspective* is the deceptive perspective of desire which is full of illusions regarding the possibility of the hero to fulfill himself through desire. It is the perspective that imprisoned him in a sterile process of jumping from one frustrated desire to the next over a period of many years. Everything the narrator could not acquire, he desired; everything he acquired, he immediately ceased to desire, until he fell into a state of ennui that could be called a state of post-mimetic desire.

The *second perspective* is one that comes from the end of the novel, from the omega point of conversion, which is a liberation from desire. This perspective enables the novelist to rectify the illusions of the hero and provides him with the creative energy he needs to write his novel. The second perspective is highly critical of the first but it is not resentful. Even though Proust never resorts to the vocabulary of sin, the reality of sin is present. The exploration of the past very much resembles a discovery of one's own sinfulness in Christianity. The time wasted away is full of idolatry, jealousy, envy, and snobbery; it all ends in a feeling of complete futility.

The word *conversion* is indispensable because Proust is describing, on the whole truthfully, the personal upheaval in his life and the great surge of creativity that enabled him to become the great novelist he could not have been earlier. Everything in the life and legend of Marcel Proust fits the conversion pattern. He enters great literature just as, earlier, he might have entered the religious life. There is something quasi-monastic about the partly mythical but nevertheless authentic account of his spending the rest of his life isolated from the world, in his cork-lined bedroom, waking up in the middle of the night to write his novel, just as monks wake up to sing their prayers.

There are many indications of a great change in Proust. The people who have worked in the Proustian archives say that one can distinguish at a single glance the post-conversion writing from the pre-conversion writing. His great novel is entirely written in the converted handwriting. The interpretation of the great Proustian creation as conversion was propounded by some of the first interpreters of his work, especially Jacques Rivière. All I did was go back to that theory armed with more biographical facts, with *Jean Santeuil* and, of course, with the mass of writing Proust produced at that time and then discarded. The major difference between *Jean Santeuil* and the later masterpiece is the author's unawareness of his own mimetic desire.

I do not claim that Proust became a saint after his conversion or even that he had a religious conversion. He did not. It is unquestionable, however, that at that time and for the only time in his life, he became interested in Christianity. He felt it could be relevant to his transformation. He sought advice and being totally ignorant about the subject, he had the curious idea of consulting, of all people, André Gide, a lapsed Protestant. André Gide discouraged him from investigating the matter any further.

What I really claim is that the creative experience of Proust is truly comparable in most respects to a religious conversion which cannot be said to have failed but which bore only esthetic fruits and never resulted in a religious conversion. It functions like a religious conversion and certainly there is no reason to disregard the voice of the novelist himself, especially in the mass of now published manuscripts which he wrote during the *Time Recaptured* period.

Before his great change, Proust was a talented amateur. His conversion turned him into a genius. When André Gide read the manuscript of Proust's first volume for his publishing house, he rejected it out of hand. The author, in his eyes, was an intellectually insignificant social butterfly who had not turned into a major writer overnight. This sort of metamorphosis is very rare indeed, and Gide was statistically correct in choosing not to believe it. He was a busy editor; but in this case he was wrong.

My insistence on the word *conversion* is like a red flag to a bull. In my first book, I did not wave one red flag at the bull but five, since I applied this notion not only to Proust, but to the four other novelists I was studying, Cervantes, Stendhal, Flaubert, and Dostoevsky. Take Don Quixote, for instance. On his deathbed he repents and says he wishes he had time to read good books instead of the novels of chivalry that had turned him into a lunatic, a puppet whose strings were pulled by a puppeteer who did not even exist, Amadis of Gaul. Take Julien Sorel about to be guillotined in *The Red and the Black*. Take Madame Bovary when she eats the arsenic which is about to kill her. Flaubert is already Proustian enough not only to say: 'Madame Bovary, c'est moi' but to add that during the creation of the death of his heroine he had the taste of arsenic in his mouth. In other words, he shared the creative death of his heroine. It is the same thing with the Siberian exile of Raskolnikov in Dostoevsky's *Crime and Punishment*.

In all these writers, I felt, there was a central work which is the conversion novel, *The Red and the Black* for Stendhal, *Madame Bovary* for Flaubert, *Crime and Punishment* for Dostoyevsky. In all these writers, I found the same two perspectives as in the great Proust, the pre-conversion and the post-conversion perspective that rectifies the pre-conversion perspective which is always some kind of self-deception.

I was guided by Proust when I coined the notion of a novelistic conversion. In the great mass of manuscripts associated with *Time*

Recaptured, there is a text which compares the still-to-be-written last and first volume of the great novel to the conclusions of many great novels in the past, and of some works that are not novels. Cervantes is there, and Stendhal, Flaubert as well. There are also other novelists I have not mentioned, such as George Eliot.

The notion of conversion provides the work with a past and a future, with its 'human time,' its temporal depth that unconverted novels do not have. The second perspective distances the writer from the experience he recounts. Great novels are written from both ends at the same time. We might say, there is first the perspective of the unenlightened hero, and then the omega perspective, the all-knowing perspective that comes from the end.

When I published my first book, my good friend John Freccero, now chairman of Italian studies at New York University, was quick to point out that my last chapter did not mention the most important work in connection with its thesis, the work that invented the spiritual autobiography and is based on a great experience of conversion: Augustine's *Confessions*. This work is the first and greatest example of the dual perspective in a book. It must be regarded as the first great literary autobiography in a sense that the ancient world did not really know.

Before all these examples and their ultimate model come the Gospels themselves and, if we look at them closely, we will see that we have the dual perspective in them also. In the three synoptic Gospels, but especially in Mark, the disciples are represented as unable to understand the teaching of Jesus at the time they hear it from his own mouth. They are not really converted – even Peter – though he is able to recognize Jesus as the Messiah.

The apostles do not understand much while they are listening to Jesus. They misunderstand everything. They believe in the triumphant Messiah after the Davidic model rather than the suffering Messiah after the Servant of Yahweh in Second Isaiah. Only after the death and resurrection of Jesus are they able to understand what they first heard without understanding. The resurrection to them is a conversion experience, which is the same as the descent of the

Holy Spirit at Pentecost when they were filled with a grace which was not theirs when Jesus was still alive. The real definition of grace is that Jesus died for us and even though his own people, as a people, did not receive him, he made those who did receive him able to become children of God.

Maxims of René Girard

1. All desire is a desire for being.

2. More than ever, I am convinced that history has meaning, and that its meaning is terrifying.

3. Violence is the heart and secret soul of the sacred.

4. The simplest gestures have their logic.

5. There is no such thing as a pure and simple lie.

6. When mutual love is absent, the only sentiment that can reconcile human beings is its opposite, a common hatred.

7. An outsider will never be acceptable unless and until his imitation becomes perfect. Mimesis is the only key that can open a closed community.

8. Only the most superficial forms of imitation are voluntary.

9. The current process of spiritual demagoguery and rhetorical over-kill has transformed the concern for victims into a totalitarian command and a permanent inquisition.

10. Desire has no worse enemy than its own truth.

11. Masochists are always fascinated artisans of their own unhappiness.

12. Each of us is a Herodias, afflicted with some importunate prophet.

13. In matters intellectual as well as in matters financial, danger and profit always run together

14. Democracy is one vast middle-class court where the courtiers are everywhere and the king is nowhere.

15. Violence, far from serving the interests of whoever exerts it, reveals the intensity of his desire; thus it is a sign of slavery.

16. The romantic does not want to be alone, but *to be seen alone.*

17. Choice always involves choosing a model, and true freedom lies in the basic choice between a human or a divine model.

18. The truth of metaphysical desire is death.

19. Men tend to see a miracle in everything they don't understand.

20. The best way not to be crucified, in the final analysis, is to do as everyone else and join in the crucifixion.

21. The peoples of the world do not invent their gods. They deify their victims.

22. No one ever sees himself as casting the first stone.

23. Even the most violent persons believe that they are always reacting to a violence committed in the first instance by someone else.

24. No philosophical thought will master the shift to charity.

25. We shouldn't go so far as to allow good manners to prevent us from thinking.

26. Flying saucers are the neo-paganism of the masses.

27. If the winners are always the same, the losers will eventually overturn the table.

28. People fail to understand that they are indebted to violence for the degree of peace that they enjoy.

29. There is great irony in the fact that the modern process of stamping out religion produces countless caricatures of it.

30. Few people want to be saints nowadays, but everybody is trying to lose weight.

31. Caiaphas is the incarnation of politics at its best, not its worst. No one has ever been a better politician.

32. In all aspects of life, the oscillation between all and nothing, which is the fruit of hysterical competition, is more and more visible.

33. There can be rivalries of renunciation rather than acquisition, of deprivation rather than of enjoyment.

34. As long as we are not provided with a goal worthy of our emptiness we will copy the emptiness of others and constantly regenerate the hell from which we are trying to escape.

35. If you do not have a real religion, you end up with a more dreadful one.

36. When we criticize the Bible we can only criticize it with the Bible.

37. What if the battle were worth more than the victory?

38. Everywhere and always, when human beings either cannot or dare not take their anger out on the thing that has caused it, they

unconsciously search for substitutes, and more often than not they find them.

39. Silence is the only conduct truly befitting a solipsist, the only one, however, that he cannot bring himself to adopt.

40. The above-ground tomb does not have to be invented. It is the pile of stones in which the victim of the unanimous stoning is buried. It is the first pyramid.

41. Men create their own hell and help one another descend into it.

42. Violence is like a raging fire that feeds on the very objects intended to smother its flames.

43. Choose your enemies carefully because you will become like them.

44. Progress in matters of the spirit is often a form of self-destruction. It may entail a violent reaction against the past.

45. Humankind is never the victim of God; God is always the victim of humankind.

46. The time has come for us to forgive one another. If we wait any longer there will not be time enough.

47. If all men loved their enemies, there would be no more enemies.

48. When the whole world is globalized, you're going to be able to set fire to the whole thing with a single match.

49. Because it always meets with disappointment in reality, the belief in man's natural goodness always leads to the hunt for scapegoats.

50. *On political correctness*: It's the religion of the victim detached from any form of transcendence.

51. In general, history is written by the victors. We're the only society that wants history to be written by the victims, and we don't see the unprecedented nature of the reversal.

52. Christ didn't write, but he is identical with his word. He dies for the reasons that cause him to speak. He speaks for the reasons that cause him to die.

53. It's not enough to put people on the same social level because they'll all find new ways of excluding one another.

54. Either we surrender and join the persecuting crowd, or we resist and stand alone. The first way is the unanimous self-deception we call mythology.

55. Myths are religions of victorious false accusation.

56. When you take sexual liberation far enough you come to the last taboo, which is the other's lack of desire.

57. The imperative of originality at all costs has killed creativity.

58. To have a scapegoat is to not realize you have a scapegoat.

59. Scapegoating is effective only if it is nonconscious. Then you do not call it scapegoating; you call it justice.

60. Intellectual life is nothing more than a series of frantic infatuations.

61. To be the first to leave a crowd, to be the first not to throw stones, is to run the risk of becoming a target for the stone-throwers.

62. We must see that there is no possible compromise between killing and being killed.

63. The one who believes he can control violence by setting up defenses is in fact controlled by violence.

64. Desire has its own logic, and it is a logic of gambling. Once past a certain level of bad luck, the luckless player does not give up; as the odds get worse, he plays for higher stakes.

65. Men are never condemned by God: they condemn themselves by their despair.

66. There is no desire except desire for absolute difference, and the subject always lacks this difference absolutely.

67. Academia, that vast herd of sheep-like individualists.

68. Modern political thought cannot dispense with morals, but it cannot become purely moral without ceasing to be political.

69. Political answers are one of the ways in which our insatiable appetite for differences satisfies itself.

70. Like every object of desire, history is ephemeral.

71. The person who hates first hates himself for the secret admiration concealed by his hatred.

72. Nothing is more difficult than admitting the final nullity of human conflict.

73. Everything, in fact, is false, theatrical, and artificial in desire except the immense hunger for the sacred.

74. Theories are expendable.

75. History is a test. Mankind is failing it.

76. Christianity will be victorious, but only in defeat.

77. War is the most extreme form of competition.

78. In intense conflict, far from becoming sharper, differences melt away.

79. Christians are unfaithful to Christianity.

80. Christianity is not teaching collective violence – it is devouring it.

81. Why is Christianity so unpopular? Instead of incriminating a single person – it indicts all of us.

82. Without a theory, facts don't mean anything.

83. The reason we talk so much about sex is that we don't dare talk about envy.

84. Desire is not of this world.

85. The distance between Don Quixote and the petty bourgeois victim of advertising is not so great as romanticism would have us believe.

86. The more one approaches madness, the more one equally approaches the truth, and if one does not fall into the former, one must end up necessarily in the latter.

87. In myth, violent death is always justified.

88. The children repeat the crimes of their fathers precisely because they believe they are morally superior to them.

89. A non-violent deity can only signal his existence to mankind by having himself driven out by violence.

90. If we respected the tenth commandment, the four commandments that precede it would be superfluous.

91. Humanity results from sacrifice; we are thus the children of religion.

92. Christianity is the only religion that has foreseen its own failure. This prescience is known as the apocalypse.

93. Revelation is dangerous. It's the spiritual equivalent of nuclear power.

94. Christians don't see that they have at their disposal an instrument that is incomparably superior to the whole mishmash of psychoanalysis and sociology that they conscientiously feed themselves. It's the old story of Esau sacrificing his inheritance for a plate of lentils.

95. What motivates Pilate, as he hands Jesus over, is the fear of a riot. He demonstrates 'political skill,' as they say. This is true, no doubt, but why does political skill almost always consist of giving in to violent contagion?

96. There's no need to refute modern thought because, as each new trend one-ups its predecessors, it's liquidating itself at high speed.

97. The good son imitates the father with such passion that father and son become each other's chief stumbling block – a situation the indifferent son more easily avoids.

98. The well-adjusted person is thus one who conceals his violent impulses and condones the collective's concealment of them. The 'maladjusted' individual cannot tolerate this concealment.

99. The Word that states itself to be absolutely true never speaks except from the position of a victim in the process of being expelled.

100. Not only is the revolt against ethnocentrism an invention of the West, it cannot be found outside the West.

101. All modern ideologies are immense machines that justify and legitimate conflicts that in our time could put an end to humanity.

102. *On the human sciences and academia*: I cannot see in this anything more than a huge unionization of failure. We must perpetuate at any cost the interminable discourse that earns us a living.

103. Christ reveals and uproots the structural matrix of all religion.

104. Instead of reading myths in the light of the Gospels, people have always read the Gospels in the light of myths.

105. Fascination is always an indication of mimesis at work.

106. Mimesis learns fast and, after only one single try, it will do routinely and automatically what seemed almost unthinkable a moment before.

107. Interpreters never notice that they are themselves invariably understood and explained by the text that they pride themselves on understanding and explaining to us.

108. Current thought is the castration of meaning.

109. Desire is responsible for its own evolution.

110. Micro-eugenics is the new form of human sacrifice.

111. We no longer protect life from violence, instead we crush life with violence, to try to appropriate for ourselves the mystery of life for our own benefit.

112. Desire bears light, but puts that light in the service of its own darkness.

113. Fighting over prestige is literally fighting over nothing.

114. The invention of science is not the reason that there are no longer witch-hunts, but the fact that there are no longer witch-hunts is the reason that science has been invented.

115. The apocalypse does not announce the end of the world; it creates hope.

116. It is the crowd's role to throw stones.

117. Men cannot confront the naked truth of their own violence without the risk of abandoning themselves to it entirely.

118. Whatever the Church may have lost by its compromises with the world, its enemies now give back by obliging it to play the same role as Christ. This is its true vocation.

119. The principle of originality at all costs leads to paralysis.

120. So-called postmodernism is even more sterile than modernism, and, as its name suggests, also totally dependent on it.

121. Mimetic desire enables us to escape from the animal realm. It is responsible for the best and the worst in us, for what lowers us below the animal level as well as what elevates us above it.

122. Our unending discords are the ransom of our freedom.

123. Vengeance succeeds in spanning generations and encompassing the world. It transcends time and space. One should not be surprised that in the ancient world vengeance was taken to be sacred.

124. The word 'theory' has been so fashionable in recent years that, in the near future, it will sound horribly dated and ridiculous.

125. A search for truth is necessarily violent since it may lead to some definite stance regarding what is true and what is false.

126. Whenever people really believe in some truth larger than the academic world, they do not dedicate themselves to the pursuit of academic success with as much ferocity as the people who believe absolutely nothing.

127. It seems to me that, far from making people more relaxed and generous, the current nihilism has made academic life harsher and less compassionate than before.

128. Our ideas are less and less lovable and, as a result, they are no longer loved.

129. When the ordinary people and the intellectuals do not agree, it is safer to go with the ordinary people.

130. The idea of renunciation has, no doubt, been overdone by the Puritans and the Jansenists, but the blanket hostility that now prevails against it is even worse. The idea that renunciation in all its forms should be renounced once and for all may well be the most flagrant nonsense any human culture has ever devised.

131. To understand human beings, their constant paradox, their innocence, their guilt, is to understand that we are all responsible for this state of things because, unlike Christ, we're not ready to die.

132. It is absolute fidelity to the principle defined in his own preaching that condemns Jesus. There is no other cause for his death than the love of one's neighbor lived to the very end, with an infinitely intelligent grasp of the constraints it imposes.

133. The intensity of conflicts has nothing to do with the reality of differences.

134. The victims are always there, and everyone is always sharpening his weapon for use against his neighbor in a desperate attempt to win himself somewhere – even if only in an indefinite, Utopian future – a plot of innocence that he can inhabit on his own, or in the company of a regenerate human race.

135. Recipes are not what we need, nor do we need to be reassured – our need is to escape from meaninglessness.

136. I hold that truth is not an empty word . . . I hold that everything capable of diverting us from madness and death, from now on, is inextricably linked with this truth.

137. Unanimity in accusation is in itself a cause for suspicion. It suggests that the accused is innocent.

138. We must place our bets either on the total disappearance of the human race or on our arriving at forms of freedom and awareness that we can hardly imagine.

139. *On Foucault*: One day, he told me that 'we shouldn't invent a philosophy of the victim.' I replied: 'No, not a philosophy, I agree – a religion! But it already exists!'

140. In our era many people think that they're breaking with tradition when in reality they're repeating it, but without the elegance displayed by their ancestors.

141. Our world is succumbing to the allure of sham complexity. It establishes your reputation as a researcher, gives you a scientific air. 'A mathematical model for everything – or death!' That's our motto!

142. The cult of the obstacle drives human beings from their human condition toward what is most against them, toward what hurts them the most, toward the non-human, toward the inert, toward the mineral, toward death . . . toward everything that goes against love, against spirit.

143. You can already sense the spirit of May '68 at its most comical in their behavior: the bourgeois parents who say 'Don't forget your scarf!' to their children as they go out to play revolution . . . Revolution as an article of consumption.

144. Marxism wants of course to save victims, but it thinks that the process that makes victims is fundamentally economic.

145. Denying the spiritual dimension of Evil is as wrong as denying the spiritual dimension of Good.

146. We still protect crippled people, handicapped people, but in the center of it all we find a sort of cancer growing, which is the return to infanticide.

147. What people call the partisan spirit is nothing but choosing the same scapegoat as everybody else.

148. The fundamentalists often defend ideas that I deplore, but a remnant of spiritual health makes them foresee the horror of the warm and fuzzy concentration camp that our benevolent bureaucracies are preparing for us, and their revolt looks more respectable to me than our somnolence.

149. In an era where everyone boasts of being a marginal dissident even as they display a stupefying mimetic docility, the fundamentalists are authentic dissidents.

150. It's now no longer possible to persecute except in the name of victims.

151. The aggressor has always already been attacked.

152. The way in which we intellectuals seek to differentiate ourselves from one another by ceaselessly inventing pseudo-differences, revolts that are even more radical than the ones that came before, leads to avant-garde fashions that are ever more sheep-like, ever more repetitive.

153. Tourism, too, is mimetic and a source of undifferentiation.

154. We are ready to deconstruct anything except the idea that we are self-directed and that the persecutors are always the others.

155. The mimetic system, in its eternal return, enslaves humanity.

156. In imitating my rival's desire I give him the impression that he has good reasons to desire what he desires, to possess what he possesses, and so the intensity of his desire keeps increasing.

157. Unlike the modern gurus who claim to be imitating nobody, but who want to be imitated on that basis, Christ says: 'Imitate me as I imitate the Father.'

158. The rules of the Kingdom of God are not at all utopian: if you want to put an end to mimetic rivalry, give way completely to your rival.

159. If someone is making excessive demands on you, he's already involved in mimetic rivalry, he expects you to participate in the escalation. So, to put a stop to it, the only means is to do the opposite of what escalation calls for: meet the excessive demand twice over.

160. If we don't see that the choice is inevitable between the two supreme models, God and the devil, then we have already chosen the devil and his mimetic violence.

161. The myth-making machine is the mimetic contagion that disappears behind the myth it generates.

162. We are living through a caricatural 'ultra-Christianity' that tries to escape from the Judeo-Christian orbit by 'radicalizing' the concern for victims in an anti-Christian manner.

163. The imitation of Christ provides the proximity that places us at a distance. It is not the Father whom we should imitate, but his Son, who has withdrawn with his Father. His absence is the very ordeal that we have to go through.

164. *On comedy*: In order to be successful an artist must come as close as he can to some important social truth without inciting painful self-criticism in the spectators.

165. The refusal of the real is the number one dogma of our time.

166. Our world produces and saves more victims than any other. The two things are true at once. There is more good and more evil than ever before.

167. The unfortunate man is not stoned because he is monstrous; he becomes a monster because of the stoning.

168. There is never anything on one side of a rivalry which, sooner or later, will not be found on the other.

169. Beyond a certain threshold of excitement, almost any human group will focus on almost any victim.

170. Evil is the mystery of a pride which, as it condemns others, unwittingly condemns itself.

171. It is because we have wanted to distance ourselves from religion that it is now returning with such force and in a retrograde, violent

form ... In this, it will perhaps have been our last mythology. We 'believed' in reason, as people used to believe in the gods.

172. The question about our world is not really why so much violence, but why so little? Why are we not always at each other's throats?

Chronology

1923

On December 25, René Noël Théophile Girard is born in Avignon, the second of five children, to Marie-Thérèse de Loye Fabre and a notable historian of the region, Joseph Frédéric Marie Girard, curator of Avignon's Musée Calvet and later the city's Palais des Papes, France's biggest medieval fortress and the pontifical residence during the Avignon papacy.

1939

On 1 September, Germany invades Poland, leading Britain and France to declare war on Germany in retaliation.

1940 and 1941

Girard receives two *baccalauréats*, the first the one common for all students, the second in philosophy, with distinction.

In 1941, he travels to Lyon to prepare for the entrance exam for the École Normal Supérieure, the foremost among the *grandes écoles*, but leaves after a few weeks. Instead, he prepares at home for entry into the École des Chartes, a training ground for archivists and librarians.

On 14 June, the Germans occupy Paris without a struggle. On 22 June, France is partitioned into an occupied zone and an unoccupied zone (Vichy France).

1942–45

In November, 1942, the Germans extend their full occupation to the south of France, with the Italians occupying the small portion of France east of the Rhône.

Girard is appointed to be a student at the École des Chartes in Paris in December 1942, and moves to Paris before his classes began in January 1943. He specializes in medieval history and paleography.

Paris is liberated during a military action that begins on 19 August 1944, and ends when the German garrison surrenders the French capital on 25 August 1944.

On 2 May 1945, the German capital of Berlin surrenders to Soviet forces. On 30 April, Hitler commits suicide, along with other members of his inner circle. On 8 May, an unconditional surrender is officially ratified.

1947
Girard finishes his dissertation on marriage and private life in fifteenth-century Avignon, and graduates as an archiviste-paléographe in 1947.

In the summer, he and a friend, Jacques Charpier, organize an exhibition of paintings at the Palais des Papes from 27 June to 30 September, under the guidance of Paris art impresario Christian Zervos. Girard rubs elbows with Pablo Picasso, Henri Matisse, Georges Braque, and other luminaries. French actor and director Jean Vilar founded the theater component of the festival, which became the celebrated annual Avignon Festival.

In September, Girard leaves France for the United States to teach at the University of Indiana in Bloomington. He is first an instructor of French language, and later teaches French literature as well.

1950
He receives his PhD with a dissertation on 'American Opinion on France, 1940–1943.'

1951
Girard marries Martha McCullough on 18 June. They will have three children: Martin on 8 April 1955; Daniel on 3 January 1957 and Mary on 16 May 1960.

1952–53
Girard becomes instructor of French literature at Duke University for one year.

1953–57
Girard becomes assistant professor at Bryn Mawr College.

1957
Girard assumes the post of associate professor of French at Johns Hopkins University in Baltimore, where he is eventually promoted to full professor and chair of the Romance Languages Department. While there, he receives two Guggenheim Fellowships, in 1959 and 1966.

1958–59
While finishing his first book, published in English as *Deceit, Desire and the Novel*, Girard undergoes two conversion experiences from the autumn of 1958 to Easter, on 29 March 1959. The Girard children were baptized, and René and Martha renew their wedding vows.

1961
Girard publishes *Mensonges romantique et vérité romanesque* (*Deceit, Desire and the Novel: Self and Other in Literary Structure*, published in English by Johns Hopkins University Press, 1965), which introduces his theory of mimetic desire.

He is promoted to Professor of French at Johns Hopkins University.

1962
Girard publishes an edited volume, *Proust: A Collection of Critical Essays*, with Prentice-Hall (Englewood Cliffs, NJ).

1963
Girard's *Dostoïevski, du double à l'unité* is published by Éditions Plon (Paris), later in English as *Resurrection from the Underground: Feodor Dostoevsky* (Crossroads, 1997), reissued by Michigan State University Press in 2012.

1966
With Richard Macksey and Eugenio Donato, Girard organizes an international symposium from 18 to 21 October: 'The Languages of Criticism and the Sciences of Man.' Lucien Goldmann, Roland Barthes, Jacques Derrida, Jacques Lacan, and others participate in the standing-room-only event. The conference marks the introduction of structuralism and French theory to America; it marked Derrida's debut in America.

1968
Girard is appointed Distinguished Professor at the State University of New York, Buffalo, in the Department of English. He begins a lifelong friendship and collaboration with Michel Serres. These years also mark the beginning of what would be a lifelong interest in Shakespeare.

1972
Girard publishes the groundbreaking *La violence et le sacré* (Grasset) developing the idea of scapegoating and sacrifice in cultures around the globe (published as *Violence and the Sacred* by Johns Hopkins University Press in 1977).

1976
In September, he returns to teach at Johns Hopkins University as the James M. Beall Professor of French and Humanities, with an appointment to Richard A. Macksey's Humanities Center.

1978
With the collaboration of French psychiatrists Jean-Michel Oughourlian and Guy Lefort, Girard publishes *Des choses cachées depuis la fondation du monde* (Grasset), published as *Things Hidden since the Foundation of the World* in English (Stanford University Press, 1987), a book-length conversation in which Girard promulgates mimetic theory in its entirety. The book sells briskly in France – 35,000 copies in the first six months, putting it on the non-fiction best-seller list.

Johns Hopkins University Press publishes *To Double Business Bound*, a collection of ten essays – seven of which Girard had written in English. The book of essays is selected by *Choice* as one of the outstanding academic books of the year, along with *Violence and the Sacred*, newly published in English.

1979
Girard is elected as a fellow of the American Academy of Arts and Sciences.

1981
On 1 January, Girard assumes the post of inaugural Andrew B. Hammond Chair in French Language, Literature and Civilization at Stanford. With Jean-Pierre Dupuy, he organizes the 'Disorder and Order' symposium at Stanford, which links disciplinary domains previously thought to be separate. Partici-

pants included Nobel Prize-winning scientist Ilya Prigogne and Nobel economist Kenneth Arrow, Ian Watt, Henri Atlan, Isabelle Stengers, Cornelius Castoriadis, Michel Deguy, Heinz von Forster, Francisco Varela, and others.

1982–85
Girard publishes *Le Bouc émissaire* in 1982 with Grasset (published in English as *The Scapegoat*, 1986) and in 1985 *La Route antique des hommes pervers* (*Job, the Victim of his People*, 1987), developing his hermeneutical approach to biblical texts based on premises of mimetic theory.

He receives first *honoris causa* from Frije University of Amsterdam in 1985.

1988
Girard receives an honorary degree from the faculty of the University of Innsbruck in Austria.

1990–91
Girard publishes *Shakespeare: les feux de l'envie* (*A Theatre of Envy: William Shakespeare*), the only book he conceived and wrote in English. The earlier French edition, *Shakespeare: les feux de l'envie*, received France's Prix Médicis in 1990.

1995
Girard receives an honorary degree from the University Faculties Saint Ignatius, Antwerp (Belgium).

1999
Girard publishes *Je vois Satan tomber comme l'éclair* (published as *I See Satan Fall Like Lightning* in 2001).

2001
Girard publishes *Celui par qui le scandale arrive* (published as *The One by Whom Scandal Comes* in 2014).

2003
A series of lectures at the Bibliothèque Nationale de France considers the Vedic tradition and eventually becomes a small book of about a hundred pages, published as *Le sacrifice*, and in 2011 in English as *Sacrifice*.

Girard receives an honorary degree in arts from the Università degli Studi di Padova in Italy.

2004

Stanford University Press publishes *Oedipus Unbound: Selected Writings on Rivalry and Desire*, a collection of Girard's essays.

He is awarded the literary prize 'Aujourd'hui' for *Les origines de la culture* and receives an honorary degree from Canada's Université de Montréal.

2005

Girard is elected to the Académie Française, an honor previously given to Voltaire, Jean Racine, and Victor Hugo. He takes the 37th chair, vacated by the death of Ambroise-Marie Carré, a Dominican priest, author, and hero of the Résistance.

The Association Recherches Mimétiques is founded in Paris.

2006

The University of Tübingen awards Girard the Dr. Leopold Lucas Prize.

2007

With Italian philosopher Gianni Vattimo, Girard publishes a series of dialogues on Christianity and modernity as *Verita o fede debole? Dialogo su cristianesimo e relativismo* (published in English in 2010 as *Christianity, Truth, and Weakening Faith: A Dialogue*).

Éditions Carnets Nord publishes his last book, *Achever Clausewitz: Entretiens avec Benoît Chantre* (*Battling to the End: Conversations with Benoît Chantre* in English, 2010).

2008

Scotland's University of St Andrews awards Girard an honorary degree.

On 28 December, he receives a lifetime achievement award from the Modern Language Association in San Francisco.

2009
On 8 December, Girard receives a *doctorat honoris causa* from the Institut Catholique de Paris.

2013
On 25 January, King Juan Carlos of Spain awards him the Order of Isabella the Catholic, a Spanish civil order bestowed for his 'profound attachment' to 'Spanish culture as a whole'.

2015
On 4 November, Girard dies at his home on the Stanford campus.

Books by René Girard

Note: Works are given first in English translation, but are in chronological order of original publication.

1961 *Deceit, Desire and the Novel: Self and Other in Literary Structure* (Baltimore, MD: Johns Hopkins University Press, 1965). (*Mensonge romantique et vérité romanesque* [Paris: Grasset]).

1962 *Proust: A Collection of Critical Essays* (Englewood Cliffs, NJ: Prentice Hall).

1963 *Resurrection from the Underground: Feodor Dostoevsky* (New York: Crossroad, 1997). (*Dostoïevski, du double à l'unité* [Paris: Plon]).

1972 *Violence and the Sacred* (Baltimore, MD: Johns Hopkins University Press, 1977). (*La violence et le sacré* [Paris: Grasset]).

1976 *Critique dans un souterrain* (Lausanne: L'Age d'Homme).

1978 *To Double Business Bound: Essays on Literature, Mimesis, and Anthropology* (Baltimore, MD: Johns Hopkins University Press).

1978 *Things Hidden since the Foundation of the World: Research Undertaken in Collaboration with J.-M. Oughourlian and G. Lefort* (Stanford, CA: Stanford University Press, 1987). (*Des choses cachées depuis la fondation du monde* [Paris: Grasset]).

1982 *The Scapegoat* (Baltimore, MD: Johns Hopkins University Press, 1986). (*Le Bouc émissaire* [Paris: Grasset]).

1985 *Job, the Victim of his People* (Stanford, CA: Stanford University Press, 1987). (*La Route antique des hommes pervers* [Paris: Grasset]).

1991 *A Theatre of Envy: William Shakespeare* (Oxford and New York: Oxford University Press).

1994 *When These Things Begin: Conversations with Michel Treguer* (East Lansing, MI: Michigan State University Press, 2014). (*Quand ces choses commenceront . . . Entretiens avec Michel Treguer* [Paris: Arléa]).

1996 *The Girard Reader*, ed. James G. Williams (New York: Crossroad).

1999 *I See Satan Fall Like Lightning* (Maryknoll, MD: Orbis Books, 2001). (*Je vois Satan tomber comme l'éclair* [Paris: Grasset]).

2001 *The One by Whom Scandal Comes* (East Lansing, MI: Michigan State University Press, 2014). (*Celui par qui le scandale arrive*, ed. Maria Stella Barberi [Paris: Desclée de Brouwer]).

2003 *Sacrifice* (East Lansing, MI: Michigan State University Press, 2011). (*Le Sacrifice* [Paris: Bibliothèque nationale de France]).

2004 *Evolution and Conversion. Dialogues on the Origins of Culture*, with Pierpaolo Antonello and João Cezar de Castro Rocha (London: Continuum, 2008). (*Les Origines de la culture. Entretiens avec Pierpaolo Antonello et João Cezar de Castro Rocha* [Paris: Desclée de Brouwer]).

2004 *Oedipus Unbound: Selected Writings on Rivalry and Desire*, ed. Mark R. Anspach (Stanford, CA: Stanford University Press).

2006 *Christianity, Truth, and Weakening Faith: A Dialogue* (New York, NY: Columbia University Press, 2010). (*Verità o fede debole: Dialogo su cristianesimo e relativismo*, with Gianni Vattimo, ed. Pierpaolo Antonello [Massa: Transeuropa]).

2007 *Battling to the End* (East Lansing, MI: Michigan State University Press, 2010). (*Achever Clausewitz* [Paris: Éditions Carnets Nord]).

2008 *Anorexia* (East Lansing, MI: Michigan State University Press, 2013). (*Anoréxie et desir mimétique* [Paris: Éditions de L'Herne]).

2008 *Mimesis and Theory: Essays on Literature and Criticism, 1953–2005* (Stanford, CA: Stanford University Press).

Acknowledgments

René Girard was fortunate in many ways. Here's one: in his first year at Indiana University, the Frenchman stumbled on a Scottish name during roll call – Martha McCullough. He solved the problem when he married her in 1951, and she became Martha Girard. His choice was a blessing that would have far-reaching consequences for his legacy.

My personal gratitude to Martha Girard is longstanding. Her calm, courtesy and common sense were a consistent source of support for my earlier books, including *Evolution of Desire: A Life of René Girard*; *Conversations with René Girard: Prophet of Envy*; and now this one, *All Desire Is a Desire for Being*.

French academician Michel Serres addressed these words to her at the Académie Française in 2005:

You embody the virtues we admire over the centuries, in the culture of your country: faithfulness, constancy, strength, fair-mindedness, fineness in sensing the feelings of others, devotion, dynamically and lucidly facing the things of life. Few people know that without you, without your inimitable presence, the great theories . . . assuredly would not have seen the light of day.*

There are many others to thank for this volume, published on the centenary of the French theorist's birth. Stefan McGrath, managing

* Michel Serres, 'Receiving René Girard into the Académie Française', trans. William A. Johnsen, in *For René Girard: Essays in Friendship and in Truth*, ed. Sandor Goodhart, Jorden Jørgensen, Tom Ryba and James G. Williams (East Lansing, MI: Michigan State University Press, 2009), 14–15.

director of Penguin Press, extended the invitation to create this anthology for the Penguin Classics series, and Emmy Yoneda, publishing coordinator at Penguin Press, labored alongside me throughout the process. Editorial manager Anna Wilson also has my gratitude. It was a pleasure to be on the Penguin team.

I owe personal thanks to Stanford's Prof. Robert Pogue Harrison, a longtime friend of René Girard and a wise expositor of his work. I am also grateful to Dana Gioia, whose encouragement and guidance has been a steady light for more than two decades.

Thanks also to Mary Pope Osborne, Paul Caringella, Luke Burgis, William Johnsen and Artur Sebastian Rosman.

Edward Haven, chair of philosophy in Los Medanos College, helped me winnow the René Girard maxims during a long weekend in the East Bay – a task that included three others: Mark Anspach, who weighed in from far away Bologna (while also translating his essay and interview for this volume); Trevor Cribben Merrill in Los Angeles; and also George A. Dunn in Indianapolis, who worked heroically on the index as well. I am indebted to all for judicious suggestions and insight.

Finally, appreciation always to Imitatio for its financial support for this endeavor.

Cynthia L. Haven
Stanford, California
25 November 2022

Sources and Copyright

Index

animals 5, 29, 132, 147, 190, 192, 194, 197, 246, 282
  animal images and metaphor 81–82, 83, 91–2
À bout de souffle (film) 69
À la recherche du temps perdu/In Search of Lost Time (Proust) 214, 268
Abel *see* Cain and Abel
Abraham 20
Académie Française xii
Acts of the Apostles 186
Aeneid (Virgil) 261
Aeschylus 168
  The Persians 168
  The Suppliants 168
Ahriman 53
Ahura Mazda *see* Ormazd
Alison, James 185
Amazonian myth 18–19
America *see* United States of America
Anaximander 265
Anderson, Peter S. 110
Annunciation 236
Anspach, Mark 15–20
  Œdipe mimétique 9
anthropology x, 13, 35, 246
  the art of the novel as x

Antichrist 171, 180
The Anti-Christ (Nietzsche) 37
Antigone (Sophocles) 153–4
anti-Semitism 217, 218
Antony and Cleopatra (Shakespeare) 250
apocalypse 40, 172, 179, 253, 280, 282
Apocalypse (Book of Revelation) 238
Apollo 11, 83
Aristotle 137, 149
art 56, 60, 61, 68, 116, 126, 137, 220,
  for art's sake 46, 54
  and mimesis/imitation 128
  of the dance 125, 127
  of the novel x
  of oratory/preaching 228, 232
  of the writer 267
  and ritual 134–5
As You Like It (Shakespeare) 251
atheism 22–3, 27, 31, 37, 188,
Auerbach, Eric 138, 139–140, 149
  Mimesis 138
Auden, W. H.: *Horae Canonicae: Nones* viii
Augustine of Hippo 186, 261, 264, 265
  Confessions 271
Avignon vii, ix, xvi
Aztecs ix, 34

Bacchae (Euripides) 32
bad faith 45, 52, 53, 54, 68, 70,
Balthazar, Hans Urs von 185
Balzac, Honoré de 68
Barabbas 223
Barber, C. L. 87–88
Baudelaire, Charles 137
Bernanos, Georges 172
Bible/biblical tradition xii, 7, 13–14,
    149, 257, 261, 275
    Hebrew Bible 13, 195, 198
    and modernity 197–200
    see also Gospels *and* Old
        Testament
Bosch, Jerome 220
Bosnian war 213
Bossuet, Jacques-Bénigne 228
Burning Man Festival ix
Byzantine world 257

Caiaphas 133, 275
Cain and Abel xv, 14
Camus, Albert xii, 41–7, 49, 50, 52–
    68, 70–3
    Discours de Suède 57
    La chute/The Fall 42–6, 52, 53–4,
        56, 61, 67, 68, 70–73
    L'étranger/The Stranger 41–2, 45,
        47–72
    L'homme révolté/The Rebel 57
    Le malentendu/The
        Misunderstanding 45
    Le mythe de Sisyphe/The Myth of
        Sisyphus 41, 45, 61, 63, 64, 68
    La peste/The Plague 44, 45
Candide (Voltaire) 208, 245
Caravaggio, Michelangelo Merisi
    da 220
Carré, Ambroise-Marie xii, 227–43

The Catcher in the Rye (Salinger) 42
Catholic Church/Catholicism 184,
    185, 228–30, 235
    see also Church *and* Second
        Vatican Council
Cervantes, Miguel de x, 68, 78,
    262, 270
    Don Quixote 261, 270, 279
charity 170, 274
Chateaubriand, François-René de 44
Chatterton (Vigny) 57–9, 63
Chenu, Marie-Dominique 232
Cheval, Ferdinand 180
Christianity 5, 7, 13, 36–7, 38, 145–6,
    165, 167, 170, 172, 173, 177, 180,
    187–8, 212, 221, 225, 259, 263–4,
    266, 268, 279, 280
    Christian apocalypse 40
    Christian God 36, 37, 39, 168
    Christian knowledge 40, 160
    Christian revelation 159, 166,
        168, 185
    Christian story 254–7
    Christian theology 170
    and conversion 265–71
    Girard's 184–5
    historical Christianity 185
    and literature 259–72
    and modernity 172
    and mythology 7, 13–14, 20, 196,
        224, 255, 256, 258
    Nietzsche's critique of 37–40, 188
    and sacrifice 36, 38, 146–147, 166–7,
        171, 172–3, 185, 198, 212
    post-Christian era 259, 260,
        261, 263
    ultra-Christianity 287
    see also Bible/biblical tradition
        and Gospels

Church 185, 235, 266, 282
  French Church 230
Church of Laodicea *see* Laodicean
  Church
The City of God (Augustine) 264
Claudel, Paul 44
Clausewitz, Carl von xii
Cold War 170
The Comedy of Errors (Shakespeare) 88
communism 171, 213
Comte, Auguste 189
concern for victims 199, 273, 287
Confessions (Augustine) 265
conflict vii–xiii, 3–4, 10, 90, 98, 104,
    105, 109, 116, 117, 124, 128, 190,
    206, 207, 215, 216, 251, 178, 279,
    281, 284
  international 157
  mimetic 11–12, 78, 99, 100, 105, 121,
    128, 132, 136, 138, 148, 153, 194,
    207–10, 213, 214, 216, 251, 278,
    279, 281
  Shakespeare and 85–7, 88, 90, 98,
    99, 100, 104–5, 109, 117
  tragic conflict 57, 67, 98, 99
conversion xi, 248, 264–72
  Augustine's 265, 271
  existential 55
  Girard's 182–4
  novelistic 270
  Proust's 169
Corbin, Michel 185
Coriolanus (Shakespeare)209
Corneille, Pierre 166
Crime and Punishment (Dostoevsky)
    xii–xiii, 41, 60, 270
Cro-Magnon man 189
crowd vii, 7, 12, 15, 18, 22, 31, 33, 58,
    99, 133, 161, 168, 175–77, 194,

    197–8, 222–3, 224, 255,
    257, 277
  in *Julius Caesar* 103, 107, 108,
    115, 117
  in Peter's denial 140, 142, 145
  in the story of woman taken in
    adultery 174–75
Crucifixion xii, 13, 145, 197, 198, 219,
    220, 221, 223, 274
Cuban missile crisis 253

dance 134–5
  Salome's xii, 119, 122–3, 124, 125–6,
    127, 129, 130, 131, 132
  and scandal 125–6, 132
Dante Alighieri 261–2
  Divine Comedy 261
Darwinism 5, 190
de Rougement, Denis 80
death of God 24–27, 31, 32, 39
degree (ladder/system of) 89–90,
    93, 96, 97, 100, 107, 119, 112,
    114, 117
democracy 128, 215, 274
Derrida, Jacques 148
desire vii, x–xi, 4, 9–10, 16, 17, 26, 35,
    76, 78, 80, 82, 94, 96, 110, 123,
    124, 126, 128–9, 130–1, 133–5,
    190–1, 249–50, 263, 273, 274,
    277, 278, 279, 281
  liberation from 268–9
  metaphysical 76, 274
  see also mimetic desire
Dickens, Charles 68
differentiation and undifferentiation
    86, 87–88, 89, 91,100, 105, 116,
    117, 118, 213, 286
Dionysus 37–9, 187–8
Donatist heresy 266

Don Quixote 261, 270, 279
Dostoevsky, Fyodor x, xv, 41, 57, 60.
    68, 71, 72, 78, 262
    Underground Man 57
doubles 90, 99, 104, 105, 109, 116,
    124, 154
    in *The Comedy of Errors*
        (Shakespeare) 88
drama *see* tragedy
Dupuy, Jean-Pierre 194

Each Day I Begin / Chaque jour je
    commence (Carré) 231, 233, 234,
    238, 239
economy / economics 205, 252, 285
Elihu 153–4, 155
Eliot, George 271
Eliphaz 161, 162
Empedocles 265
'The Emperor's New Clothes' (Hans
    Christian Andersen) 16
Enlightenment, philosophers of
    27, 145
envy and jealousy vii–viii, 41, 76,
    103, 110, 145, 151, 268, 279
epistemology 36, 117, 237
Epistles of Paul 72
egalitarianism / equality 10, 237, 138,
    207, 210
Esau 280
eternal return / recurrence 24, 35, 36,
    37, 39, 40, 51, 265
Eucharist 32, 256
Euripides: *Bacchae* 32
evil 72, 152, 285

faith 7, 182, 184, 231, 233, 235, 236, 239,
    264, 266
    in historical progress 138

in science 136
Peter's confession of 147
see also bad faith
fate (*fatum*) 48, 49
Flaubert, Gustave x, 119, 126, 262,
    270, 271
    Madame Bovary 271
flying saucers 275
France 170, 189, 204, 210, 216, 227, 228
Francis of Assisi 261
freedom 104, 125, 173, 200, 203, 218,
    282, 284
    mimetic desire / mimetic models
        and 173, 177, 178, 274
French Academy 227–8, 240–1
French Church 230 *see also* Catholic
    Church
French résistance 294
French Revolution 216, 2228
Freud, Sigmund 4, 12, 16–18, 36, 122,
    191, 209, 250, 263
    Freudianism 255
    Freudian unconscious 130
    Moses and Monotheism 17
    Oedipus complex 17
    Totem and Taboo 17, 36
Freudianism / Freudian 79, 98, 255

Gal Foundation 227
Galilee / Galilean 131–2, 139, 142,
    143, 144
Gauchet, Marcel 173
The Gay Science (Nietzsche) 22, 33
Gibson, Mel xii, 117–225
Gioia, Ted viii–ix
Girard, René vii–xvi, 165–188
    Battling to the End xvi
    change of mind on the meaning
        of 'sacrifice' 166–7

Christian youth 181
conversion experience 182–184
*Deceit, Desire and the Novel
    (Mensonge romantique et
    vérité romanesque)* x, 10
experience of reading
    Shakespeare 165–6
'the new Darwin of the human
    sciences' ix
*Things Hidden since the Foundation
    of the World (Des choses
    cachées depuis la fondation du
    monde)* xi, 189
*Violence and the Sacred (La violence
    et le sacré)* xi, 16
Violent Origins 18
Giroud, Françoise 186
globalization 205, 213, 276
God 20, 49, 172, 173, 181, 184, 189, 205,
    231, 236, 233, 234, 235, 236–7, 239,
    241, 242, 254, 257, 264, 265, 272,
    276, 277, 286
    death of 25–37, 39–40
    Kingdom of 212, 286
    lamb of 257, 172
    and retribution/vengeance 163, 169
    and sacrifice 174–3
Goethe, Johann Wolfgang von:
    *The Sorrows of Young
    Werther* 44
Golgotha 217
Gospels 38,119, 122, 134, 140, 146,
    147–8, 168–9, 173, 179, 185, 197,
    225, 233
    Auerbach on 138
    and conversion 264–5, 271–5
    and mythology 7, 13–14, 133, 145–6,
        188, 195–186, 288, 212,
        255–6, 281

and *The Passion of the Christ*
    (Gibson) 217, 219–20,
    222–5, 224
and scandal 124, 125
see also John, Luke, Mark *and*
    Matthew
Greek mythology 36
Greek religion 6–7, 232
Green, Julien 239–40

Hamlet (Shakespeare) 209
Hebrew Bible 13, 195, 198 *see also*
    Bible/biblical tradition
Hebrews, ancient 229
Hegel, Georg Wilhelm Friedrich
    13, 134
Heidegger, Martin 10, 23, 25, 37, 187
    Holzwege 23
    Mitsein (being-together) 141,
        143, 146
Heraclitus 265
Herod 119, 120–1, 122, 123–5, 126,
    127, 128, 129, 130–2, 133,
    134–6, 137
'Herodiade' (Mallarmé) 119, 120–1,
    122, 123, 124, 125, 126, 129,
    130–2, 133
Herodias 123, 124–5, 126, 127, 128–9,
    130, 131–2, 133, 134, 135–6,
    137, 278
'Herodias' (Flaubert) 119
hierarchy 203 *see also* degree
Hinduism 6, 183
    Puranas 265
history xii, xiv, 3, 13, 30, 35, 36–7, 40,
    108, 118, 137, 138, 156, 159, 167,
    169, 170, 171, 172, 170, 185, 194–5,
    198–9, 206, 214, 224, 248, 273,
    277, 278, 279

history – *cont'd*.
 Christian 37, 168, 221, 225, 266
 medieval x
 pagan conception of 265
 Roman 114, 115
 and totalitarianism 160
Hobbes, Thomas 252–3
 war of all against all 5, 253
Hofmannsthal, Hugo von 119
Holy Spirit 186, 272
 Paraclete 177
Holy Week 184, 232
Homer 224
hominization 5
Hosea 198
Hudon, Louis 47
Huitzilopochtli ix

identity 204–5, 251 *see also*
  differentiation and
  undifferentiation
Imago Christi 39
imitation vii, xi, xiv, 17, 71, 77, 90,
  176–7, 192, 196, 197, 206, 210,
  213, 219, 246, 273, 280
 in Aristotle 137, 149
 of Christ 166, 264, 286, 285
 and literature 45–6
 and Oedipus 11, 17
  in art 137
  See also mimesis *and* mimetic
   desire
imperialism 169, 170
India 35
Indiana University x
injustice 162, 225
 of the mob 197
 political, social, and racial 207
 see also justice

Isaiah 149, 195, 224, 271
Islam 167
Italy 203–4, 210

Jackson, Michael 19
Jansenists 183
jealousy *see* envy and jealousy
Jesus Christ 125, 130, 131, 166, 167–9,
  172, 184, 187, 195, 198, 235, 254,
  256, 277, 280, 281, 282, 283,
  286, 287
 and the woman taken in adultery
   173–5, 177–8
 crucifixion xii, 13, 145, 197, 198,
   119, 221
 and mythology 6–7, 146, 196, 277
 passion of 130, 133, 212, 255
 and *The Passion of the Christ*
   (Gibson) 217–8, 219, 221, 222,
   223, 224
 and Peter's denial 138, 139, 141, 143,
   144–5, 147, 149, 197, 255, 266
 and Suffering Servant 14, 195,
   196, 271
 see also Passion of Jesus Christ
Jewish state (under Rome) 196, 254
Jews and Judaism xii, 13, 37, 40, 72,
  140–1, 167, 187, 195, 212, 221, 217,
  222, 223, 224, 225, 263
Job xii, 20, 151–163, 195, 196, 223,
  224, 225
Joel 186
John, Gospel of 133, 138. 140, 141, 142,
  173, 256,
John Paul II 230
John the Baptist 23, 119–22, 124,
  126–33
Johns Hopkins University x
Jonah 172

Johnson, Ben: *Timber: Or, Discoveries* 73
Joseph and his brothers 195, 196
Josephus, Flavius 120
Joyce, James 179
Judeo-Christian tradition 20, 35, 37, 72, 159, 224, 287
Julius Caesar (Shakespeare) 98–118, 165–6
Jung, Carl 250
justice 41, 72, 92, 154, 155, 156, 160, 161, 277
   see also injustice

Kafka, Franz 44
Keynes, John Maynard 252
Kierkegaard, Søren 62–64
   The Sickness unto Death 62–3
King Lear (Shakespeare) 168
Kingdom of God 168, 212, 286

La chute/The Fall (Camus) 42, 43–6, 52, 53–4, 56, 61, 67, 68, 70–3
L'étranger/The Stranger (Camus) 41–2, 45, 47–72
L'homme révolté/The Rebel (Camus) 57
Le malentendu/The Misunderstanding (Camus) 45
Le mythe de Sisyphe/The Myth of Sisyphus (Camus) 41, 45, 61, 63, 64, 68
La peste/The Plague (Camus) 44, 45
La table ronde (Sénart) 56
Lacordaire, Jean-Baptiste Henri 228
Laodicean Church 238–9
Leibniz, Gottfried Wilhelm 208
Lent 184, 228
Levinas, Emmanuel xv

Leviticus 174
L'homme révolté/The Rebel (Camus) 57
liberalism (economic) 210
literature x, 45–6, 53, 57, 59, 61, 67, 80, 137–8, 149
   and Christianity 269–72
   prophetic literature 195, 198
   trial literature 71–2
   tragic literature 117
Lohfink, Gerhard 185
Lot, nephew of Abraham 20
Love in the Western World (de Rougement) 82
Lukács, Georg 138
Luke, Gospel of 142, 173, 297
lynching viii, 5, 6, 7, 116, 157, 237

Machiavellianism 217
Madame Bovary (Flaubert) 270
Mahler, Gustav 182
Mallarmé, Stéphane 119, 125
Manicheism 55
Mantegna, Andrea 220
Maoism 237–8
Maquet, Albert 46
Marcel, Gabriel 72, 240
Mark, Gospel of 119–35, 140, 142, 271
The Marriage of Figaro 182
Marx, Karl 4, 13
Marxism 117, 138, 285
Mary, Virgin 236
Matisse, Henri 290
Matthew, Gospel of 33, 119, 123, 125, 142, 143, 236
Mauss, Marcel 36
Metamorphoses (Ovid) 92
metanoia 64, 265 *see also* conversion
metaphysical desire 76, 274

micro-eugenics 281
A Midsummer Night's Dream
    (Shakespeare) 73–97
Middle Ages 15, 175, 198, 261
Milomaki *see* Amazonian myth
mimesis x–xi, xv, 10, 12, 105, 109,
    128–9, 138, 139–40, 144, 148, 159,
    163, 193, 210, 273, 281
    conflictual 105, 214
    good mimesis xv, 149
    ritual mimesis 133
    and literature and art 137
    Plato and 148, 149
    Aristotle and 137, 149
    see also mimetic desire
Mimesis (Auerbach) 138
mimetic desire 9, 10, 13, 21, 76, 105,
    132, 148, 173, 177–9, 207–9,
    251, 263–4, 282, 268, 269, 282,
    286
    in the Gospels 121, 123–4, 126, 130,
    131–2, 134, 138, 145, 148, 149
    in Shakespeare 75, 76–77, 78–9, 81,
    82, 86, 91, 99, 100–01, 105,
    108, 165, 168, 249
mimetic rivalry *see* rivalry
models/mediators 9, 10, 16, 17, 58,
    78, 81, 86, 87, 98, 100, 101, 105,
    107–8, 121, 124, 125, 126, 128, 174,
    176, 178, 190, 206, 208–9, 210,
    212, 215, 230, 234, 251, 262–3,
    264, 271, 274, 286
    model-obstacle 121, 129, 209
Modern Language Association 261
Molière (Jean-Baptiste Poquelin) 78
Monsieur Teste (Valéry) 59, 60, 61, 62,
    63, 64
Montaigne, Michel de 118, 166
Mosaic Law 72, 173–4

Moses 173
Moses and Monotheism (Freud) 17
mysticism/mystics 225, 238
    mystical awakening 181
    mystical experience 233–4, 235,
        239–40, 241, 242
    Oriental 264
    and Passion of Christ 221
myth vii, x, 18–19, 29, 35–6, 57, 59, 71,
    119–20, 138, 154, 162, 163, 179,
    185, 186, 191–2, 224–5, 252–3,
    265, 269, 277, 279, 286
    and Christianity 7, 13–14, 37–8,
        188, 194–198, 212, 224, 254–57,
        281
    foundational 5–7, 145, 191, 223
    and literature 261
    and *A Midsummer Night's Dream*
        77, 79, 82, 84, 85, 91–2, 93–4,
        95, 69
    Oedipus 5, 11, 14, 16–19, 20, 188,
        191, 192, 212, 256
    and ritual viii, 12, 35, 149
    and scapegoating 7, 12, 133, 152,
        162, 163, 212, 256

Nazareth 139
Nazi occupation of France 228
Nemesis 48
Neuilly 234–5, 236, 237, 239, 241, 242
New Yorker 217
Nietzsche, Friedrich xii, 21–40, 58,
    62, 238
    and *amor fati* 62
    The Anti-Christ 37
    and Christianity 38–40, 169, 178,
        187–88, 198
    and eternal return/recurrence 35,
        36, 37, 39, 40, 58

The Gay Science 22, 33
and death of God 24–27, 31, 32, 39
and *ressentiment* 101
Thus Spoke Zarathustra 37
Twilight of the Idols 39
The Will to Power 37–8
Noah 224, 261
Nobel Prize 57, 73
Notre-Dame Cathedral 228
novelistic truth 10, 11

Oedipus viii, 11–12, 14–15, 19–20, 71,
    152, 188, 224
    complex 9, 17, 23, 181
    and mimetic desire 11, 12–13, 16, 17
    myth 5, 12, 14, 16, 17–18, 19, 191,
        255, 257
Oedipus at Colonus (Sophocles) 11, 20
Oedipus the King (Sophocles) 9, 11, 16,
    257
Old Testament 7, 185
    see also Bible *and* Hebrew Bible
Ormazd (Ahura Mazda) 53
Orwell, George 89
Ovid 82, 92
    Metamorphoses 92

paganism 7, 37, 38, 146, 233, 265
    conception of history 265
    neo-paganism 266
    gods 212
Paraclete *see* Holy Spirit
Pascal, Blaise 28, 44, 82, 118,
    170, 263
Passion of Jesus Christ 7, 14, 27, 39,
    130, 134, 174, 177, 184, 187, 212
    and ritual 35–6
    and Dionysus 37–8, 188
    and Peter's denial 145, 146

The Passion of the Christ (Gibson)
    xii, 217–25
    and portrayal of Pilate 223
    realism of 219, 220, 224
    and violence 218, 221, 222, 223–4
patriotism 215
Paul the Apostle 248, 264–5, 266
    Epistles 72, 186
Pax Romana 111, 223
Pentecost 272
The Persians (Aeschylus) 168–9
Peter the Apostle 186, 271
    betrayal of Jesus xii, 138–49, 197,
        248, 255, 266
Phaedrus (Plato) 167
Pharisees 33, 42–3, 173, 185
Philippi, Battle of 104, 109, 110, 115
Pilate 131, 133, 145, 197, 222, 223, 280
plague xiii, 15, 161, 188
    and Oedipus myth 5, 11, 15–16, 20,
        188, 191, 255, 257
philosophy 24, 162, 180, 257, 284
    of the Enlightenment 27
    Greek 225, 265
    pre-Socratic 35, 36, 265
Plato / Platonism 167, 224–5
    and mimesis 129, 137, 148, 149
    Phaedrus 167
    The Republic 148
Plutarch 103, 114, 165
Pope viii, 230
political correctness 227
Poquelin, Jean-Baptiste *see* Molière
positivism 36, 38, 69, 94, 188
post-Christian era 259–64, 263
pre-Socratic philosophy 35, 36, 265
Protestant Reformation 216
Proust, Marcel x, xii, 181, 214, 215,
    216, 262, 267, 268–71

Proust, Marcel x – *cont'd.*
  *À la recherche du temps perdu/In
    Search of Lost Time* 214, 268
Psalms 7, 191, 195, 223
Puranas 265
Puritans 283

Racine, Jean 44, 166
rationalism 5, 27, 36, 93, 97, 99
rationality 48–9, 104, 105,
reciprocity 36, 58, 71, 74, 86, 88, 128,
    168, 190, 246–9, 251
  of forgiveness 239
  mimetic reciprocity/reciprocal
    mimicry 117, 124
Reformation *see* Protestant
    Reformation
religion 6, 16, 22, 27, 29, 30, 34, 35, 38,
    145–6, 151, 158, 165, 172–3, 187,
    188, 189, 190, 199, 200, 201, 203,
    218, 223, 257, 263, 275, 277, 280,
    281, 284, 287
  archaic 13, 14, 166, 190, 191, 194,
    195, 196, 198, 201, 211,
  of the book 167
  mythical 212
  primitive 159–60, 162
Renaissance 137, 220, 221
The Republic (Plato) 148
ressentiment 101
retaliation *see* revenge, retaliation,
    and retribution
retribution *see* revenge, retaliation,
    and retribution
revelation xii, 38–40, 115, 133, 149, 159,
    162, 165, 162, 164, 166, 171, 172,
    176, 185, 225, 253, 280
  Christian 166, 168, 185,
  Judeo-Christian xii, 159

Revelation, Book of *see* Apocalypse
revenge, retaliation, and retribution
    5, 88, 108, 109, 112, 121, 130, 153,
    162, 179, 212, 221, 246, 248
  God of vengeance/divine
    vengeance 153, 161, 168
Richelieu, Cardinal (Armand Jean
    du Plessis): *Spiritual
    Writings* 228
Rimbaud, Arthur 44
ritual viii–ix, 29, 30, 31–6, 39, 132, 137,
    156, 163, 174, 185, 198
  and art 134
  Hebrew 12
  in *Julius Caesar* (Shakespeare) 112,
    114, 115
  and myth viii, 12, 35, 149
  and Nietzsche 33, 35, 39
  and Peter's denial of Christ 141,
    147, 149
  and religion 6, 32, 212
  and sacrifice xi, 13, 112, 114–115,
    132, 193–5, 211–14, 256
  and Salome's dance 129, 132–4
  and scapegoat 12–13, 132, 133,
    212, 214
rivalry ix, 5, 6, 7, 10, 11, 13, 17, 119,
    121, 134, 144, 148, 151, 190, 192,
    193, 194, 199, 200, 207–11,
    212–3, 215, 234, 252, 275,
    286, 287
  in *As You Like It* 251–2
  in *Julius Caesar* 100, 102, 104,
    112, 118
  in *A Midsummer Night's Dream*
    74, 75, 77, 78, 79, 85, 86,
    90, 99
Rivière, Jacques 269
romantic lie x, 10, 11

Romanticism 57–60, 61, 62, 69,
    205, 279
Rome / Romans 96, 99, 100, 103, 104,
    105, 106, 110, 112, 113, 115, 116,
    117, 137, 165, 166, 169, 170, 196,
    221, 222, 223, 264
    Pax Romana 111
    Roman Empire 111
    Roman Republic 100, 114
Rousseau, Jean-Jacques x, 3
Russia 3, 170, 253

the sacred 29, 30, 34, 39, 273, 278
    primitive sacred 33
    archaic sacred 211, 254
sacrifice viii–xi, 35, 59, 155, 156,
    165, 171, 188, 199–203, 119,
    279, 292
    and Christianity 36, 38, 145–6,
        166–7, 171, 172–3, 185, 198,
        200, 212
    and dance 134–5
    and God 172–3
    human xii, 33–4, 39, 132, 156,
        171, 285
    in *Julius Caesar* (Shakespeare) 111,
        112, 113, 115–17–19, 169
    and myth 146, 198
    and ritual 6, 13, 112, 114–5, 132,
        193–5, 211–14, 256
    sacrificial victim 86, 146
    and tragedy 115
    see also sacrificial crisis
sacrificial crisis 21, 28–9, 36, 153
sado-masochism 222
Salamis, Battle of 168–9
Salinger, J. D.: *Catcher in the Rye* 42
Salome (Hofmannsthal) 119
Salome (Strauss) 119

Salome (Wilde) 119
Salomé, Lou 22
Sartre, Jean-Paul 44, 52–3, 125
Satan 3, 56, 133, 172, 180, 265
Savonarola, Girolamo xv
scandal 46, 92, 235, 237, 253
    and Job 153
    and Nietzsche 33
    and the Passion of Jesus Christ
        219
    and Peter's denial 141
    and Salome 119–135
    and the woman taken in adultery
        174, 175
scapegoating vii–viii, xi–xii, xiii–xiv,
    5–6, 24, 32, 39, 124, 163, 170,
    201, 211–12, 214, 215, 254–56,
    276, 277
    in the Bible 13–14, 132, 133, 145, 147
    and Jesus Christ 7, 14, 145, 147, 172,
        175, 212, 255, 256
    Job as scapegoat xii, 151, 152–4,
        156, 157, 158, 159, 160–2,
        163,195, 196, 223
    in *Julius Caesar* (Shakespeare)
        103, 165–6
    and myth 7, 12, 133, 162, 192,
        214, 256
    Oedipus as scapegoat 14–16,
        20, 154
    and ritual 12–13, 134, 135, 212, 214
    see also scapegoat mechanism
scapegoat mechanism xi, 132, 133,
    151, 152, 157, 159, 161, 162, 163,
    165, 175, 210–11,
Schwager, Raymund 185
science 10, 138, 220, 245, 246, 252, 282
    hard sciences xii
    human sciences ix, 281

science – *cont'd.*
  sciences of man 124
  social science 172, 180, 213, 214
  see also sociology / sociologists
Scriptures 5, 224, 261 *see also* Bible
Second Vatican Council 183, 228, 230
Sénart, Philippe 56
Sertillanges, Antonin 232
sexuality 17, 263, 279
  homosexual desire 17
  sexual dominance 75
  sexual liberation 277
  sexual rivalry 190, 209
The Sickness unto Death
  (Kierkegaard) 62–3
Shakespeare, William xii, 29, 74–81,
  83, 84–5, 87–9, 92, 95–7, 253,
  263, 291
  Antony and Cleopatra 250
  As You Like It 251
  The Comedy of Errors 88
  Coriolanus 209
  Hamlet 209
  Julius Caesar 98–118, 165–166
  A Midsummer Night's Dream 73–97
  Troilus and Cressida 89, 100–1
  The Two Gentlemen of Verona 249
  'Shakespeare's Caesar: The
    Language of Sacrifice'
    (Anderson) 110
Simon of Cyrene 217
Sisyphus 64
Situations (Sartre) 53
sociology / sociologists x, 107,
  213, 280
Socrates 167
Sodom 20
Sophocles xii, 11–12, 16, 19–20,
  153, 257

Antigone 153–4
Oedipus at Colonus 11, 20
Oedipus the King 9, 11, 16, 257
Stalinism 159
Stendhal x, 10, 262, 270, 271
  The Red and the Black 270
Stravinsky, Igor 182
structuralism 137
Suffering Servant 14, 195, 196, 224, 271
The Suppliants (Aeschylus) 168
Swift, Jonathan 209

Tantalus 64
Tarquin 112–3, 116
technology 10, 201, 220
Tertullian 266
Thebans 9, 152, 154, 191
Thebes 11, 15–16, 19, 20, 191, 257
Teresa of Ávila 265
theology 5, 36, 145, 162, 170
  of the Church fathers 232
Thérèse of Lisieux 236
Thomas the Apostle 23
Thus Spoke Zarathustra (Nietzsche)
  37
Tocqueville, Alexis de 252
totalitarianism xii, 151, 155, 156, 157,
  158–61, 163, 215, 273
tourism 286
Teilhard de Chardin, Pierre 232
tragedy 32, 58, 89, 113, 139, 160, 221
  and myth 29
  Oedipus and the Theban plays
    9–14, 16, 19, 152, 153, 154
  Shakespearean 113, 114–6
Troilus and Cressida (Shakespeare)
  89, 100–1
Troyes, Chrétien de: *Yvain, the
  Knight of the Lion* 209

Twilight of the Idols (Nietzsche) 39
The Two Gentlemen of Verona
    (Shakespeare) 249

undifferentiation *see* differentiation
    and undifferentiation
United States of America ix–x, 170,
    200, 204, 252
    judiciary 247
    medical system 183
    and Russia 3

Valéry, Paul 59, 60, 61, 63
Vatican II *see* Second Vatican
    Council
vengeance *see* revenge,
    retaliation, and retribution
Vercingetorix 170
Viggiani, Carl 48
Vigny, Alfred de 57, 59, 60, 63
    Chatterton 57–9, 63
violence vii, viii, xii, xiii, 38–9, 59,
    75, 81, 88, 94, 110, 111, 112, 117,
    133, 144, 148, 154, 156, 168, 171,
    178, 298–9, 245–6, 262, 274,
    275, 279, 278, 279, 280, 281,
    282, 287
    and Christianity 254–7, 279, 280
    collective 12, 19, 21–2, 23–4, 26–8,
        29–30, 31–2, 34, 35, 36, 37–40,
        108, 115–16, 129, 130, 133, 166,
        175–6, 187, 191, 224, 279
    and foundational myths 6, 111–15,
        188, 191, 223–4
    and mimesis 96, 104, 123, 131, 147,
        153, 174, 177, 192, 193, 194, 196,
        198, 210, 212, 246–7, 249–50,
        251, 252–4, 274, 276, 286
    and Oedipus myth 11, 255, 257

and *The Passion of the Christ* 217,
    218, 221, 222, 223
and relationship of belonging
    206–7, 209, 210, 211, 212–13,
    215–16
and ritual sacrifice xl, 35, 147, 174,
    198, 200, 211, 212
and the sacred ix, 29, 34, 189–91,
    212, 273
and the scapegoat xiv, 12–13, 124,
    147, 156–7, 159, 162, 254–5
Virgil: *Aeneid* 261
Voltaire: *Candide* 208, 245

Wagner, Cosima 22
war 50, 80, 209, 237, 279
    civil 99, 106, 109, 116
    god of ix
    of all against all 5, 253
    See also Bosnian war, Cold War,
        World War I, *and* World
        War II
the West 15, 18, 119, 160, 168, 169, 170,
    198, 220, 234, 266, 280
    history of 37
    literature/literary theory of
        137–8
Wilde, Oscar: *Salome* 119
witchcraft 255
witch-hunts 15, 282
World War I 216
World War II 217, 260
Wotan 6

Yahuna *see* Amazonian myth
    (Yahuna)
Yahweh 198, 271
    see also God
Yom Kippur 12